Reckoning with Spirit in the Paradigm of Performance

Reckoning with Spirit IN THE *Paradigm of Performance*

Donnalee Dox

University of Michigan Press
Ann Arbor

Published in the United States of America by the
University of Michigan Press
Manufactured in the United States of America
♾ Printed on acid-free paper

2019 2018 2017 2016 4 3 2 1

A CIP catalog record for this book is available from the British Library.

Dox, Donnalee.
Reckoning with spirit in the paradigm of performance / Donnalee Dox.
pages cm
Includes bibliographical references and index.
ISBN 978-0-472-07297-2 (hardcover : alk. paper) — ISBN 978-0-472-05297-4 (pbk. : alk. paper) — ISBN 978-0-472-12157-1 (ebook)
1. Performing arts—Religious aspects. 2. Performing arts—Moral and ethical aspects. 3. Spirituality. I. Title.
PN1590.R45D69 2016
791—dc23

2015031789

This book is dedicated to
Professor Emeritus Louis J. Hamman of Gettysburg College

Acknowledgments

This book owes the greatest debt to Martin Klabunde and Dunya McPherson, who allowed me to write about their practices. Their generosity of spirit cannot be matched by words of acknowledgment. This book is written in a language that is not necessarily theirs. I trust that the effort to bring their voices into conversation with critical discourses has not compromised their words or the ways they engage the world. At Texas A&M University, two colleagues, Marian Eide (English) and Ashley Currier (Sociology), were rigorous readers of early drafts. Independent of one another, they identified the same paragraph in the first draft of what became chapter 1 as the core of the project. Over a period of eighteen months, they saw gaps and possibilities I would not otherwise have seen. Joseph Jewell (Sociology), Joan Wolf (Women's and Gender Studies) and Cara Wallis (Communication) read and critiqued chapters 3 and 4 in later stages. Chapter 4 owes a great debt to discussions with N. Fadeke Castor (Anthropology and Africana Studies). I first discussed spirituality as a topic with Hilaire Kallendorf (Hispanic Studies) in 2002. Hilaire brought me back to the matter of spirit again and again until the ideas found form in this project.

LeAnn Fields at the University of Michigan Press recognized the challenges of this project. Her support has been unwavering from our first conversation. For that I am profoundly grateful. Also at the Press, Kevin Rennells handled the manuscript with grace and patience. Deborah Streahle and Elizabeth Grumbach edited the manuscript and corrected numerous technical errors in earlier drafts. In the later stages, Bridget Liddell brought not only sharp editorial skills but a critical sensitivity to the project itself. Her contribution was significant. Any remaining errors are my own.

Many scholars in theater and performance are grappling with the issues raised in this book from many points of view. Conversations with Josh Edelman, Jill Stephenson, Lance Gharavi, Claire Marie Chambers, Edward Lingan, and David Mason have been especially rewarding. To physicians Dr. Jon Bergeron and Dr. James Sterling I extend personal thanks for their skill and compassion in medical practice.

Over a period of five years, Texas A&M University provided financial support. The Glasscock Center for Humanities Research (College of Liberal Arts), a university-level grant through the Program to Enhance Scholarly and Creative Activity, a University Faculty Development Leave, and travel funds from the Department of Performance Studies supported this project at various stages.

Contents

Preface: Disorienting Performance

SPIRIT AND PERFORMANCE

That performance has become a paradigm for interpreting the world around us does not surprise. Performance shapes our perceptions and tells us what is real. Every day we watch people perform in multiple forms of media, from films to YouTube. We recognize advertisements, political speeches, sports events, and news broadcasts as crafted performances. In everyday life, we consciously or unconsciously perform our identities through dress, speech, gestures, and social behavior. "Performativity" has emerged as a critical stance that analyzes the power of performance to produce knowledge. The purpose of this book is to open space for discussing the kinds of knowledge produced by spiritual practices in a paradigm rooted in the social construction of reality.[1]

As neuroscientist Sam Harris suggests, the very idea of spirituality and a spiritual life as a topic for critical discussion is off-putting to many people (Harris 6). Yet people continue to explore and express a sense they can only describe with a language of "spirit." Here that language and the sensibilities people claim along with it invite curiosity rather than animosity. From the critical stance of performativity, spirituality appears as a kind of representation. People perform rituals and ceremonies. Politicians use religious rhetoric to perform their ideological positions. People reenact religious stories through theater, convey religious emotions through music, and describe religious experiences in writing. From this stance, performances are the *matter* of spirit: performance makes deities, spirits, mystical experiences, religious belief systems, and transcendent wisdom visible in material forms such as myths and rituals. We study these forms as performances.

Within these performances, however, people may claim that there is more going on than meets the eye of an observer: a dimension of spirit. What to do with those claims in a paradigm like performance studies, which is firmly rooted in the observable, material, and social world of human communication, is the subject of this book. How might people's sense of spirit inform the materiality of performance?[2] This question troubles the paradigm of performance in productive ways.

People continue to sense an ineffable, ephemeral reality they call "spiritual" in the modern, industrial world. Paul Heelas observes that spirituality "has run riot" in the modern West ("On Making Sense" 3). Accounting for this sense of spirit in the paradigm of performance has become an increasingly relevant topic.[3] The word "spirit" invokes a reality that does not depend on the material world. What happens when the visible materiality of bodies, objects, and texts that constitute performance collides with people's sense of a numinous, ineffable, invisible presence?[4]

Today people describe spirituality broadly and do not always connect spirituality with religion. Believing in higher or supernatural powers, perceiving matter as pulsing energy, experiencing self as spirit, or awakening to a new consciousness are but a few ways people might describe spirituality. Certainly such descriptions are bound to culturally specific patterns of meaning-making and belief systems. However, taking spirituality as a cultural construction, discursive formation, or perceptual error might limit a complex aspect of performance.[5] When spirituality informs people's performative practices, how do we read the materiality of the performance?

Performance has been a powerful critical paradigm for humanities and social science inquiries. Spirituality tests the limits of the paradigm. There are certainly risks to venturing into the elusive and suspect domain of spirituality and to taking people's descriptive experiences seriously.[6] The language of spirituality is far less comfortable than the analytical and critical terms of performance theory. Spirituality is disorienting. Theorizing the intersection of spirituality and the materiality of performance (not necessarily through Christian theology) means putting people's sense of the ineffable into play with familiar critical terms and concepts that ground a view of the social world as performance: presence, visibility, embodiment, textuality, authenticity, material culture, and representation.[7] The willingness to question terms that structure the paradigm of performance opens space for different interpretive and analytical question.

A personal anecdote here illustrates how the paradigm works. Many years ago I told a colleague that I had hung a bird feeder in my backyard. The response was this: "Oh, you are *performing nature*." In the paradigm of performance, "performing nature" makes all human action a kind of theater and the social world a place for watching people perform identity. The statement implies that an affinity for birds is not an inherent quality, but is shaped by cultural forces that can be observed in the act of hanging a bird feeder. Thus, my act of hanging a bird feeder becomes a performance of nature.

The performance paradigm, by design, "troubles" human actions. The paradigm opens the act of hanging a bird feeder to a critical reading. A critical reading of this act assumes, for example, that nature is real only insofar as a discourse (a collection of ideas, images, practices, and texts that constitute knowledge or reality) on nature *makes* nature real. The performance (hanging the feeder) makes nature real by marking nature as distinct from the socially constructed world of house, fenced backyard, hammer and nails, and stores that sell manufactured birdseed.

In the paradigm, a critical reading of "performing nature" might then take apart the way nature is constructed (a deconstruction). Nature becomes the referent for the action of hanging the feeder; the feeder becomes a prop that signifies nature. The body that hangs the feeder becomes the object of a gaze (perhaps that of the speaker, my own internal representation of myself to myself, an unseen spectator watching me hang the feeder, or the doves in the trees).

Such a critical reading of hanging a bird feeder might point out that my purchase of the feeder and birdseed makes me complicit in consumer capitalism, or that my desire for these goods—feeder and seed—substitutes for my desire to experience nature (which, in this logic, is a discursive construction that covers the loss or lack of nature as a reality). In such a reading, my fenced backyard might indicate my class status and attitudes about privacy and property. The feeder's design (handcrafted, rough-hewn wood) might suggest my self-identity as eco-friendly or faux rustic, even as I participate in the economic and social systems that make it possible for me to buy a mass-produced bird feeder. The internal inconsistencies of my self-performance become immediately apparent to a critical observer (although the birds quite likely do not care). This is a familiar line of critique in the paradigm of performance, though somewhat simplified here for purposes of illustration.

Introducing spirituality on its own terms does not aim to reject the paradigm, but to explore its borders. Uncritical acceptance of this stance is, I suggest, one of the reasons spirituality is difficult for performance theory.

Performance theory privileges doing (action) over being (essence) and material forms over people's subjective sensibilities.[8] Performance theory also eschews ontological truths, such as the existence of a stable self or deity. The logic of performativity thus understands spirituality as the construction of historical, cultural, and discursive forces. According to this logic, performers' sense of spiritual presence cannot be the starting point for interpreting performance. What happens if we do make spirituality the starting point for theorizing performance?

When I undertook this project more than eight years ago, scholarly literature generally distinguished spirituality from religion along two axes. In general, religion referred to the doctrines, beliefs, and rituals of monotheism, whereas spirituality referred to beliefs and practices that fell outside the purview of religion, labeled variously as unchurched, New Age, alternative, non-Western, premodern, and so on. Along the axis of human experience, spirituality referred to some internal sense of the divine or sacred (for example, the mystical writings of Thomas Merton), whereas religion referred to the ways belief in a deity played out in social or institutional ways (such as a Christian church service or faith-based charity).

More recently, the lines between secular, religious, and spiritual have been questioned and blurred. "Spiritual, not religious" as a sociological category has been released from its artificial binary and replaced by "nones" (no declared religion). The term "postsecular," introduced by Jürgen Habermas, now describes the contemporary condition in which notions of spirit and divinity are inextricable from the materiality of human culture.[9] Still, as Courtney Bender concludes, studying spirituality is like shoveling fog (182). What can we make of people's claims that the materiality of performance is infused with spirit and emerges from their sense of a numinous, divine, or ineffable presence? How do we interpret performances that begin in this sense when the epistemological assumptions that govern performativity do not account for spirituality?

The seeds of these questions, which grew into this project, were planted over a decade ago at a theater conference on the topic of theater and "the real." There a prominent theater theorist and scholar of Chinese literature observed that in seventeenth-century European plays such as *Hamlet* or *The Spanish Tragedy*, a ghost is a staged fiction. Ghosts in Chinese plays of the same period were understood to be part of the everyday world, as real as people.[10] What, I wondered at the time, is the status of spirits in an intellectual tradition that relegates ghosts to the machinery of representation? If a ghost in the European tradition is an imaginary "thing," then theatrical performance calls ghosts into being as things on the stage, where they are visible in material form. Stage ghosts can exist even if ghosts do not really exist in the material world. In the conventions of performance theory, the stage makes a ghost present as matter, and as matter the ghost is seen and known.

Ironically, the legacy of hauntology, introduced in Jacques Derrida's *Spectres of Marx*, remains a prominent metaphor in performance studies. Hauntology opened the materiality of performance to absence and the "Other," loss and lack, mourning and irony. The ghosts that now haunt performance are ever-receding referents that make direct knowledge of any thing (including the self) impossible except through performance.[11] Making sense of spirits, ghosts, gods, the ineffable, the divine, the sacred, and numinous or other nonmaterial phenomena, however, has not been the business of performance theory.

This particular absence is evident in, for example, the three-volume collection *Performance: Critical Concepts in Literary and Cultural Studies*, which brings together foundational theoretical essays in performance theory. This thorough compilation establishes performance as a critical perspective on culture, bodies, and language. It constructs performance as an interpretive paradigm that puts embodied culture and expressive forms into dialogue with discursive knowledge. The topics span the far reaches of what constitutes performance: play, ritual, theatricality, written language, spoken language, everyday life as performance, the audience, the body, gender construction, spectatorship, morality, representation and reproduction, acting and role playing, and cultural difference.[12]

Spirituality is not part of this discourse on performance. The materiality of ritual and ceremony accommodates whatever people might sense as spirituality. Perhaps the lack of a theoretical text on spirituality and performance is an apophatic statement, asserting that the numinous can only be known by what it is not (spirituality is *not* performance). More likely, however, the absence of spirituality as a critical category in these volumes indicates that spirituality has simply not been a theoretical concern.

More recently, the October 2012 issue of *Theatre Journal*, devoted to "Theatre and Material Culture," makes clear that the business of performance theory is to move back and forth from embodiment to text, from page to stage, from thought to material culture. Performance theory "wrestles with translating *material presence* into *discursive terms*" (Sofer 323, italics added). This wrestling has been enormously valuable. But what happens when we go beyond this limit and try to translate *spiritual presence* into the material terms of performance and discourse, and back again? Is there new epistemological territory to explore if we let go of the hold on visibility and materiality?

Spirit as a kind of felt presence, however, vexes a belief that performance testifies to what is missing, or that spirits cannot *be* except when they are made present by performance.[13] As Heelas points out, vernacular culture abounds with practices through which people know spirit as *presence*, not absence—from spiritual dance to spirit channeling to Corpus Christi processions to speaking in tongues. This sense of spirit as presence may well constitute performance in very different terms than those that organize the critical project of the performance paradigm. We can certainly insist on reading expressions of felt spirituality as marking absence, but can we allow spirit into the paradigm as presence? How does the paradigm of performance shift if we give people's spiritual perspectives credibility? Spirituality forces this reckoning in and with the paradigm.

IN THE BEGINNING

This project did not set out to question the paradigm, or even with the critical distance to reflect on the ways the paradigm constructs a way of thinking. In the beginning, my goals fit comfortably and predictably within the performance paradigm. The project began as a study of vernacular culture, which is the lifeblood of performance studies and a research emphasis in my university department.[14] I started with the assumption that discourses on spirituality construct people's beliefs, and that people "perform spirituality." In the framework of familiar terms, I assumed that performance theory would "trouble" contemporary spiritual practices (though ultimately spirituality troubled performance).

Early on I decided to write about "spiritual, not religious" practices. Excellent studies were already under way on religious performance, religion as performative, and the politics of religious performance. Spirituality apart from religion seemed amenable to the fluidity of social identity that performance theory celebrates and critiques. Resistance to institutionalized religion also seemed aligned with the value performance theory places on activism and challenging social norms. I assumed normative discourses on ethnicity, gender, and class would emerge as well.

The analysis I set out to do was along the lines of the bird feeder anecdote above. I expected to show how people "perform spirituality" in practices such as neopagan drum circles, ecstatic dance, or yoga. I expected to show how these practices were embedded in Western liberal humanist discourses on health and well-being, as well as how people's beliefs were shaped by discourses on an autonomous self and reliance on scientific discourses to validate subjective experience. I expected also to show that in unchurched spiritual practices people performed countercultural identities through romantic imaginings of non-Western cultures and nostalgic reconstructions of premodern spiritualities. The performance paradigm made such critical readings logical.

I anticipated that reading spirituality as performance would show what Wade Clark Roof famously identifies as the "spiritual marketplace" of modern American culture. My critique, so I imagined, would expose purportedly universal spiritual experiences—such as the feeling of universal oneness—to be rooted in an unacknowledged monotheistic worldview. Tracing the legacies of American spiritualism and the human potential movement would help me demonstrate the processes by which esoteric beliefs in spirit guides, afterlives, past lives, and out-of-body travel were performed as truths. I would show how New Age books, lectures, workshops, and self-help CDs domesticated historically radical practices such as Indic Tantra for easy consumption. Such an approach would reveal the neo-Orientalism and latent primitivism in borrowings from non-Western, archaic, and indigenous cultures. Thinking with the intellectual conventions of performance theory, I expected to parse narratives of spiritual selves, divinity, ghosts, transcendence, and the sacred as the desire for new mythologies. These mythologies would account for a real sense of lack, loss, and longing for authenticity.

The task was set, the terms known, the analytical machinery already working. At first the project lined up nicely (meaning predictably). Heelas was right: spirituality was running riot in the modern, urban, affluent West. The expressive forms of contemporary spirituality seemed perfectly suited to an analytical paradigm designed to read the social world as performance.

As this early vision of the project came into focus, examples appeared as if by magic. A colleague sent me a flyer for a two-day workshop titled "Dance as Trance / Dance as Ritual." This dance practice seemed to be a rich site for a critique of cultural appropriation in its amalgamation of shamanism, Sufism, Buddhism, and yoga as well as a critique of spirituality as an accessible consumer experience. The flyer proclaimed in capital letters:

"THIS IS IT—THE ONLY DANCE THERE IS." For $250, the workshop offered "elements of 'Core Shamanism'" combined with "practices of Sufi, yoga and Buddhism" by practitioners whose "spiritual practices have come out of dance." The flyer asserted that "dance artists of all decades have evolved deeply personal relationships to movement often expressing ritualistic and symbolic transformations of experience" and that "by working with performance as ritual," participants "will observe how the expression of the 'spiritual' manifests both reverently and irreverently." From the comfort of critical distance, performance theory would reveal this practice to be a discursive construction of spirituality as non-Western, personal, ritualistic, artistic, and embodied.

Another example appeared in a popular catalogue of "Inspiring Gifts and Natural Living": "The Healing Drum Kit: Drumming for Personal Wellness and Creative Expression," offered for $49.95. Eureka once again. The spiritual valences were unmistakable and again the framework of performance seemed to expose its construction. The catalogue's description invoked an imperialist narrative in which indigenous cultures have special wisdom, which Westerners can discover and put to use for their own instrumental benefit. The instructional CD promised a collection of "world rhythms," including Brazilian samba, defining the entire world outside the modern, global North-West as "indigenous." The text fit a pattern observed by critiques of cultural appropriation in performance analysis as well as critiques of New Age and alternative spiritualities. The description invited an analysis of how the performance of cultural privilege turned back on itself in an image of spiritual deprivation: "Indigenous peoples have always drummed in daily life, and we deprived ones of the Western world are now catching on to the incredible benefits and fun such practices can be."

In the familiar terms of the critical paradigm, the description created a lack then filled it with the promise of a consumer capitalist fetish object. An hour of drumming, the description assures the buyer, is "*scientifically proven* to enhance one's immune system, lower blood pressure, reduce stress and help one get in touch with one's feelings." Here was a conflation of well-being, physical health, self-transformation, secret spiritual wisdom, and nature all reassuringly backed up by the reality check of modern science. The narrative constructed Western identity in its identification of "indigenous" cultures' spiritual wisdom, then its focus on self-improvement, construction of the self by the consumption of goods, and medicalization of spirituality.

My critical mind homed in on these, and numerous other, examples of vernacular spirituality. A two-year search took me to forgiveness workshops and energetic healing demonstrations, psychic fairs and kirtans, yoga demonstrations and Hari Krishna dances. The hermeneutic hype, slippage of terms, cultural borrowings, spiritualizing of art, and the mix of emotional affect with embodied experience in these practices seemed like perfect subjects for the critical lens of performativity. That lens showed contemporary spiritual practices performing cultural Otherness and the individuality of the Western self. Spirituality became a consumer product. The counterculture of the 1960s had been reconstituted as mainstream holism (not the Holy). Western selves had appropriated and represented indigenous and ancient spiritualities. People linked spirituality to nature in resistance to urban modernity. Utopian visions of a peaceful, harmonious social world emerged out of personal growth and well-being as an evasion of genuine political engagement. Fairly quickly, a thesis emerged. Contemporary Western spirituality touted by middle-class spiritual seekers could be interpreted as a modern folk idiom that had been absorbed and reconstituted in the most iconic attribute of postmodern culture—performance.

REVERSAL

Discovery begins with the sense that something is not right. Something was definitely not right about this approach. As I moved into it, the project began to refuse the paradigm. Chapter outline after chapter outline failed. The material kept pulling against my theoretical orientation. Eventually, I saw the problem. The events and texts I wanted to analyze were already structured as performance by the paradigm. Performance revealed only and exactly what the paradigm promised. Spirituality became the ever-receding referent in the interplay of symbolic codes, frames, and bodies. There was no scholarly obligation to reckon seriously with people's spirits, gods, energies, or mystical experiences. There was no imperative to engage with whatever people thought they were doing in relation to some sort of numinous presence beyond what could be observed and rendered as performance. The critical terms of performance had made spirituality material, and manageable. I began to wonder how taking spiritual practitioners on their own terms would change the assumptions I so uncritically imposed on them. I was compelled to ask a different question: *What if spirituality structured performance, not the other way around?*

RESISTING PERFORMANCE

Patrick McNamara observes, "We have before us a set of human experiences reported by otherwise rational, sane, accomplished, smart, creative people. It's time that those experiences and the individuals who report them are taken seriously" (20). Even as I planned, in the beginning, for a more comprehensive critical analysis of spirituality-as-performance, McNamara's call to take spiritual experience seriously suggested exploring how spirituality might constitute performance.

Thinking about performance as a function of spirituality, rather than spirituality as a function of performance, became the project. What was going on in the interaction between the sense of spirit and the materiality of performance? What might the array of theories that constitute a discourse on performance limit in explorations of spirituality?

With new questions forming, I turned to studies of religion and spirituality as lived experience. Charles Taylor's widely influential *A Secular Age* had already shown me how secularity, religion, and spirituality operate as interdependent categories. Courtney Bender's critical sociology in *The New Metaphysicals: Spirituality and the American Religious Imagination* provided inspiration on the complexity of spiritual practices in material culture. Anne Taves's *Religious Experience Reconsidered* offered a reevaluation of methods for analyzing religious experience. Edward Slingerland's *What Science Offers the Humanities* addressed the limits of the postmodern orientation of performance theory. Meredith McGuire's rich ethnography in *Lived Religion: Faith and Practice in Everyday Life* brought out the complex, subtle ways people engage spirit as experience in and outside religion. As this book goes into its last revisions, spirituality is taking a legitimate place in scholarly inquiry. Linda A. Mercadante's ethnographic analysis of "nones" in *Belief without Borders: Inside the Minds of the Spiritual but Not Religious*, Kelly Besecke's nuanced exploration of reflexive spirituality in *You Can't Put God in a Box* and Barbara Ehrenreich's personal reflections in *Living with a Wild God: A Nonbeliever's Search for the Truth about Everything*, all published in 2014, speak to the scholarly and popular efforts to reckon with spirituality in contemporary societies.

If performance theory looks to the materiality of texts, bodies, and objects for presence, what is its critical language for people's sense of spirit? What do these spiritual sensibilities offer to familiar critical strategies that insist on performance as materiality and the discursive or social construction of experience? At the end of this book, there is still no exact language for the sense of spirit. There is, however, an opening for recognizing that those sensibilities warrant consideration on their own terms, which creates a space for reckoning with the ways experiential spirituality reconfigures notions of performance and performativity.

ENCOUNTERS WITH SPIRIT

There are many sites from which to rethink the paradigm of performance through the sense of spirit. Some are within religious traditions, some involve belief systems, some have valences of cruelty or engage cultural taboos. I chose to focus on two practices for this study: Collective Awakening, a neoshamanic drumming practice developed by Martin Klabunde (Tucson, Arizona) and Dancemeditation, a trademarked movement-meditation practice developed by Dunya Dianne McPherson (Manhattan). McPherson and Klabunde are the "rational, sane, accomplished, smart, creative people," whose experiences McNamara suggests we should take seriously.

These two practices are nodes in a network of spiritual drumming and dance practices. Neoshamanic/sacred drumming and ecstatic/contemplative dance have their own status as genres of alternative spiritualities. Music played on non-Western instruments and fusions of Western and Middle Eastern dance idioms have generic characteristics as vernacular or folk art. Practitioners' writings deploy tropes found in many spiritual self-help traditions (such as an embodied sense of universal love that transcends nature and culture).

My questions, however, focus not on the genres and their discursive/performative constructions, but on the sense of spirit people cultivate in the practices. Of the many practices I observed in the early stages of the project, these particular practices raised most clearly the issue of how people's sense of spirit shapes what we see as performance, and how the conventions in which we think about performance are proscribed by expectations for material presence, action, and observation. I decided to take Collective Awakening and Dancemeditation on their own terms.

Why these two practices? Collective Awakening and Dancemeditation resisted the assumptions about performance I brought to the project. The terms that structured their understanding of performance—for example, love—were not those of performance theory. Their terms came from a sense of spirit; the materiality of their performance also came from and invoked that sense. The "performance of spirituality" was thus not *only* representational, discursive, symbolic, material, and affective, but grounded in practitioners' embodied sense of an ineffable presence.

These two practices drove a wedge into the theoretical orientation to the social world as performative. Klabunde and McPherson have both analyzed how performance works as spiritual practice and how spiritual practice works as performance. Both practitioners started out as professional performers and found performance to be an inadequate framework for what they sensed. Each transformed an artistic practice into a spiritual practice. Drumming and dancing yielded knowledge of spirit, not of the social world around them. This is a very different orientation to performance than that assumed by the critical performance paradigm.

Certainly, their practices are performative. The workshops, ceremonies, and classes as well as websites, blogs, and online stores they produce can certainly be analyzed for how they "perform spirituality." But these activities are also part of practitioners' cultivation of a sense of spirit, which for them is very real. What interpretive language for that sense is possible in a paradigm that translates material presence into discursive terms and discourse into embodied doing?

The interplay between material culture and spirituality presents challenging problems for the critical project of theorizing performance. One problem is their engagement with cultural difference (see chapter 4). These practices fuse indigenous instruments with electronic amplification (Klabunde) and combine Middle Eastern dance traditions with Western modern dance (McPherson). They ground the sensations of spirituality in African shamanism (Klabunde) and the Islamic mystical tradition of Sufism (McPherson). Their writings rely on personal, subjective experience, and their epistemologies are organized around self-knowledge and perceptions of truths they understand to be universal (see chapter 2).

The paradigmatic critical response to cultural difference emphasizes cultural appropriation and the imposition of Western values. From a critical perspective, these practices raise the questions: Why is spiritually so often a mark of cultural difference? Why is spirituality accepted, even respected, in Western analyses of performances such as a South Indian *râs lila* (see David V. Mason), a Balinese *Topeng Pajagen* (see Jane Turner), or the Yaqui Easter pageant (see Richard Schechner), but not in the practices of middle-class Americans performing, for example, a Christian Nativity play or a neopagan solstice ceremony (see chapter 1)? What borders protect Western modernism from spirituality?

Another way these practices problematize the interplay between material culture and spirituality is along the axis of consumerism.[15] The standard critique focuses on how spiritual practices like these produce the desire for spiritual experiences by making products and constructing experiential events for a marketplace of uncommitted spiritual seekers. (Religion is not immune to this critique: witness the transformation of Christian church parishes into megachurches with Jumbotrons and the migration of Christian preaching into coffee shops.) Again, Collective Awakening and Dance-meditation challenge this critique. These practitioners are socially, educationally, and economically privileged in the sense that they had employment opportunities and social mobility. These are not stories of social marginalization. Again, this would seem a site for critique, either of the social status that affords the luxury of spiritual explorations or, conversely, of the credulity of people in this demographic who should know better than to believe in spirits.

At the same time, access to the advantages of the dominant culture makes their life choices significant in a different way. For this demographic, career is a primary mark of identity, as is financial security. Both practitioners made a spiritual life a financial and social commitment comparable to that of a priest, minister, rabbi, missionary, monk, nun, or other professionally committed religious person. Their engagement with consumer culture as spiritual practitioners marks a risk along a fairly significant axis of value in their particular demographic (see chapter 4).

Finally, even as these two practices engage cultural valences of Africa and the Middle East, they also critique the culture in which they are situated. Resistance to the dominant culture is evident in their founders' writing (see chapter 2): both suggest that turning internal experience outward as a spiritual practice (which we habitually read as performative) is a way of negotiating the material world, the physical body, and some understanding of self that is not entirely hooked on social identity. I observed that these spiritual practices pressed performance into the service of spirituality, rather than expressing spirituality by means of performance. That shift turns the critical lens on the performance paradigm itself. Vernacular practices may not reinforce the paradigms we, as critical observers, want to uphold. In this case, practitioners' orientation in a deeply felt internal sense of spirituality offers a critical perspective on performance that is worth considering.

How might spirituality be the impetus for performance? How do people translate embodied sensibilities into knowledge? How does that knowledge structure what we see as performative? How do people come to identify certain mental and somatic sensations as spiritual? How do people come to value such sensations and cultivate them in practices? How does a view of the world from an orientation in spirituality challenge the view of performance as material, visible, and audible? We might ask, if spiritual practitioners put expressive forms into the social world, what political or social work do those forms do? Is that work distinct from other kinds of action in any substantive way? How does a sense of spirit orient a person to a world of matter? What would it be to read practitioners' texts as if their sense of the numinous mattered? What would performance look or feel like if it were not grounded in the materiality of culture? How can we take people's embodied sensations of spirituality as if those sensations were as real as the drums, veils, bodies, and books we understand to be performing?

Critical distance and rigor distinguish scholarly analysis from advocacy. I am not arguing here that two vernacular practices define spirituality, or proposing some sort of transhistorical, transcultural spirituality. The critical project here asks *how people's sense of spirit affects the interpretive frame of performance.* When spirituality is taken seriously as a set of human experiences, how does the paradigm of performance expand to accommodate those experiences? How might people's sense of spirit reorient a perspective that constructs the world as performance? Imagining that reorientation is the task of this book.

Introduction

At the Borders of Performance

THE PROBLEM OF SPIRIT AND PERFORMANCE

Today, the shelves of mainstream bookstores offer an array of books on spirituality, from writings on Buddhism, Christianity, and physics by His Holiness the Dalai Lama to *Spirituality for Dummies* and, with no irony intended in the title, *The Complete Idiot's Guide to Communicating with Spirits*. Outside religion, spirituality may be defined variously as New Age, alternative, inner-life, unchurched, or "none."[1] In vernacular practice, lived spirituality may be as readily associated with self-improvement, esoteric knowledge, non-Western philosophies, the holistic well-being of mind and body, health and longevity, and scientific discoveries, as it is with the institutions, rituals, and doctrines of religious traditions.[2] Modernity did not render religion obsolete, and spirituality now occupies a place in vernacular culture as internal, subjective, and personal experience—an open-ended sense of the sacred (Zinnbauer and Pargament 25–26).[3] At the level of people's experience, the categories are convenient but artificial. What matters is that people sense something that is not of the material world, yet fully present to consciousness, mind, and body. This is the presence that troubles performance.

A sense of spirit meets material culture in this-worldly practices (Heelas, *Spiritualities of Life* 174), which can be read as performative. Theories of performance provide a lens for viewing spirituality across a wide range of social and discursive practices: institutions, organizations, communities, belief systems, texts, dress codes, festivals, rituals, myths, public ceremonies, political ideologies, performed religiosity, and so on.[4] The frame of performance positions the viewer as a critical observer of material culture who need not accept people's beliefs or experiences as evidence that gods, spirits, a numinous domain, or ghosts exist. The frame also shows a social world in which religion, spirituality, and secularity are now mutually dependent categories.[5]

The proliferation of spiritual practices in the United States has without question opened social space for "interaction and communication" around spirituality (Besecke, "Seeing Invisible Religion" 91), where practices can be analyzed as a function of social conditions and discourses (Hammer 52).[6] People's claims to the authority of subjective experience, reliance on the self as a source of spiritual knowledge, and the feeling of direct contact with the divine or sacred have little status in critical strategies that privilege observation of the material social world.[7] Yet people may sense material culture, language, and bodies upon which performance depends as infused with spirit. Countering the idea that the structuring power of religious belief and ritual mitigates confusion, spirituality in practices such as neopagan earth worship or channeling spirit guides may rely on the ambiguity of their sensed experience (rather than received doctrine) for knowledge of the sacred, divinity, or a dimension of spirit. Theories of performance can easily situate this "open-ended spirituality" in the materiality of culture and social practices, but how can the view of material culture as performative access spirituality?[8]

I want to suggest that we consider how people's sense of *an ultimate, ineffable, unseen presence of some kind* informs the bodies, texts, and objects we take as performing. Here is a more concrete example of the problem spirituality poses to performance. A valued sense in kundalini yoga is that of a strong energy twisting upward from the base of the spine. A critical observer of a kundalini practitioner might construe the gestures, physical movements, facial expressions, gong, and white clothing as performative. A critical observer might understand the practice as a repeatable "performance of kundalini rising" that references other kundalini "performances" and is constructed by a discourse on kundalini yoga. However, what the practitioner's body looks like to others or in a reading of kundalini yoga practice as performative might be irrelevant to the spiritual practice. Whereas an observer sees reality in the material presence of the body, the sense of energy rising confirms a reality of energetic presence for the practitioner. How might incorporating this experiential presence alter the conventional view of bodies in performance?

Embodied practices such as tai chi, yoga, kirtan, sacred drumming, ecstatic dance, energy healing (e.g., Reiki), and meditation techniques (e.g., Vipassana) might all appear to "perform spirituality." Yet the very idea of "performing" might be anathema to a spiritual practice. The materiality and visibility of the body we call "performance" may in fact be a by-product of the particular sense of spirit practitioners cultivate. Another example of the interpretive problem spirituality poses to performance might be a public afternoon tai chi practice in an American city park. This public practice can easily be read as performance. It makes a statement about Chinese cultural identity (whether as cultural authenticity or as "performing China"). The practice might be read as evidence of globalization or cosmopolitanism (cultural hybridity), or as a demonstration of resistance to the presumed stress of modern, urban life (an exotic mind-body-spirit amalgam). Participants doing a public tai chi practice could be read as performing their own social identities in the clothing they wear—the casual shorts of a passerby, the business suit of an executive on a break, or the yoga gear of someone with time and money to cultivate a style of alternative athleticism. In the logic of performativity, a popular book on tai chi in the health and well-being or New Age section of a chain bookstore performs a particular formation of tai chi for its market: pastoral imagery, health benefits, and a description of it as an ancient path to spiritual wisdom in the modern world. A cultural critic might read the tai chi participants' bodies as texts, their half-closed eyes and slightly downturned mouths as affected sincerity communicating a culturally constructed desire for sensations of "bliss" or "inner peace."

What the performance paradigm does not see, and what I want to bring into discussion, is the embodied sensibilities the practice cultivates. However rich an analysis of the performative aspects of a public tai chi practice might be, the practice itself might engage people's physiological and cognitive capacities in ways that are no less important simply because they cannot be seen. How might people's sense of chi, or "energy," be incorporated into discussions that rely on visibility and materiality?

The question asks for reconsideration of embodiment and performance in relation to people's sense of spiritual presence. The actions we observe and read as performative are not only written *on* the body, but *from* people's bodies. Certainly, the observable effects of internal sensations associated with spiritual experience can be codified and reproduced as theatrically inflected performances of spirituality, absent any internal sensation at all. In the example of tai chi above, people perform cultural codes and constructed meanings at the same time they may or may not sense what might be described as "spirit" in the slow patterns of movement. This is the classic problem with taking the body's external signs as evidence of any kind of "true" spiritual experience (see chapter 1). Bodies falling into trance, seeing visions, or communicating with spirits can all be observed as performances, and the paradigm can dismiss experiences such as communicating with spirits in a séance or faith healing as performative fakery.

However, there is also a possibility that bodies we observe as performing may be responding to something observers cannot detect by sight. If we assume people's sense of spirit might infuse performance, then what we observe as performative—the head rolling back in trance, a person's gaze fixing on an invisible ghost, eyelids fluttering in meditation, for example—might be interpreted as a body's observable response to that sense. The responses may be no more or less performative than a body responding to a muscle cramp or nausea. What, then, does performance tell us about spirituality?

THE PROBLEM OF BINDING KNOWING TO SHOWING

Performativity, as an interpretive or analytical paradigm, binds *knowing* to *showing* (see chapter 4). Knowledge, performativity insists, comes from what we can see, hear, touch, and perhaps taste or smell. Performance asserts that we know by doing, by observing, what people do and by reading what we observe. By binding *knowing* to *showing*, performativity sees matter, but not what people sense as spirit. Rather, the performance paradigm constructs spirituality in its own image: as material form.

This construction is evident various ways. As the domain of the expressive rather than the rational, the performing arts (dance, music, theater, and by extension, painting, sculpture, literature) have been interpreted as the material forms of internal experiences.[9] Aesthetics, for example, renders spirituality as a particular kind of affect produced by artistic performance.[10]

Modern theater practitioners have long explored the potential for performance to reconstitute religious rituals and beliefs, in the process sacralizing theater without affirming the sacred. Peter Brook's Holy Theatre, Jerzy Grotowski's Paratheater, Eugenio Barba's cross-cultural preexpressive psychophysical techniques, and numerous other modern theatrical theories (many in the legacy of Antonin Artaud) impart a metaphysical quality to theatrical performance. Modern techniques for realistic acting that emphasize actors' "inner work" similarly serve the act of performance, the investment in being seen.[11] These approaches to theater locate meaning in the shared performer-to-audience relationship and the material presence of actors' bodies. Still, knowing spirituality remains bound to the theatrical showing.

The theoretical frames provided by postmodernism and poststructuralism also contribute to an approach to performance as visible and material by calling attention to how performance structures knowledge. In the gap between representations and referents, for example, analysis privileges language and expressive forms but eschews knowledge people might derive from a sense of connection with the sacred, received knowledge, or inner wisdom. Psychoanalysis, another prominent frame for performance analysis, constructs people's inner lives in a language of divided subjects, projected egos, and repressed desires rather than inner wisdom or insight. In these frameworks, the futility of longing for unmediated access to truth deconstructs claims to authentic experience, including those of spiritual experience.[12] Even the postmodern effort to replace positivist objectivity with neutrality establishes expectations for what constitutes knowledge and rejects what falls outside those expectations.[13]

Performativity, as a strategy for interpretation and analysis with roots in practice and theory, pries art and aesthetics away from spirituality. Performativity focuses on how performances and texts *do* things in a culture, how language and performances construct knowledge, how events and texts signify in relation to each other, how personal experience is performed through politics and identity markers, and how bodies function in signifying systems. The materiality of religion's texts, rituals, buildings, and social organization can be analyzed productively as performative, even theatrical, across multiple genres in multiple registers. Painting and paintings, sculpting and sculptures, singing and songs, writing and poetry, preaching and sacred texts, walking a labyrinth and the labyrinth itself, dramas and theatrical performances, attending a religious theme park and the theme park itself, and rituals are all recognizably performative.

By binding the possibility of internally sensed spirituality to the interplay of words, objects, and bodies, and then positing that interplay in the materiality of culture, performativity constitutes the real in what is observable.[14] It provides a lens for interpreting religious art—the emotional effect of a Christian Easter pageant or the otherworldly sounds of Tibetan Buddhist overtone singing.[15] Through this lens, people's dress, gestures, physical postures, body markings, behaviors, customs, rituals, and symbolic systems all perform religious identity. Wearing a hijab or a cross in Paris, for example, takes on political, social, and historical significance as a performance of religious belief. This lens sees how religious institutions reproduce power relations in political systems in the performance of rising smoke that signals the election of a new pope, the display of a Nativity scene on public ground in the United States, or the sale of objects sacred to Hopi people as art.

A critical observer looking through this lens need not accept religious or spiritual beliefs to study them. Observations such as "Witches *believe* that spells can cure or cause illness," "Charismatic Christians *believe* that Jesus has saved them from sin," or "The Yolma people *believe* they can talk to the spirits of their ancestors" slip easily into analytical or interpretive writing as descriptions of others' cognitive leaps into domains of spirit. Acknowledgment of someone else's belief does not require an observer to accept whatever sensibilities might accompany those beliefs (the sense of connecting with supernatural forces to cast a spell, the ecstasy of divine love, the sense of a spirit presence, and so on).

By focusing on words, actions, and objects (chanting spells, falling into trance, a sacred drum) rather than the internal sense that moves the action, the lens of performativity renders those sensibilities unimportant. With the surety of religious conviction, the theoretical frame of performativity shows representational strategies, asserting that there is no real to be represented, and that performance itself constitutes presence. In the wake of postmodernism, performance testifies to a lack, something absent; it is a reminder that something has slipped out of range of consciousness and must be recouped. The presence of performance is always that which it is not.

What is known and knowable in the paradigm of performativity, then, is performance. Theories of antimimesis, the death of theatrical character, and the collapse of representation have tried to work out of or against this problem. Still, the radical presence of human bodies performing in a social world remains invested in the referential capacities of representation and the mental processes that make critical distance and representation possible, necessary, and ultimately desired. The paradigm of performance first produces vernacular culture as an object of study, then reifies its own privileged status when it insists on material presence. How does the insistence on material presence meet the ineffable sense of spirit?

PRESENCE AND REPRESENTATION: A KOAN

Theoretical moves in performance studies have introduced embodiment into the logocentric orientation of Western culture, focusing on performer-spectator interaction as mutually constitutive of performance and exploring performance's cognitive dimensions. These approaches to performance have helped shift the representational model. However, I would argue that a representational model of the mind still supports a view of the social world as performative (see chapter 3). Familiar formulations "performing spirituality," "spirituality as performance," and "performance of spirituality" seem to accommodate people's sense of spirit. These formulations rely on a representational model, which may occlude serious consideration of spirituality as a component of performance. However, as philosopher Alva Noë suggests, "The idea that presence is representation is a bad idea" (*Varieties of Presence* 30).

A model of a mind that projects and interprets representations of an external world has long been under revision. Francisco J. Varela, Evan Thompson, and Eleanor Rosch have noted a gradual reorientation in Western thinking "away from the idea of the world as independent and extrinsic to the idea of a world as inseparable from the structure of these processes of self-modification," and toward mental processes that "do not operate by representation" (139–40). The model of the mind as a theater has given way to models of consciousness in which people's mental processes are not separate from the body that gazes at a world of material forms.[16] An embodied mind interacting with the world proposes that the experiential "inside" of mental processes is as present as the material forms we observe around us. Philosophical or theological frameworks, as well as vernacular spiritualities, might well identify this sense of presence as spirit (Rolston 29).

Vernacular culture has not abandoned the metaphysics of presence, even when spirituality goes against cultural norms that emphasize materialism, social performance, critique, and skepticism (Irwin 198).[17] Against the conventional critical orientation toward human experience as culturally, socially, and discursively constructed, the ways people experience spirituality refuse to be bound (at least at the level of experience) by sensory data and material conditions. People find the supernatural in nature, metaphysics in the materiality of culture, and the numinous within the self. Vernacular practices may not hinge spirituality on the axis of representation. The sensibilities they cultivate may not align with readings of people's bodies, texts, and staged events as representational performance.[18] Taking the presence of spirits seriously thus requires thinking at odds with most critical strategies.

The independent existence of spirit is intellectually difficult for most critical perspectives. Inquiries into spiritual practices need not defend, define, or explain spirituality. Interpretive projects need not argue for the reality of the sacred or divine, or that spirituality exceeds or eludes representation and therefore cannot be discussed productively. Inquiry need neither become advocacy nor abandon analysis for description. The question is how people's internal sense of the divine, sacred, or numinous as presence can be *performative* if it cannot be made present in material terms (performed) and observed. Conversely, how can this sense of spirit be *observed* (and therefore known) if it cannot be performed?

As a way of investigating spirituality and religion in the paradigm of performance, I want to suggest that insofar as people continue to cultivate a sense of spirit in performance practices, material form need not constitute all possibilities for presence. We narrow our options when "performance" is bound *only* to what can be shown and described in the terms of matter and perceptual data. Expressive forms informed by a sense of spirit might add to the ways aesthetic traditions constitute music, dance, visual art, and theater, and the ways theory constitutes performance as cultural politics and representational practices.[19] People's sense of the numinous might constitute what we see and hear in terms other than those of the observable, material world. Expressions of spiritual experience may not be motivated by the theoretical drive of the theatrical avant-garde to shatter aesthetic consciousness or sacralize theater. Spiritual practitioners' language might not be a discourse on the spiritual in art but the movement of a sense of spirit into communication.

At the very least, we limit the possibilities for performance if we dismiss outright what people sense as spirit on its own terms in service of habitual skepticism of spirituality and religious belief. How can we engage critically with practices that do not depend on the five external senses, representational mental processes, and symbol systems to construct knowledge? We might seek how people's sense of spiritual presence comes *through* the materiality of performance, through the cultural signs and codes, and expressive forms we observe and analyze.

BODIES, DISCOURSE, AND SPIRIT

The last three decades of performance theory have shown that bodies are always enmeshed in economic and political forces, informed by culture, and written over by discourses of power. The awareness that we participate in and engage discourses is often taken to mean that we are constructed by them. Spirit, from the perspective of people invested in cultivating the sense of the numinous, is not necessarily limited to distinctions such as "internal" and "external" or "self" and "other." Taking spirituality not as symbolic representation but as a kind of corporeal engagement with a sacred or divine dimension thus gives spirituality a double presence in the performance paradigm: both a material performance and the practitioners' sense of an ineffable, spiritual presence.

If performance that originates in people's sense of spirit is not just hermeneutic hype and heightened emotional affect, then there is no lack or absence in a performer's body and the materiality of a spiritual practice. A body in performance can be acknowledged as "a medium for the divine" if we are willing to ask how that works (Sachs Norris, "Examining the Structure" 184). We must be willing to ask *how* a shaman's drum is a conduit for spirit communication or *how* a dancer's silk veil engages maya (the veil of reality) in addition to recognizing that performers believe their practices involve the presence of spirit.

The practitioners of music and dance discussed in chapter 2 do not try to work outside of representation in any theoretical way: representation simply is not an issue for them. Their practices, texts, and framed performances are the means by which they cultivate the capacity to sense a numinous dimension. The presence of spirit is understood to be in the body but not of the body, in the mind but not of the mind.

Interpreting practices that are informed by spiritual presence, whether within or outside religious traditions, requires attention to the ways people cultivate spirituality and articulate the knowledge they derive from practice. What do they do (dance, drum, chant, sit still, pray, etc.)? How do these actions generate the sense of the numinous? For practitioners, spirituality may be real but not material; spirit may not be limited to embodied processes such as thinking or feeling; knowledge outside the perceptible world of matter may be accessible via thought, feeling, and experience; and there may be no presumed gap between knowledge derived from an internal sense of spirit and its material expression.

Richard Schechner identifies the "main characteristic" of performance as behavior recovered from an originary moment and reproduced in an already existing form ("Restoration of Behavior" 442). Many vernacular spiritual practices describe the experiential collapse of corporeality and cognition, even when the culture otherwise separates them (for example, physical exercise vs. mental work). In many vernacular spiritual practices this collapse is a primary marker of spiritual experience: the experience of body-mind uniting with spirit. How does this sense of spirit, which is grounded in practitioners' experiences but unlikely a critical observer's, affect readings of spiritual practices as performative? How might we imagine such a sense of spirit as a characteristic that renews each performative moment rather than referring to an originary moment, and re-creates itself in every gesture, word, sound, and image of a performance?

CRITICAL APPROACHES TO THE SENSE OF SPIRIT IN THE MATTER OF PERFORMANCE

Taking people's internal sense of a numinous, ineffable presence seriously reorients how we view texts, bodies, and objects to include people's sense of a very real nonmaterial dimension to performance practices without resorting to mind-body dualism or religious advocacy. Theoretical reorientations to person-world interaction and the significance of internal experience are evident in several fields upon which this study draws.

The model of the human mind as an internal theater that represents reality has given way. Newer models broaden our understanding of how seemingly oppositional mental capacities—such as computational thinking, flights of imagination, and a sense of spirit—might share common neurological processes rather than occupy regions of the brain (see chapter 3). Mark C. Taylor advocates shifting to a "hierarchical yet nonlinear" model of cognition that incorporates "intuition, perception, consciousness, self-consciousness, and reason" equally and without prejudice (18). Such approaches to theorizing cognition open space in humanities inquiries for considering people's sense of spirit in general. To the point of this project, they open space for how people's sense of spirit informs the materiality of performance.

An integrative approach to human thought, culture, and behavior such as Taylor's suggests a more tolerant approach to spirituality within analytical and critical frameworks, which is the project here as well. Taylor proposes theorizing religion with a critical perspective that can "bring together structuralism and poststructuralism through an appropriation of the theory of complex adaptive systems to interpret the emergence, development, and operational logic of religion" (12). Rather than taking performativity as a paradigm that shows spirituality to be a discursive or cultural construct, integrative approaches such as Taylor's invite a perspective that understands the material forms of performance as emergent from people's internal sense of spiritual presence. Spirituality, in this way of thinking, might be treated as a human capacity on the order of cognition or emotion; spirituality need not be bracketed as antithetical to rational inquiry. Rather, the sense of spirit people experience, and from which they develop knowledge, might be integrated into studies of how human minds and bodies creatively *produce* culture (as opposed to assuming spirituality is a cultural or discursive construction).

The nondualist, nonrepresentational account of human-world interaction, subjective experience, and meaning-making proposed by Maurice Merleau-Ponty in his later works moves toward embodied spirituality. The approach through phenomenology allows for an ephemeral aspect of human experience in the interplay between bodies and culture by working out relationships between corporeal sensation, perception, rational thought, and the material world (Gibbs 25; Slingerland 88). Phenomenology offers one point of entry for performance theory and spirituality, though as a philosophical system, it does not posit a dimension of spirit or lapse into theology (Barua 27, 41).[20] As an antidote to a theological interpretation of human being and interaction with the world, philosophy does not move into the territory of the numinous, the sacred, the divine, or spirit. The "theological turn" in the work of philosophers such as Jean-Luc Marion moves phenomenology toward that border.

Religious studies has wrestled with spirituality in many of the same frameworks that structure performance studies: cultural materialism, biological determinism, naturalism, mind-body dualism, and internal sensation. From religious studies, Anne Taves's summary below traces the main approaches to studying spiritual experience and the material world, and the consequences of their logic:

> If language, tradition, and culture constitute experience, then experiences could be explained in socio-cultural terms; if some of the more unusual experiences are cross-culturally stable, then more unusual psychological processes and brain states presumably play a causal role as well. Scholars in the humanities generally valued linguistic and cultural explanations because they emphasized cultural differences that psychological and neurological explanations tended to obscure. In arguing for the cross-cultural stability of certain types of experiences that they construed as mystical, the neo-perennialists bucked the dominant

> trend in the humanities. They did so, not because they were eager to embrace the naturalism or, as they would say, the "materialistic reductionism" of the sciences, but because they were sympathetic to the idea that consciousness itself might be separable from matter and able to exist independently. In this view, consciousness itself is potentially very special, perhaps so special that it exists as an absolute apart from the body, mediated by—rather than a product of—brain processes, and highly amenable to mystical or spiritual ascriptions. (Taves, *Religious Experience Reconsidered* 88)[21]

From this labyrinth of competing theoretical positions, an approach to spirituality emerging in religious studies speaks to the kind of critical engagement with material culture and embodiment that already characterizes performance studies.

Jeffrey Kripal calls for "radical critical thought and normative debate about religious and spiritual matters, linked to a deep appreciation for and dialogue with the experiential resources of the traditions themselves" (*The Serpent's Gift* 13–14). Kristy Nabhan-Warren asks that scholars of religion "turn to their bodies as sources of deep knowledge" and "take embodied ethnography seriously when they write up their findings" toward scholarship that does not privilege "spectatorship only" (381). Kimerer LaMothe points out that scholarly writing about spirituality and religion requires engaging one's body, just as religious practices require bodily engagement. Her critique of disembodied scholarly practice, like the critique offered in this book, seeks "the possibility of attending to moments of religious life that have been traditionally left behind in the search for phenomena that look and act and can be translated like texts" ("What Bodies Know about Religion" 580). These approaches suggest a willingness to allow alternative modes of knowledge to inform scholarly praxis, which is the project undertaken here.

Still, taking spirituality seriously reveals deeply held biases in critical work and presses the boundaries of reasoned inquiry. It destabilizes the privilege of observation and the authority of interpretation. As Robert Orsi writes, scholarly inquiries into religion and spirituality require "experiencing one's own world from the disorienting perspective of the other . . . and this necessarily entails risk, vulnerability, vertigo; it invites anger and creates distress" (204). Anger and distress might indeed be a fitting response to an inquiry that allows people's sense of spirit to orient an understanding of performance.

CRITICAL LANGUAGE AND THE LANGUAGE OF SPIRIT

Studying religious texts (including doctrines, dogma, histories, narratives, myths, lyrics, proclamations, wisdom writings, and scriptures) has traditionally provided an entry point into spiritual experience. Language, a form of symbolic logic, remains the most prominent medium for critical analysis and abstract, conceptual knowledge. The language of critique assumes representation and interpretation. Even critical studies of New Age and alternative spiritualities rely primarily on spoken language and written texts to identify a contemporary discourse on spirituality.

The affective, subjective, and participatory turns in humanities scholarship recognize that life praxis requires multiple modes of knowledge—corporeal, experiential, nonlinguistic, imagistic, and sensory. These turns are reintroducing possibilities for better understanding how language works as a conduit for engagement with knowledge rather than its final (if contingent and contested) form.

The easy assumption that language expresses people's spiritual sensibilities reinforces the logocentricity that characterizes Western thought. However, there is an important shift to be urged here. If spirituality is sensed in the body and language emerges from an embodied mind, spoken and written language might also be interpreted as embodiments of spirituality. This is a very old notion of sacred words, reimagined from modern ideas of neuroplasticity and person-world interaction. If the mental processes of cognition work jointly with bodily senses and feelings, languages of spirituality might not only be symbolic, representational, signifying, reporting, metaphoric, or descriptive. Language might literally emerge from a sense of spirit, impossible without that sense (see chapter 3).

The connection of language to the sense of spirit requires attention in a paradigm that separates representation from referent. A critical approach to spiritually informed performance might consider that language (even when it is poetic or metaphorical) can function for people in one-to-one correspondence with the sense of spirit. There may be no irony or critical distance; sincerity in expression might not mark naïveté, but wisdom and truth. The language of spirituality puts performance in tension with what *real* means, thwarting expectations for material evidence and threatening to substitute feeling for thinking by insisting on presence that cannot be observed. Language might be a way for practitioners to cultivate as well as articulate their sense of spirit. The language of their texts may function no less experientially than the physical practices of drumming and dancing. The specificity and ambiguity of the spirituality may require, then, a shift in how we "read" practitioners' texts as well as observe or participate in their practices (see chapter 2).

A nonhierarchical approach to knowledge can account for the overlap between the sense of an embodied self and the presence practitioners experience as spiritual. Though the formation of concepts in language has had a privileged position in Western culture, the hierarchy is much less evident within the human brain (see chapter 3). From the point of view of fMRI (functional magnetic resonance imaging), the primacy placed on language and symbolic logic in critical analysis is somewhat artificial (perhaps culturally constructed).

What happens when we treat cognitive processes normally associated with logic and language on the same level as those that produce the images, sounds, gestures, and physical movements that cultivate people's sense of spirit? If we take people's internal sense of spirit as the foundation for a performance practice, and that sense involves cognition and corporeality collapsing into each other, how then do we read practitioners' language of spirituality (see chapter 2)? If the human brain's capacity for symbol-making is inextricable from the neural activity involved in emotions, feelings, and other noncognitive sensations, what is the relationship between a person's internal sense of spirit and language, which we read as performative?

In experiential practice, an embodied sense of spirit narrows the theoretical gaps between representation and referent, external and internal, subjective and objective so easily assumed in the paradigm of performance. The sense of spirit as presence may render the conventional, poststructuralist understanding of language in completely different colors. Lee Irwin observes that this sense throws those theoretical gaps into stark relief:

> By excluding the subjective and private from the discourses of empirical analysis, metaphysical claims by members of various world religions have been marginalized by many academic scholars as myth and fantasy or characterized as mere "folklore" and often dismissed as the detritus of misguided subjectivisms, no longer relevant in a rational, public, measurable, externalized world of observable facts. (197)

Here we come to a juncture. We can critique experiential spirituality through performance theory and reproduce the paradigm, or we can ask what value people's experiences hold *for* performance theory. This productive tension is heightened when we are willing to confront phenomena that do *not* make sense in our analytical paradigm and we refuse to let the paradigm explain those phenomena. What relationship does an inner, spiritual life have with what is available for observation as performance? What happens when spirituality "by means of performance" becomes performance "by means of spirit"?

MIND IN BODY IN SPIRIT IN PERFORMANCE

Today, an "inner life" is visible. With modern technology, we look inside the human body for the physiological workings of people's mental—and spiritual—experiences. As Taves points out, pictures or graphs of brain activity alone cannot tell us how people interpret certain experiences as specifically spiritual (see chapter 3). Culture and discourse help us there. Conversely, if we reduce people's spiritual experience to cultural and discursive constructions, we do not account for spirituality as an embodied, and frankly real, experience (see chapter 4). Yet, if we posit spirit as some kind of consciousness that is separable from the body, or as a transcendental realm accessible to human consciousness, we end up right back in some kind of subject dualism (see chapter 1).

While we analyze the diversity of cultural and social identities with gusto in the exhaustive parsing of cultural difference, the diversity of people's inner worlds is rarely acknowledged. How can we talk about spirituality as and in performance without reducing it to the familiar terms of the material world we so easily observe and parse? One way is by thinking of performance as a membrane between the interior of the human body (the site of sensation and its interpretation) and observable, material reality (culture, social interaction).

What happens when we give people's inner lives ontological status in the body's materiality without dismissing that interiority as the naive construction of an imaginary self? Might there be other kinds of relationships between performative signs and people's claims to experience of a numinous dimension? What can we ask about the relationship between sensations people experience within their bodies and what those bodies *do* in culture? And what kinds of epistemologies are emerging in this postsecular condition to accommodate whatever it is in people's brains that keeps seeking—perhaps finding—the numinous? How does the performativity of bodies and texts contribute to the ways people experience spirituality as an inner life, or an inner life as spiritual? How do bodies and texts perform spirituality as an internal experience if that experience is ineffable? How is the complex of internal sensations that coalesces into spiritual experience affected by the materiality of cultural environments?

These questions begin to shift focus from how performance indexes spirituality, spiritual experience, or discourses on spirituality to (1) how framed performances and texts allow people to make sense out of sensations and identify them as spiritual experiences and (2) how performance allows people to develop and disseminate epistemologies that originate in internal sensation by engaging material culture in the practice of spirituality.

Situating performativity within the subjective, affective, and participatory turns in recent humanities inquiries, which attend to an inward-facing tendency in vernacular culture, opens possibilities for expanding the performance paradigm.[22] Performativity can become a strategy for exploring the exchange between people's internal sensations (awareness, thoughts, consciousness, physical feelings) and the expressive forms that define human culture (symbol systems, images, artistic performances, texts, practices, discourses, etc.). "Performance" might be reimagined as a permeable, vibrating membrane between people's internal sense of spirit and the materiality of culture.

INEFFABILITY IN THE MATERIALITY OF PERFORMANCE

The effort to bring people's inner, spiritual experiences into the critical perspective of performance analysis does not seek to recoup the specter of the spiritual in art, rehearse an apologia for the authority of mystical experience, or spin more narratives of haunting. Nor does this effort try to reclaim the metaphysics of presence, revive transnormative notions of an essential self or soul, or reconstruct the autonomy of the Western ego-self. The discussion here does not advocate the perennialist orientation of transpersonal psychology or reify subjective internal experience. After this litany of apophatic statements, the positive theoretical move is to expand what performativity can do as a strategy for inquiry into material culture.

Rethinking performativity from the practitioners' point of view may reveal performance as a process by which people negotiate their inner lives, the material worlds they live in, and their bodies. How can performance theory expand to include the ways people formulate knowledge from internal sensations and allow that knowledge to structure performance? How do we connect the emphasis on interiority in so many spiritual practices with how verbal and bodily expressions perform actions? Rethinking requires in part becoming comfortable with analogous, ambiguous, and imagistic modes of thinking.

The ontological status of spirituality is outside the scope of this book, but there are three guiding premises for the approach. First, spirituality (the sense of spirit or spiritual experience) can be thought of nonreligiously as the internal sense of something ineffable, numinous, or divine in the world. How one person can know exactly what another person is feeling, thinking, or experiencing internally is, of course, well-explored territory. Because the performance paradigm privileges observation, the second premise is that people's bodies respond to internal sensations (such as the grip of a strong emotion or the struggle to form an abstract thought in words) in ways other people can observe. Internal sensations may motivate gestures, facial expressions, and bodily movements independent of reference to the cultural norms that would render them performative.

Given the first two premises, the third is that spiritually can originate in internal sensations even as practitioners engage in the meaning systems of culture and discourse we are accustomed to reading as performative. I am willing to define spirituality as an internal sense of something people identify as distinct from the material world and to assume that their bodies in action (here, drumming and dancing), their words (written or spoken), and the objects with which they cultivate spirituality (drums, veils) emerge out of that sense. In this way, spirituality constructs performance.

CHAPTERS

Chapter 1 analyzes the impediments to taking spirituality on its own terms as a kind or quality of internal experience in the Western orientation to knowledge. If spirits cannot exist in epistemological paradigms, such as performativity, that are dependent on observation and analysis of matter, what happens when we encounter framed performances and texts shaped by epistemologies of spirit? One response to this question proposes that what is available for observation as performance is the visible evidence of internal, physiological processes. A body-in-performance is responding to internal sensations, even as we interpret a body as performing cultural codes. Chapter 2 responds to this question with descriptions of two contemporary vernacular spiritual practices. The question becomes, how do we incorporate an orientation to knowledge that recognizes that people's inner lives and a nonmaterial reality are crucial to studying human culture as performative?

Chapters 1 and 2 take spirituality seriously as a way people orient themselves to and in the material world of bodies and culture, positing knowledge as an internal sensibility of a nonmaterial reality. Chapter 3 starts with the materiality of the body, looking to the interior for the processes by which what we take as performative (in some representational or referential engagement with culture) can also be understood as coextensive with the neurological conditions practitioners cultivate. Neurological correlates to spirituality alone do not explain how people translate internal sensations into meaningful spiritual experiences. At issue are the internal, primarily neurological processes associated with spirituality that undo the representational and referential processes associated with performance.

Chapter 4 looks at the cultural resources practitioners draw on to define sensations as spiritual and communicate in meaningful ways. How do people use the conventions of performance, including its materiality, reliance on observation, and traditional techniques of representing and referencing, as a means of putting spirituality into the immediate culture? Chapter 4 reverses chapter 3's analysis of how internal sensations generate and inform performance by examining how cultural resources identify internal sensations as spiritual and ascribe meaning to the experience of those internal sensations. Spiritual performance emerges not as a hermeneutic process of expressing what people feel inside and "press out" by performing it for others with affective intentions; rather, spiritual performance emerges in the interplay between what is internal and external to the body. Performance becomes the process of that exchange between internal sensations of the numinous and embodied engagement with culture. Chapter 5 brings the alterity of spirituality into the framework of performance analysis.

TAXONOMY

Words perform differently in different academic domains. Working cross-disciplinarily often involves stretching or contesting the assumptions held in one field or another, while changing or narrowing the accepted meanings of particular terms for others. In the interest of clarity, I have tried to be consistent in the use of terms that might otherwise shift meaning as they migrate across disciplines and traverse the chapters of this book. The taxonomy below may help ameliorate, though not entirely avoid, problems of clarity.

Spirituality refers to people's internal sense of a divine, numinous, sacred, or ultimate reality. Spirituality, as practitioners encounter it, is ineffable. For the purposes of this study, spirituality felt as nonmaterial yet experientially present is the main quality of interest. Vernacular spiritualities at one extreme can involve antisocial or destructive behavior, and purportedly spiritual experiences can be classified as mental aberrations when they manifest in delusional or disruptive social behavior. The practices considered here are oriented around a positive, socially engaged ethics grounded in a spiritual sensibility. Part of their relevance as a site of inquiry is the ease with which they operate in contemporary Western culture. *Spiritual practices* are the actions people do, including writing and reading, to cultivate spirituality as an internal experience. *Spiritual experience* refers to people's awareness of internal sensations as specifically spiritual (rather than, for example, emotional or psychological affect) and the basis for knowledge about the world and themselves as spiritual.

Interiority refers to physiological processes of human bodies and the sensations people identify as experiences or experiential knowledge. In practice, interior sensations might include a wide range of sensed mental and physical processes: linguistic thoughts, images, emotions, body awareness, or feelings. All of these might constitute people's sense of an *inner life*. *Inner* and *internal* throughout this study thus refer to what people sense as within themselves, not the traditional boundary between the inside of the body or the contents of the mind and the external world. *Interior* refers specifically to the interior of the physical body (see chapter 3). *Inner*, *internal*, and *interiority* all presume that what different discourses and disciplines call consciousness, awareness, mind, and spiritual or mystical experience are embodied, and that the body is situated within and engaged with its surroundings.[23]

Sensation and *sense* refer to what is happening within people's minds and bodies. I include physical sensations associated with emotions and feelings as well as interoceptive sensing of interior biological processes, proprioceptive sensing of muscles and the body in space, and the more familiar exteroceptive perception of information accessed by the five sense organs. Sensation also includes mental processes, which encompass representational thinking and reasoning, processing sensory information, nonlinguistic awareness, recognition of emotions and feelings, and observation of the self. Mental sensations can also include the more general sense of being conscious or aware, processes such as relaxing the mind, releasing mental constructs, "letting go," watching one's thoughts, and witnessing one's self.

Expression, meaning "to press out," can suggest that a performance practice is an individual's personal experience pressed out in some performative way as an articulation of the experience or insight. *Expressive forms* are the objects, events, texts, and so forth that practitioners produce. In performance studies, *expressive forms* are by definition performative. I am avoiding referring to practitioners' concerts or events as performances in favor of the more inclusive and less confusing term *expressive forms.* The limits of *expression* for this project, however, are twofold. First, expression is generally understood as unidirectional, moving from a person's internal experience into a form. Second, expression assumes the primacy of individual experience and its reception. Though individuality and internal experience have, since James, distinguished spiritual experience from the institutional, doctrinal, performative, and historical characteristics of religious traditions, I reinforce in this project that contemporary vernacular spiritualities can be social and communal. *Expression* is also easily confused with creative expression, which is not what either of the practices discussed here are about (though spirituality and creativity are often linked in other practices and discourses). The term *expression* is thus used sparingly and specifically.

Affect, as noted above, refers to emotional responses to configurations of visible and audible stimuli, such as those produced by framed performances.[24] Affect in an older usage implies an internal, individual response to a work of art's aesthetics (as in Suzanne Langer's *Feeling and Form* [1953]). The current use of affect looks for the ways performances move people to social or political action (as in Jill Dolan's *Utopia in Performance: Finding Hope in the Theatre* [2005]). Affect is grounded in emotion, which can be a component of spiritual experience but does not completely cover the range of sensations people associate with spirituality. It also implies the desire of a performer to elicit a response from observers. Affect may be the connective tissue between a performer and an audience, but because it preserves an observer-observed binary and limits interiority to emotional or intellectual responses, affect does not go far enough to get at spirituality as a kind of internal experience.

Formulations of spiritual knowledge or *formulations of spirituality* refer to articulations of spiritual experience as epistemologies for life praxis (as distinct from Foucauldian discursive formations). The formulations of knowledge these practitioners derive from internal experiences make spirituality normative. Formulation here refers primarily to linguistic articulations of spirituality such as aphorisms, narratives, or statements of fact (for example, "You are a child of the universe"). Language takes responsibility for articulating what the shared or individual experience means, and presenting the performance practice as embodying a kind of spiritual knowledge. Formulations of spirituality, as I use the phrase here, come from the sensations of the practice. *Discourse* is used in the Foucauldian sense. A discourse on spirituality brings spirituality into existence as a thing or object in the public domain, and formulations of spiritual knowledge can be read as discursive formations. However, the formulations of spiritual knowledge articulated by practitioners generate discourses *from*, rather than *on*, spirituality. This is a critical point of difference in how this study frames spiritually informed performance.

Culture is used here not in the sense of a civilization but in reference to the orientations (traditions, customs, languages, beliefs) held in common by social groups. Culture here refers not only to literary and artistic traditions through which practitioners formulate and cultivate spiritual epistemologies or to the myths and rituals associated with religion. Culture refers to socially transmitted ideas, practices, ways of perceiving and sensing, patterns of symbolic meaning, and assumptions of value. In keeping with the emphasis in performance studies, culture refers to material objects, practices, and the effects of power expressed in discourses and institutions. *Western* means a source of culture and intellectual tradition that derives from Europe and the United States. Unless otherwise indicated, "Western culture" or "the West" thus refers not to a specific geographic region, but to a system of meaning-making that positions spirituality (Campbell 44) (see chapter 4).

Throughout this book, I refer to human bodies holistically, assuming that the distinction between mind and body is a convention. *Body* here encompasses mental processes and physiological processes. The interior processes of human bodies and the internal sensations people experience as spirituality are in dynamic relationships with material culture; however, these relationships are not performative in the sense that culture and discourse make spirituality real or present. Performativity becomes the membrane across which the internal sensations of a body and cultural idioms interact.

CHAPTER I

Situating Performance in Spirit

I. The Trouble with Spirit

The effort to understand religious experience on its own terms in the Western thought tradition has established vocabularies for talking about spirituality. In the modern western tradition, spirit has been discussed as a numinous mystery, the Holy (Rudolph Otto); as a domain of the Sacred (Mircea Eliade); and as the private experience of the ineffable (William James), to give just three taxonomic frameworks.[1] Today, the most salient characteristic of spirituality unaffiliated with religion is the reliance on the self for the wisdom, ethics, and truths.[2] This sense of spirit is the conceptual and sensory foundation from which many people navigate the material world and social identities.[3] Performance offers a vocabulary of matter, physical space, and bodies to the study of spirituality.

However, this sense of spirit, if taken seriously, makes the materiality of performance an imperceptibly thin edge where matter meets the possibility of a numinous, ineffable, sacred domain. The habits of a critical stance toward performance interpret discourses *on* spirituality, read artistic expressions as performances *of* spirituality, or analyze spiritual practices *as* performance. This stance privileges representation over people's sense of spirit, while in practice that sense may govern the very logic of performance. How can we think about this edge from a perspective on the matter of performance as visible, material presence? The answer requires examination of the ways modern Western thought rejects or brackets spirituality, the topic of section 1 of this chapter.

EPISTEMOLOGICAL TROUBLES WITH SPIRITUALITY

From Descartes in the seventeenth century, to Kant a century later, and to contemporary investigations in phenomenology and neuroscience, Western thinking tends to posit spirituality as a phenomenon of the mind, not as an inquiry into transcendent realities.[4] Nineteenth-century psychoanalysis offered modern thinking a method that objectifies peoples' inner selves for scientific observation.[5] Spirituality as private experience can be traced through the Protestant emphasis on personal faith and unmediated connection with God.[6] Religious experience interpreted as feeling or emotion follows a trajectory from Friedrich Schleiermacher in the late eighteenth century.[7] The now iconic view of spirituality, as internal, private experience, which synthesizes all three trajectories, comes from William James's famous lectures on psychology, *Varieties of Religious Experience* (1902).[8]

Western modernism's emphasis on empirical observation shifts the kind of internal sensing associated with spirituality (feeling, intuition, insight, imagination) into aesthetics and affect.[9] In modernism, which has no place for spirits or the numinous,

> Rationalization substitutes mastery for mystery; it standardizes rules and procedures, thereby creating formal structures called bureaucracies; it encourages instrumental criteria and approaches to life; it favors rational and scientific-technical ways of knowing and ordering experience at the expense of the intuitive and non-empirical; it privileges mind over body, the cognitive over the imaginative and the emotional; its hold upon the individual is far-reaching and threatening to the human spirit. (Roof 61)

Postmodernism's assault on rational thought, syllogistic reasoning, and the power of science to reveal a natural world (including a biological body independent of culture) produced a dialogic play between solid matter and the representational capacities of the mind to break modernism's hold, but not to open space for spirituality in the boundaries of reasoned inquiry and analysis.[10]

This legacy yields analytical and interpretive methods for studying spirituality that vacillate between critical reduction and sympathetic description from a critical distance. As Jeffrey Kripal points out, the study of spirituality qua spirituality has been

> defined by a kind of Ping-Pong movement between two modes of human functioning, two sides of the brain, as it were, analogous but not identical to those associated with faith and reason. Thus, we are told that the study of religion should be about the faithful description and comparison of worldviews as members of those cultures might recognize them—a kind of cultural cheerleading. Or we are told that the study of religion should be about explaining religious myths, rituals, and beliefs in the nonreligious terms of the natural and social sciences, that is, reduced to the entirely secular processes of the psyche, society, and political control—a kind of heartless deconstruction. (*The Serpent's Gift* 12–13)[11]

Kripal's point that spirituality need not be "a zero-sum game, an either-or choice that must conclude either on the side of a faithful description of revealed truths or on the side of a materialistic reductionism," is well taken (13). Even in a materially oriented discipline like performance studies, we can think about performance in the space between describing spiritual "truths" and reducing those truths to the visible matter of performance and affect. However, the terms of spirit—ineffability, ephemerality, invisibility, sensation, insight, experience, the numinous—are not easy in any analytical paradigm invested in observing the workings of the material, social world.

THE SAFETY OF CRITICAL DISTANCE

What assumptions about spirituality does performativity, as an interpretive or critical strategy, impose on people's sense of spirit (especially people in mainstream American vernacular culture)?[12] Janelle Reinelt's broadly applicable summary of the three categories of performance shows some of those assumptions. Performance is, first and foremost, material and social and virtually everything people do, say, and write is performative (201–3).[13] Into the first category fall events people frame as performances: those that script, choreograph, paint, and otherwise represent everyday life. The frame of performance sets performers' actions apart from everyday behavior. Framed performance, even when disguised by realism or aimed at shattering social conventions, exaggerates everyday life. The framing allows for critical distance as well as aesthetic appreciation. Second is everyday life itself: practices and identities that appear to be "natural" or "normal" activities are in fact performances. Performances of everyday life can be analyzed to reveal the social norms they encode or contest. Third is language: language is the performative mechanism through which people construct reality. Language allows us to inscribe and enact normative values. Language, like framed performances and the performance of everyday life, can also be a method for analyzing and interpreting the social world. Language in particular is the means by which we translate the material presence of performance into discursive knowledge. Hence, in the study of performance we "read" vernacular culture and the products of human culture."[14]

In Reinelt's elegant summary of performance as social practice, spirituality is a ghost no one can see except those who can.[15] Theories of performance allow us to "see" and "read" spirituality in material practices such as rituals, but limit the extent to which people's sense of spirit can be incorporated into reasoned inquiry.[16] Spirituality, in or outside religion, sits beyond the conventions of thinking that bind performance to matter and knowledge to language.[17] These conventions have deep roots.

Modern thought keeps spirituality at a critical distance. Performance studies, and disciplinary methods from which it draws, can navigate around spirituality with no obligation to incorporate the knowledge people derive from spiritual traditions, practices, or experiences into reasoned inquiry. Anthropology and ethnography, for example, acknowledge the hermeneutic and functional aspects of spiritual experience. Analyses of religion and politics can reveal the role of religion in state institutions and government systems, as well as how political systems affect religious practices and beliefs.[18] Sociology and folklore can posit spirituality as a function of religious traditions, institutions, and cultural forces.[19] These methods can attend to the material effects of religious belief on social organization without directly engaging spiritual experience or belief.

As noted in the introduction, phenomenology ventures into the ephemeral aspects of first-person experience by analyzing human experience in the interplay between corporeal sensation, perception, rational thought, and the material world but does not posit spirituality as a metaphysical reality (Gibbs 25; Slingerland 88–89).[20] The discipline of religious studies, too, navigates around spirituality.[21] Religious studies can share theology's vocabulary for spirituality (the divine, the sacred, the numinous, the daimonic, mystery, transcendence, and mysticism)[22] while maintaining a critical distance that brackets spirituality as an ontological condition or foundation for knowledge-making.[23]

The sense of spirit people cultivate and express in practices such as those described in chapter 2 pushes against the borders that prescribe how we constitute knowledge from a critical distance. If we are willing to look at rituals, ceremonies, and other practices that involve people's spiritual sensibilities, we might begin by asking what knowledge derived from a sense of spirit offers interpretive and analytical methods. The question opens reasoned inquiry to influence by the knowledge people derive from a sense of spirit. This openness may be welcome, productively destabilizing, or downright dangerous, but it does expand possibilities for examining how we construct and value knowledge.

Spirituality pushes against the borders of performance studies in specific ways. Performance studies reads cultural dynamics with a "materialist concern for exposing the operations of power and oppression in society" (Carlson 184); performance studies sees not "individual expression or formal concerns but the 'making of culture'" (Carlson 178). As a paradigm for cultural analysis, performativity takes the subjective, internally sensed content of people's minds and bodies as a screen upon which people project socially grounded identities from the resources and discourses of their sociocultural environments (Carlson 51).[24] In the classic definition by Richard Schechner, performance is behavior that is replayed, restored, remembered, and reconstructed. If performance is restored behavior, it is outside the self, always in culture. "Restored behavior," Schechner writes, is

> "out there," distant from "me." It is separate and therefore can be "worked on," changed, even though it has "already happened." . . . Restored behavior is symbolic and reflexive: not empty but loaded behavior multivocally broadcasting significances. These difficult terms express a single principle: The self can act in/as another; the social or transindividual self is a role or set of roles. Symbolic and reflexive behavior is the hardening into theatre of social, religious, aesthetic, medical, and educational process. Performance means: never for the first time. It means: for the second to the *n*th time. Performance is "twice-behaved behavior." (*Between Theatre and Anthropology* 36)

The study of performance as social practice is embedded in an epistemology that keeps a distance from knowledge claims informed by spirituality.[25] A critical stance is suspicious of subjective experience in general and transcendence in particular.[26] Performance studies thus readily situates vernacular spirituality in and as social action that involves repetition, role-playing, signification, and re-presentation. Spiritually informed performances such as rituals, religious theater, or sacred music appear as social practices. Though people's beliefs might be acknowledged in a reasoned inquiry, there is no critical imperative to investigate the possibility that participants' claims to knowledge of an ineffable presence or numinous reality might govern what we see and hear as performance.[27]

SPIRITUALITY FROM A CRITICAL DISTANCE

The overview of disciplinary orientations to spirituality above reinforces Edward Slingerland's point that the "ontologically unique realm of the 'sacred'" remains "foreign to scientific reasoning" and sits outside reasoned inquiry in general (228). People's professed sense of spirits, gods, spiritual energy, universal wisdom, and so on brings reasoned inquiry up against a peculiar awareness: Western thought has evolved "without a language or worldview that can conceptualise expanded states of consciousness in a healthy way" (Douglas-Klotz 49).[28] What, then, does the foreign territory of spirituality look like from a critical distance?

When spirituality suggests a rejection of institutional religion and evinces political engagement (for example, living a green lifestyle and practicing earth worship or campaigning for the liberation of Tibet and practicing Tantric chanting and breathing), interpretive paradigms can afford a cautiously sympathetic stance. Analyses might investigate the eco-friendly ethics of the Gaia movement, or the politics of Buddhist monks creating a mandala on a university campus. However, critiques of spirituality are far more prominent than affirmations.[29] As Paul Heelas notes, since G. K. Chesterton's 1909 *Orthodoxy*, "scholars have clearly enjoyed using their acerbic skills to criticize 'alternative' spiritualities," and further

> The "reduction" to consumption strategy has been their favoured tool—for some, because it can be used in their war against the increasing significance of the "sins" of capitalism; for others, to show that the sacred has taken corrupt forms under the influence of modernity. (*Spiritualities of Life* 83)

People's internal sense of spirit can be dismissed not only by strategies that privilege consumer capitalism but by those that relegate spirituality to naive folk belief or psychological illusion,[30] attribute spirituality to human biology and cultural constructions,[31] or characterize spirituality as appropriations of other cultures.[32]

Analytical and interpretive projects thus tend to discount people's claims to spiritual experience, particularly when those claims are situated in the modern West.[33] At the same time, the number of people in modern, postindustrial, technologically advanced cultures who self-identify as spiritual but not religious has been widely noted.[34] In the spirit of the methods reviewed above, their spirituality can easily be analyzed as a cultural product marketed to and consumed by educated, affluent, and culturally engaged "seekers" of meaning lacking in their personal lives and without political commitments.

The question of whether or how spirituality outside institutionalized religion can effect political or social change now that spirituality is mainstream remains vital.[35] David Tacey's reflection on the place of spirituality in modern, secular cultures suggests both the need for serious analysis of spiritual practices and attention to what people who develop spiritual practices might be contributing to the reevaluation of social norms:

> Dealing with spirituality "outside" tradition is too scary, dangerous and annoying for secular nations, for it suggests that spirituality might not be contained in its old forms, and may even be inherent in the nature of human experience. If that is true, where does this leave the secular beliefs of the state and its humanist philosophy? And what of the disruptive possibilities of free-floating spiritual urges to the social and political order? (13)

"Postmodern primitives" with cosmopolitan, choice-rich lifestyles may seek spirituality in events like California's Bhakti Fest and Arizona's Native American sweat lodges.[36] Such cross-cultural forays into an open-ended sacred appear in relief against the theological commitments, creeds, codes of conduct, and institutional organizations that bind religious communities together. Without the credibility scholarly analysis affords religion, a sense of spirit cultivated in these contexts might easily be dismissed as a useful fiction that serves people's desire for holistic well-being, personal growth, and expanded mental capacities, even a substitute for psychotherapy.[37] Without a grounding in the textually based historical religions, spirituality appears as an accommodation to secularism with its potential for disrupting social systems or political power compromised by solipsism.[38]

Another line of critique points out that spiritual practitioners in the modern West use existing institutions, economies, and social structures to support practices adapted from ancient, indigenous, occult, or otherwise "othered" spiritualities.[39] Vernacular spiritual practices readily blur traditions and synthesize ideas to create new spiritualities (Wuthnow, *Creative Spirituality* 170). This tendency leaves them open to criticism for blending decontextualized borrowings from non-Western, indigenous, and ancient cultures in order to personalize spiritual experience as ahistorical, acultural, and timeless.[40]

An interesting double standard works in this line of critique. The foreignness of spirituality to prominent styles of critical analysis that leaves the West's "spiritual seekers" and "postmodern primitives" open to criticism also protects contemporary non-Western and indigenous spiritual practices from the critiques of discursive and economic production. Spiritual practices observed in non-Western, indigenous, or ancient cultures tend to be considered with respectful tolerance, even given credibility.[41] Non-Western, ancient, and indigenous spiritualities may in fact be no less hybrid and rife with out-of-context borrowings than the spiritualities produced in the contemporary West.[42] Their Othered place outside the geographic North-West and more importantly outside Western styles of thinking, however, makes them safer for more tolerant interpretation.

The default critique of consumer culture noted above is a good example of how familiar critical stances dismiss spirituality without acknowledging the assumptions that support the critique. Critical stances that privilege the materiality of culture and the body emphasize the body as the locus for sensory stimulation associated with spiritual experience. Products from essential oils to sweat lodge retreats, as Adam Possamai points out, are marketed for the purpose of "gaining and enhancing sensations" that are promoted as spiritual experiences; in a discursive construction of spirituality, sensation is linked to personal well-being and the pleasure of consumption ("Alternative Spiritualities" 31; *Religion and Popular Culture* 49–50).[43] The resulting feelings of relaxation and emotional balance are consistent with the kind of pacific spirituality imagined in popular practices like yoga and meditation in the West (Heelas, *Spiritualities of Life* 197, 201; Bender and McRoberts 14). Critical stances like Possamai's also recognize how sensory stimulation promoted as spirituality fits into a broader category of products marketed to appeal to the senses, from energy drinks to air fresheners.

This critique assumes to some degree that participation in consumer capitalism discredits spirituality. The logic is that people consume products and services that stimulate sensations discursively constructed as spiritual. At the same time, however, the critique tacitly accepts a premise that spirituality must be disengaged from worldly things. Images of cloistered monks or mountain-dwelling yogis might confirm the ideal of "real" spirituality as invisible and renunciate, despite the historical reality that religious communities and institutions have always been invested in the materiality of commercial exchange from buying salvation through donations and selling sacred relics, to manufacturing wine, to banking. Commercial, as well as charitable, interests are essential for the survival of institutional religions as well as those practices identified in the alternative category.

Even within a critique of consumer-constructed spirituality, Adam Possamai acknowledges that in contemporary Western culture people are "feeling and confronting a religious experience they cannot always easily express" (*Religion and Popular Culture* 32).[44] Clearly, spirituality is not a simple matter. How do we find footing in the epistemological ground proposed by people whose sense of spirit shapes their knowledge of the world if spiritual epistemologies cannot participate in the critical interpretation of performance? How does a sense of the ineffable, numinous, sacred, or divine intersect with performativity's emphasis on the materiality of people's bodies, words, and actions? How can we talk about performance that does not rely on observation and materiality to constitute knowledge? Can we think of presence as spirit, as well as the materiality of performance (Noë, *Varieties of Presence* 5)? What is the critical language for accommodating spirituality in the paradigm of performance?

CRITICAL PATHWAYS INTO SPIRIT-PERFORMANCE

The commitment to an inner life puts spiritual practices at odds with the emphasis on visibility, material culture, and communication so important to theorizing performance.[45] People's desire for a private, interior self seems irritatingly aligned with the egocentric, autonomous Western self. This is the self that postmodernism critiqued to death, then resurrected in a language of subject positions and constructed identities. Subject positions, constructed identities, representation, and the imperative to perform are the invisible beams, buttresses, and girders that structure performativity as an epistemology (M. C. Taylor 10). The turn inward in vernacular spiritual practices resists reliance on representational models for knowledge and runs against the imperative to perform in a media-saturated society.[46]

Vernacular spirituality may not require unpacking as a genre preconstructed by surveys, but may instead require an investigation of exactly what people are sensing as spirit. Courtney Bender advocates "a stronger investigation of the cultural and spatial logics that render mystics' self-understandings immune from the battery of criticisms associated with cultural appropriation and religious consumerism" in order to "gain some understanding of how spiritual practitioners position themselves in the world, and how in so doing they struggle with modern and postmodern questions about the boundaries and uses of culture and peoplehood, the autonomy of individuals and their identities, and other concerns" (154). Interpretive strategies are needed that join the materiality of the body and culture with the ephemerality of the internal, subjective experiences people understand as spiritual.[47] How do the ways of knowing, seeing, and being people cultivate in spiritual practices affect the approach to performance as observable, material, communicative, and social?[48]

With language as our conduit for knowledge and culture as our text, spirituality remains bound to what we can observe and read: rituals, institutions, art forms, architecture, social structures, belief systems, doctrines, mystical writings, and so on. The relationship between these expressive forms and what they signify provides the basic structure for the paradigm of performance.[49] However, a sense of spirit may not rely on that structure at all. An experiential sense of spirit cultivated in a spiritual practice such as drumming, dancing, or doing rituals closes the gap between representation and referents. In the context of a spiritual practice, doing, being, and showing may collapse into one sense of presence. We can insist on keeping the gap pried open in service of a critical stance that eschews metaphysical presences, an essential self, absolute truths, and unmediated inner experience as perceptual fictions. What happens, however, when we do not force vernacular spiritualities into these interpretive parameters but instead seek ways to think about the intersection of people's spirituality sensibilities with the materiality of performance?

"How do we know the insides of other people?" and "How do we communicate an inner life?" asks Edward Slingerland (27, 151, 304). Anne Taves asks, "How do we know the minds of others?" (*Religious Experience Reconsidered* 67). As noted at the beginning of this chapter, the conventions of Western thought align spirituality with the mind. Thus, one pathway to the intersection of people's sense of spirit with the materiality of performance goes through theories of consciousness. Inner experience is what philosopher David Chalmers calls "the really hard problem" of getting to the "subjective aspect" of the "whir of information-processing of which the brain is capable."[50] However, the compelling paradox of an inner life, as B. Alan Wallace points out, is "that from the first-person perspective, consciousness is a prime irreducible datum, but from the third-person scientific perspective there is no way of investigating it directly. That is, brain research tells us nothing about why neural processes should give rise to mental experiences of any kind" (75).

Standard methods of looking into the biology of people's inner lives—fMRI (functional magnetic resonance imaging), SPECT (single-photon emission computed tomography), or EEG (electroencephalography)—rely on analyzing mediated representations to see what a brain is doing (see chapter 3).[51] These technologies show our brains performing. For spirituality as an experiential phenomenon and performativity as an interpretive paradigm, two overarching questions emerge about mental processes. First, what is the relationship between functions we associate with mental activity (rational and abstract thought, awareness, consciousness, sensory processing, etc.) and whatever is *not* the mind (the material world, the biological matter of the brain)? Second, is it possible for the mind to reflect on the mind, and, if so, what is the relationship between the observing and the observed? These questions drive the study of consciousness as a human capacity, which involves investigations into metacognition, the properties of consciousness, and the experiential conditions of attention and awareness (Wallace 108–9; Lyons 126).

For performance, spirituality as consciousness thus presents a tautology. Performance requires observation; therefore the inner sense of spirit cannot be observed except as some kind of embodied practice or representation (including representations of brain activity). If we cannot observe spirituality except in its performative practice or expression, how can we know anything about how a sense of spirit informs and structures performance?[52]

Another path finds spirituality performing in the theater of consciousness. Performance studies has been less concerned with meta*cognition* and the problems of self-reflexivity as an internal process than with how the capacity for reflection plays out as representational forms. Meta*theatricality* involves the ways mental constructions act on the material, social world as well as the ways consciousness refracts and represents the material world. This line of inquiry has shaped fruitful perspectives on consciousness and performance as scholars wrestle with the matter of spirit.

William Demastes and Daniel Meyer-Dinkgrafe both deal with consciousness as essentially theatrical, though not in the Cartesian sense of a "theater of the mind." Both Demastes and Meyer-Dinkgrafe start with theater as a material, observable manifestation of consciousness.[53] Demastes rightly questions and critiques the widely held belief in performance studies that culture and human behavior can be reduced to performativity. Demastes asks if mental patterns are "reflections of our own self-willed postmodern metatheatrical obsession with the nature of theatricality in our culture, merely a reflection of how everything we do in one way or another is metaphorically 'theatrical'" (8). He argues against a Western materialist approach to consciousness, proposing that the empirically real world is the foundation for rediscovering the mysterious and ineffable in human consciousness.

Meyer-Dinkgrafe critiques Demastes from the perspective of the "Vedic science" developed for a Western intellectual orientation by Maharishi Mahesh Yogi. Meyer-Dinkgrafe begins with the Vedic traditions rather than Western science: his purpose is to explain the materiality of theater by way of this particular conception of consciousness (176–96). In each of these studies, claims of internally sensed, metaphysical knowledge raise the question of what, if anything, we can observe apart from the visible, material worlds of culture and nature.

If consciousness is a hard problem for theatricality, as these studies demonstrate, spirituality is a near impossibility. Whether taken as a very particular kind of consciousness or as a phenomenon unto itself, spirituality posits a reality that exceeds what can be known with the external senses, representation, or the perceptual capacities of the mind (Wallace 118). Theatricality thus serves as a container for spirituality, a paradigm in which spirituality can be made to make sense. In Ralph Yarrow's study *Sacred Theatre*, for example, the representational function and materiality of theater make spirituality intellectually manageable. Spirituality can be understood as a quality (the sacred) and described in terms of theatrical representation. There is no need to reckon directly with spirits or with spirituality as sui generis experience structuring how representation works.

Following this path, Anthony Kubiak posits religion as a "uniquely performative issue," a kind of "ontologically charged theatricality" that hinges on appearance (271). In this line of thinking, religion performs spirituality theatrically and the theatricality of religion makes spirituality real and gives it an ontological charge (see preface). Theatricality mediates the illusion of spiritual experience and constructs that experience in the reality of social norms. Kubiak calls for attention to the epiphenomenal "ecstatic, trance, and transformative aspects" of performance (272).[54]

Critical first-person experience and ethnography is another path to articulating a relationship between the materiality of performance and the interiority of spirituality. The language of somatic awareness in acting training maps easily onto some meditation and embodied spiritual practices such as rituals or dance. When stripped of their religious or ritual contexts, the sensations of somatic awareness may also be described as spirituality, though the purpose of the awareness is to serve theatrical performance.

Deborah Middleton and Franc Chamberlain find experiential spirituality in the overlap between Buddhist-inflected meditation and acting training techniques for physical awareness. Middleton describes a lesson in Alexander technique as generating the experience of being "open, connected, receptive" that she also associates with Vipassana (insight) meditation and so with spirituality (108). Spirituality in the context of developing a performer's skill is understood as a mode of consciousness that shifts from object-oriented perception to a direct encounter with one's own body-mind. Spirituality in this experiential context is a way to "get close to the heart of the moments which precede and generate performance," where performance becomes the adjustment of "attention and psychophysical condition(s)" that "bring about an encounter with the spiritual" (110). Here spirituality is without spirits, ghosts, or gods, but experiential. The experience itself is contained and structured by what is already known: theatrical performance.

These are all bold reckonings with spirit in the paradigm of performance. The ways they make spirituality make sense within the paradigm speak to the deeply rooted difficulty with spirituality in the conventions of Western modernism and postmodernism. Spirituality is situated in relation to the mind, the body, culture, and representation; spiritual experience mapped onto performance practice. Spirituality, whether understood as conceptual or experiential, sui generis or transcendent, an epiphenomenon of the mind or a product of culture, can be an object of inquiry—but is not understood or applied as a mode of knowledge. People's claims to unmediated, purely spiritual experience have little traction in disciplinary commitments to objectivity or neutrality (Smith, *Why Religion Matters* 88–89).[55]

Spirituality and spiritual knowledge in the monotheism that undergirds the Western intellectual tradition has been traditionally achieved through representation. The critical act of looking at material culture and the body with an analytical intent immediately structures people's sense of spirit and spiritual knowledge as modes of representation. Reckoning with spirit in the paradigm of performance also means asking how people invested in spirituality reconfigure performance. Spirituality, taken seriously, requires that we ask what the materiality of performance cannot show. The presumption that the materiality of performance makes spirituality present or constructs spirituality may not be enough to open interpretive or analytical space for people's sense of spirit.

THE PRESENCE OF SPIRITUAL BODIES

Performance begins with bodies. Epistemologies of observing bodies structure performativity. The critique of presence underlying the study of the social world as performative writes out the kind of experiential, corporeal knowledge upon which spirituality relies.[56] Poststructuralist critiques reinscribe textual models on the human body, reinforcing language as the primary medium for thought and the primary model for constructing and communicating knowledge.[57] The roots of this epistemological orientation can be traced through Christian thinking, in which belief in a transcendent spirit and a telos of bodily remembering required ocular proof of the body's material presence as flesh and blood, symbolized in ritual and theatrical reenactments of Christ's bodily death and resurrection as an embodied spirit. This conceptual framework distinguishes people's sense of spirit from the body and sets both against the rational functions of the mind.[58]

For Jean-Luc Nancy, the contemporary Western body is "our old culture's latest, most worked over, sifted, refined, dismantled, and reconstructed product" (7). The theological body posited by Western modernity and postmodernity renders Descartes's pineal gland vestigial, disembodying spirituality and emptying the body of any interior life.[59] In his analysis of the mystical body in sixteenth- and seventeenth-century Christianity, for example, Michel de Certeau wrote of the early modern body as that which Christianity rejected, along with the material world, only to call it back in the incarnational statement *hoc est corpus meum*. Certeau's analysis of the interiority of religious affect and the necessity of discourse for calling the mystical body into being has been extremely influential on contemporary readings of absent bodies inscribed in and by religious discourses (80).

The body remains a discursive proposition, not an experiential site for a spiritual self or the sense of an ultimate, nonmaterial reality. "We have saved our bodies," writes Nancy, "bodies of health, sports, and pleasure. But this only aggravates the disaster, as we all know: because the body is ever more fallen, the fall being further inward, more agonizing. 'The body' is our agony stripped bare" (7). Nancy's postmodern body, inflected with the incarnational aesthetics of Christianity, has a gravitas beyond that of a sign caught signifying. This is poststructuralism's absent and abject body made wholly present in the theological statement *hoc est corpus meum* as easily as in the elongated strides of an emaciated runway model.

In a discussion of devotional objects associated with the Catholic Virgin Mary, Robert Orsi suggests that scholars reconsider one of the foundational premises of postmodern thinking: the "imposition of absence everywhere, and the insistence on absence, or lack, as the necessary origin of desire" (60). Reconsidering this premise yields a different orientation to what we see and hear as performance by allowing spirits, as well as the human body, presence. This requires a mode of seeing that is not bound to the familiar epistemological architecture of representation, vision, reflection, mirroring, and affect.

The critique of presence in the rejection of the Cartesian mind-soul turns the essential self into a conglomeration of identities constructed by culture and discourse.[60] In critical discourse, bodies perform spirituality as "passive receiver[s] of culture," the postmodern body becomes "an otherwise featureless 'site' for discursive power struggles" that does not in itself contribute "any sort of meaningful structure to human experience" (Slingerland 118). Such a perspective has structured current notions of embodiment. In practice, however, enspirited bodies are fully engaged in the felt consciousness of a numinous presence, otherwise marginalized in their culture or intellectual habits (see chapter 2 for examples). They are docile bodies only in the most reductionist and fearful of analytical perspectives.

Performing bodies—inscribed, resistant, citational, marked, mimetic, and semiotically loaded—are by convention read as making visible the ideologies that define and complicate identity in formations of race, class, gender, and religion. The idea that the internal experience of a metaphysical reality informs performances, practices, and texts rather than the other way around runs counter to the overtly performative quality that characterizes postmodernity. As Anne-Britt Gran observes, "Theatrical rhetoric is a part of postmodern self-perception," and that perception also works in analytical perspectives that construe the world and bodies as performing (252). Turning inward to the self, as these spiritual practices do, seems contrary to the kind of self-performance that marks postmodern culture and the assumptions that undergird performance theory (Roof 58). Sincerity of expression, in this perspective, seems in desperate need of a critical apparatus to dispel its unseemly naïveté.

Spirituality felt in the body can thus be more easily reckoned with as a production of cultural processes, particularly those of capitalism. As a cultural production, spirituality is more easily managed as "a merchandising label for all sorts of undefined beliefs about the inner-self, wholesomeness and quality of life" (Carrette and King 53). A critical approach to spirituality as a consumer product has immediate intellectual traction, but what about experiential spirituality does such an approach occlude?

BEYOND READING TEXTS AND BODIES

The conventions of performance theory suggest that discourses on spirituality construct people's spiritual experience. From this perspective, people experience a sense of spirit already constructed by discourses on spirituality, and therefore project inward what they expect to sense. Descriptions of spirituality, such as *Skin of Glass* and *Music as Medicine*, discussed in chapter 2, could be read as part of this discourse on spirituality. Spiritual practitioners' books, websites, blogs, and verbal instructions could also be interpreted as reinforcing a person's ideas about spirituality and predetermining the experiences people might have in a workshop, event, or ceremony (for the counterperspective, see the introduction). Bodies might be read as performing actions (such as drumming or dancing) structured by the cognitive belief that the activity is inherently spiritual or with the expectation that the action will generate certain kinds of sensations.

To the extent that postmodern spiritual selves are constituted by their consumption of popular culture, religion, and indigenous cultures, spirits as well as bodies are indeed stripped bare by reproduction and repetition (Possamai, *Religion and Popular Culture* 66).[61] In a catalog that markets provocative lingerie, for example, the image of a model in a yoga posture would seem to empty out the very possibility of an internally sensed spirituality, even comment on its irrelevance in the cultural capital of sexual desirability. This model selling yoga clothes can easily be read as performing a recognizable and reproducible image of Eastern meditation. She stands on one leg in "tree pose" with arms uplifted to display a racer-back T-shirt and cropped flare-leg yoga pants. An iconic hatha yoga posture does the cultural work in this image. It performs an Indian spiritual practice that has been recast as physical fitness in the West and fitted to the model's idealized, sexualized female body. The model is posed to signify the effects associated with yoga: relaxation and a trim body.

The photograph constructs an observer's desire: for the clothes, the body, the effects of yoga, and, in this context, the desire to be desired. The image does not sell spirituality—spirituality sells the clothing. Commerce itself takes on valences of spirituality. This complicated image of spirituality might well perform Jeremy Carrette and Richard King's observation that the "psychological individualism of capitalism creates [an] addiction to private spiritualities" (58).[62]

Reading such an image as performative situates a performance of spirituality in multiple discourses—gender, sexuality, cultural norms for beauty and attraction, self and identity construction, desire, and capitalism.[63] Situating and reading spirituality in multiple discourses in this way *should* figure prominently in analysis of spiritually oriented performances.[64] We must read spiritually oriented performances in the context of late capitalism and politics of cultural hybridity, just as we need to analyze the ways spiritual practices use the economic structures and technological resources available to them.

However, when such a reading reinforces the willingness to dismiss the *possibility* that spirituality has no experiential content or meaning outside of social locations, it is limited in its ability to address the kinds of performances, practices, and texts that take spirituality as a condition of human experience informing everything else. This easily unpacked visual image of a lingerie model in clothes designed for an athletic yoga workout is also, at some level, bound into and informed by a spiritual, mental, and physical discipline with its roots in complex religious and philosophical traditions of the Indian subcontinent. Historically, yoga as a spiritual practice involved moral action as well as mastery of thought, breath, the senses, the body, and mental capacities.

This visual example suggests that while we are busily parsing representational nuances between theatricality and performativity with the assumption that performance situates spirituality in material culture, we occlude spirituality as an experiential phenomenon from which images such as the model's "tree pose" originate (however distantly). The possibility that some internal sense of spirituality informs the image slips away because it eludes observation (Slingerland 229). Analysis or interpretation of such an image, one that "performs spirituality," need not negate the spiritual practice it references (however oblique the reference).

Just as we are obligated to deal with how performances of spirituality are situated, we also must consider the possibility that spirituality situates imagery such as this. Such imagery is informed at some level by sensibilities and practices that may not be dependent on the image's context (here, a popular retail catalog aimed at constructing women's desire to conform to standards of beauty). Those sensibilities are difficult to access in the conventional language of nontheological analysis and intellectual habits that focus on, most prominently here, the construction of gender.

Even as religion is being recouped as a site for performing identities, cultural politics, ideologies, nationalities, and social norms, the internal sensibilities that often provide the substrate for religious beliefs remain invisible to the paradigm of performativity.[65] Yet the dominant strategies deployed in the study of performance evince a suspicion of such interiority and encounter the spiritual component of hatha yoga with restless foot tapping and head scratching. Indeed, Richard Bauman emphasizes the focus on materiality as the main contribution of performance studies: "The analysis of performance—indeed, the very conduct of performance—highlights the social, cultural, and aesthetic dimensions of the communicative process," not those of the inner life or the interior of the body (41).[66]

People's sense of spirit is marked by its inexplicable Otherness, and accessed within a self that is simultaneously spiritual, mental, and corporeal. How can a knowledge paradigm constituting presence from performance as materiality and language as symbolic logic reconcile people's sense of a presence that is neither? We are like surgeons confronted with a physiological condition that cannot be fixed by surgery.

READING AND THE SUSPICION OF SPIRITUAL SENSIBILITIES

When we read them as texts, bodies can point to, symbolize, and represent spirituality. What is interior to the body remains invisible and unknown—except as an absence marked by the visibility of the body's surface. In a paradigm that insists on reading bodies as performed identities, bodies will always be something other than conduits for a sense of spirit. Indeed, as

Martin Jay observes, experience and the physical body are both suspect as impediments to reason: "Whenever experience has been in bad odor, distrusted for undermining the certain truths of deductive reason, or attacked as unreliably subjective and incommunicable, its ground in the creaturely human body is often implicitly to blame" (131).

If the goal is to think about the sense of spirit in the paradigm of performance, reading meaning *onto* performing bodies perpetuates a dichotomy between representation and experience.[67] Can we accept performance as the visible effect of an internal sense? Is it possible that a performing body is not first inscribed by codes dictating spirituality, but creates codes and language in response to internal sensations? Might such a body be indifferent to the readings and codes written upon it?

Texts, practices, and performances informed by people's sense of spirit certainly do engage symbolic systems that can be read. I suggest here, however, that their significance (and signifying power) may also be found in practitioners' knowledge that their acts and words speak *from the sense of spirit within the body*. Rather than reading performances for their citational value, can we observe people's bodies and read their words as a response to the internal sense of spirit? The next section considers experience and the body as a response to a sense of spirit.

The widespread assumption that culture and language construct our reality reflects a deeply rooted faith in empirical observation to mitigate the unknown. Yet, as performance studies scholar Dwight Conquergood observed in 2002, "only middle-class academics could blithely assume that all the world is a text because reading and writing are central to their everyday lives and occupational security" (147). Anthropologist Thomas Csordas similarly observes in anthropological methods "a strong representationalist bias . . . in the predominance of Foucauldian textual metaphors, such as that social reality is 'inscribed in the body,' and that our analyses are forms of 'reading the body'" (242). Only as a broad theoretical principle can culture and language be held solely responsible for the constitution of people's internal experiences (Slingerland 105–6). Discourses on spirituality or linguistic formulations such as "I am a spiritual person" or "feeling a spiritual presence" may in fact be insufficient subliminal priming or precognitive structuring to yield what some people sense as the irreducible presence of spirit (Wallace 119). The sense of spirit, when it is not contained by theoretical paradigms discrediting knowledge from bodily experience, moves into the unknown rather than mitigating uncertainty.

Interpretive methods in the humanities, as Anne Taves notes, tend to turn "a suspicious gaze on the concept of experience, questioning whether it was possible to speak of experience at all apart from the way it is represented in and shaped by discourse" (*Religious Experience Reconsidered* 56).[68] Raymond Gibbs points out that cultural studies' incorporation of embodiment is not focused on human bodies per se, but in the social processes bodies make visible. "Rather than being a biological given," Gibbs observes, embodiment becomes "a category of sociocultural analysis" (37). Csordas identifies this tendency as taking hold in social-science and humanities research when, during the 1980s,

> adjectives like "shared" and "meaningful" in descriptions of culture were replaced by ones like "shifting" and "fragmented." Cultural phenomena were no longer interpreted but interrogated, no longer understood in terms of community but in terms of contestation. The newly discovered immediacy of embodiment offered anthropological theory a specific appreciation of the perpetual dialectic between representation and being-in-the-world, indeterminacy and objectification, continuity and transformation, subjectivity and intersubjectivity. (3)

Anthropological studies of ritual, as Edward Schieffelin observes, see rituals "as processes of practice and performance," but the perspective remains "concerned with the experience-near aspects of *social* phenomena" (59; italics added).[69] The emphasis on social efficacy and ritual's formal and structural elements keeps at bay sensations that veer perilously toward authenticity, an inner self, or the divine.[70] These observations identify a widely accepted perspective on the social world that dismisses subjectivity from interpretation or analysis. The paradigm of performance, as discussed in the introduction, is grounded in this perspective.

This theoretical perspective can frame the subjective sense of spirit in a variety of ways: spirituality may appear as a concept, beliefs, or narratives; it may be identified as a discursive formation that constructs experience; or people's sense of spirit can be analyzed as social practices with symbolic significance. The sense of spirit becomes the external performance of spirituality. Spiritual practices then appear as processes of citation, representation, and reference situated in a social, historical context. Reading spirituality as performance exposes social relations, ideologies, and power relations by privileging the materiality of people's bodies and expressions.

Though the paradigm of performance places great value on embodiment and corporeality, its methods rely on knowledge produced by theoretical constructs grounded in language. Embodiment as a strategy for inquiry exposes the dialectic between representation and experience. Yet the semiotic, symbol-making, language, and theoretical force frameworks construing experience as socially constructed are powerful. Thus, "Though concepts such as performance and persuasion have substantial experiential force, ultimately representation appeals to the model of a text" (Csordas 3). The convention of distinguishing between knowledge as mental activity expressed as text and knowledge embodied in experience structures most inquiries into spirituality. Methods that take people's sense of spirit as a legitimate basis for interpretation might allow us to think in the interstices among the materiality of bodies, the symbol-making capacities of the mind, and the presence of spirit in performance.

STAGING SPIRITUALITY

Spirituality slips into the convenient containers of myth and ritual, which while useful can occlude discussion of spirituality on its own terms. The assumption that narrative structures action has linked myth and ritual with theatricality. In the history of theater, rituals beget embodiment in mimesis, and myth gives meaning to ritual action.[71] Religious myths and rituals shaped the theater of Europe's medieval period, and the ancient theaters of Greece, Japan, China, and India. The myth of Dionysus must be remembered in ritual, the story of Medea's escape from Corinth must be retold as civic poetry, the dialogue between Krishna and Arjuna must be danced, and the death and resurrection of Jesus must be acted out again and again to make it real in the present moment.

Modernist and postmodernist efforts to recover theater's origins in myths and rituals, from Antonin Artaud to the experimental theaters of the 1960s and 1970s, did not aim directly at spirituality as life praxis, but at investing theater with sensibilities imagined in premodern or "exotic" cultures. Spirituality functions in modern and postmodern theater as a construct that reifies performance, rather than a presence beyond the theatrical act. Peter Brook's Holy Theatre and Jerzy Grotowski's Holy Actor have little commerce with the sense of an ontological, transcendent Holy, or the practice of calling down spirits to heal a broken bone. Suspicion of spirit as real in any ontological, authentic, or epistemological way reinforces myths and rituals as performance, and performance as a material practice.

Examples of false gurus such as Marjoe Gortner, José Alvarez, and Vikram Gandhi, along with anthropological accounts of fake shamans, demonstrate for the scholarly record that performances of spirituality can indeed be nothing more than the theatrical reproduction of codes for spirituality, and that such performances have powerful affective potential.[72] Religious practices, too, may be uncoupled from their spiritual contexts to function as professional entertainment, their spiritual valences explained in program notes and accounted for in reviews. At Lincoln Center's October–November 2010 White Light Festival, for example, eighteen framed performances of "spiritual" music were as culturally and religiously diverse as Brahms's *Deutsches Requiem* and the *Manganiyar Seduction* (a touring piece performing Sufi songs with an architecture of stacked cubes representing a Manganiyar community), as well as ballads and a dance piece entitled *Sutra* based on Chinese martial arts.

The festival, intended as an "act of spirituality" in an "era of distraction," multitasking as an exploration of "our larger interior universe" in the context of New York's major concert venues, generated public discussion on what constitutes spirituality in art, modern urban life, and capitalism.[73] This discussion hinged on assumptions that spirituality is at odds with the demands of modern culture. The festival itself set spirituality apart from daily life by treating spirituality as performance on display, managed within the boundaries of darkened theaters rather than cathedrals or temples. Framing spirituality as performance in this way reinforces the alterity of spirituality to Western urban culture by situating it in the domain of high art, performance, and art criticism, rather than in everyday experience or life praxis. Performance keeps spirituality contained.

Conversely, the commitment to cultural diversity in the paradigm of performance mitigates the response to spirituality as scary, dangerous, and annoying (to use Tacey's words again). The alterity of spirituality in the Western cultural tradition is evident in theater scholar David Mason's insightful work on the *râs lila*, a ritualized theatrical retelling of Indian mythology. For Western readers, the Indian context puts an ironic twist on the critical fear of exoticizing non-Western cultures. The geographical setting in a Hindu pilgrimage site, Vrindavan, keeps spirituality at a distance: cultural alterity makes spirituality safe for discussion and much less threatening to think about as life praxis. Mason's study works through the inseparability of aesthetics and devotional spirituality, which I am suggesting is more easily tolerated in performance practices outside the boundaries of contemporary Western thought and culture.

Râs lila performers embody familiar stories of Shiva and Krishna that have been retold for centuries in dance and dramatic forms on the Indian subcontinent. Mason observes that the performers and their audiences "enter into a mutually-affirming relationship with a performance" (118). In his detailed interpretation, performers and spectators participate in something "like the religious experience that results from a person's active complicity with spiritual worldviews" (118). For devotees, on or off the stage, Shiva's stage transformation from male to female becomes "a model for the kind of inner transformation that devotion requires" (132). In the social contract of this theater, performance allows for the same "dogged disregard for the divide between the empirical world and the unverifiable" that characterizes religious experience (119). Returning to William James, Mason moves toward an acceptance of a sense of spirit in this non-Western theatrical form. He astutely suggests that religious experience and theater both require acting in the subjunctive: "as if" one were Shiva or "as if" one believed in the reality of transcendent deity (Mason 119; James 64).

What makes spirituality acceptable in the practices of cultural Others? Can spirituality be dislodged from its association with cultural Otherness and premodern ways of being in the world? Is an analysis of spirituality as an epistemological foundation for performance possible in the modern, technological, urban, global West? What might similarly close readings of spiritually informed performance in the postsecular West offer performance studies?

Without reading spirit through the lens of "what if," people's sense of spirit becomes an important, if elusive, criterion for interpretation. The body remains the starting place, as it already has a place in critical performance analysis. Because the body is the experiential locus for many contemporary spiritual practices, the necessary move for an interpretive paradigm is to accept the possibility of bodies infused with a sense of an ineffable presence. This may not be immediately accessible to critical methods.

Schechner observes, for example, that the act of spinning in one place will generate the Freudian "oceanic" sensation of feeling "good" even without the mystical aspirations or hermeneutic content of Sufism to inform ritualized whirling.[74] Discourses, rituals, or performances might identify the sensations of whirling as spiritual, but the sensations themselves do not require construction by culture or discourse (Schechner, "Living a Double Consciousness" 18). At the level of bodily sensation, Schechner writes, rituals such as dervish whirling "communicate in their own code, whether or not I understand the code" (24). What are these codes, how do they communicate, and how can we translate them? In the language of performance studies, how do we know what refuses to be theorized?

Theories of performance have not yet reconciled the ways conventions of interpretation divide human capacities into symbolic thought and embodied experience.[75] The abstractions of linguistic and symbolic representation continue to hold privileged status as the higher-order brain functions that construct patterns and narrative (myth). These are the functions of the brain generally believed to organize lower-order activities such as emotion, feeling, and bodily expressions (rituals) (D'Aquili and Newberg 17–18, 12). This hierarchy is akin to that which organizes reading bodies and embodied practices in performance theory.

Nonhierarchical views on physiological activity suggest that language and bodily action cannot be separated.[76] These views may be very useful in reorienting performance to people's embodied sense of spirit. In practice, people may actively cultivate neurological processes that intertwine symbolic thinking with physical action.[77] One of the ways into this reorientation is to take the body as a point of origin for the internal experience of spirituality, allowing what happens at the bodily level to influence how we understand the performative.[78] The paradigm of performance invokes a model of observation; for performances informed by people's sense of spirit, critical practice might shift from interpreting *what* we see to understanding *how* we are seeing.

UNSTAGING SPIRITUALITY

Framing spirituality as performance translates people's sense of spirit in reference to social or cultural contexts, linguistic and visual codes for meaning.[79] Indeed, in conventional modes of thinking, spirituality is almost impossible to talk about apart from people's situated practices and communicative expressions. Spirituality eludes even the most sophisticated efforts to theorize or define it in critical discourses. Wade Clark Roof observes that scholars "have multiple discourses about spirituality, and seldom is the term precisely defined in any of the discourses"; spirituality is at best "difficult to grasp" (34–35). Bender writes in a similar vein that spirituality "is bedeviled not by a lack of definitions but by an almost endless proliferation of them. Most definitions—including those that are . . . psychological, perennial, or neurological—have served to protect, defend, debunk, or claim certain territory for the spiritual; these definitions confound more than they illuminate" (5).[80] The situation requires, as Bender argues, a multidirectional approach to the study of spirituality, "historically, institutionally, and imaginatively without pulling it completely together into a single thing" (6). The ways spiritual practitioners identify spirit as a sense of presence, however, moves the interpretive horizon beyond a model of observation, representation, and performativity (Taves, *Religious Experience Reconsidered* 11–12, 56; Slingerland 228; McGuire 98).[81]

Spiritually oriented performance practices may involve experiential nuances that elude the visibility of performance and discursive construction. Taves proposes studying spirituality as "the processes whereby people sometimes ascribe *special characteristics* to things that we (as scholars) associate with terms such as 'religious,' 'magical,' mystical,' 'spiritual,' et cetera" (*Religious Experience Reconsidered* 8). These processes may involve what we conventionally view as performative. Meredith McGuire locates people's sense of spirit not in symbol systems or abstract concepts but in "the everyday ways ordinary people attend to their spiritual lives" (98). Spirituality may not be marked by exceptional or transcendent experiences, but experienced as an aspect of everyday life. The material conditions of everyday life, *including what we constitute as performance*, may be part of that elusive sense of spirit.[82] How can we allow that sense of spirit to influence how we see the social world as performance?

In addition to the status of spirituality as a topic, this chapter has introduced another difficulty: the sheer variety of phenomena the sense of spirit can include. Spirituality can include experiences from lucid dreaming to hallucinations, to spirit possession, trance, and the sense of one's spirit leaving the physical body (Taves, *Religious Experience* 11–12; *Fits, Trances* 7–8). People might identify a spiritual experience as a particular state of consciousness, communicating with spiritual beings, cognizance of universal laws or ethical principles, a feeling of sacredness or mystery, a sense of overwhelming awe, connection with supernatural forces or powers, miracles or inexplicable occurrences, radical self-transformation, the perception of unseen forces at work in the world, the ability to alter the material world through magic or prayer, or most broadly as the sense of something real beyond the material world. While spiritual practices, discourses, and communities give value to certain kinds of experiences, it is also important to recognize that people create meaning from experiences that seem to have no context, explanation, or value except as spirit.

The impediments to taking spirituality seriously are many, as this chapter thus far has shown. Spirituality, taken on its own terms, complicates the epistemological foundations of performance as a paradigm for critical and interpretive work. Taking spirituality at face value as a particular kind of engagement with the material world and the body's physicality presents some challenges. Doing so, however, opens possibilities for understanding many social practices as ways in which people cultivate a sense of something that is outside human concepts, constructs, and culture. Practices as diverse as gardening and séances, home altars and drum circles, prayer meetings and dance improvisation sessions, political rallies and tai chi, Reiki healing and tarot reading can be interpreted as particular configurations of a sense of spirit.

Spirituality, following Taves, is an "embodied and interactive" process (*Religious Experience Reconsidered* 4). Performance is also an embodied and interactive process. Can performance accommodate claims to a sense that has no referent in the material world? What happens to interpretations of discourses, cultural idioms, performance conventions, imagery, and objects? In the performance paradigm, these questions seem to create a tautology: performing spirituality defines what we can know about people's sense of spirit because performance as materiality gives us an object to see. These questions also seem to set up a linear trajectory: people press an internal sense of spirit out into material forms that can be seen through critical lenses. Performance may be the very process by which people who sense spirit negotiate that internal sense and external world of culture and societies. Spirit must thus be sought in the interplay of the human bodies, material culture, and discursive formations that constitute performance.[83]

II. Taking Spirit Seriously

The previous section worked through the conundrum of spirituality as an internal sense in an intellectual and cultural tradition that privileges the representational power of the mind over the sensations of the body. The issue thus far has been how to take people's internal sense of spirit seriously and connect that sense with what is visible as performance. The focus of this next section is how taking spirituality seriously alters performance as a framework for interpreting culture, observing human behavior, and understanding human action, language, and expressive forms. The basic question is this: how can the sense of something nonmaterial be understood as the generative source for the materiality and representational logic of performance? In this section, the relationship between embodiment and textuality turns on the pivot of spirituality. Vernacular spiritual practitioners can be interpreted as *creating* culture even as they consume it, and read as writing *from* the body even as social norms write race, class, religion, artistic idioms, and gender onto their bodies.

SIGNS OF SPIRIT WITHIN THE BODY

Even when religious belief requires denying or transcending the body (as in out-of-body experiences or fasting), the body is always essential to spiritual experience (McGuire 98–99). Embodiment, as Csordas posits, is the phenomenological equivalent "to the semiotic paradigm of culture as text" (241). McGuire, like Csordas, acknowledges that critical inquiry is doubly biased against taking the body as the point of origin for abstract or symbolic knowledge, as well as against taking subjective claims of internal experiences as epistemologically credible. The body, like the sense of spirit, always appears lacking when it does not have language to give it meaning. Even as performance theory moves back and forth between text and embodiment, the critical framework that supports the theory shows

> spirituality and materiality as dichotomous, in tidy binary opposition. Accordingly, those individuals who wanted to enhance their spirituality would have to overcome the burden of their materiality, deny their material urges and concerns, and transcend the limitations (perhaps also the pollution) of the material body. (McGuire 97)

At its root, this perspective is a variation on the theology of transcendence prominent in Christianity. Robert Wuthnow observes that recent scholarship sometimes overcompensates for the failure to give the body proper attention and often ends up sanctifying corporeality rather than dealing directly with spirituality in or of the body (Wuthnow, *Creative Spirituality* 170).[84]

Giving spirit a place in the body, however, opens a critical space for more intricate connections between the materiality of products, expressive forms, practices, and people's sense of an ineffable presence. Practitioners in a trance dance ceremony, for example, might sense the smoke of burning sage as cleansing the air, purifying their lungs, and/or carrying prayers to spiritual entities. As a practice, repeatedly focusing on the sensation of the smell might help cultivate the sense of spirits present. Sensory stimulation may shift and heighten people's engagement with their bodies, creating more options for processing sensory data.

Many physical expressions give spirituality recognizable form—for example, singing, ecstatic shaking, fingering prayer beads, swaying, speaking in tongues, bowing before sacred objects. These appear to be performative insofar as they are culturally constituted *signs of* spiritual experience. Conventional performance studies logic says that performance constructs spirituality (as in the example of the White Light Festival above), represents spirituality (see Kubiak above), or produces a spiritual affect (see Middleton and Chamberlain above). Engagement with cultural codes, symbol systems, and material objects provides a mechanism by which people identify spirituality, making spirituality available on the terms of performance theories—however, this may also be the means through which people attend to, cultivate, and privilege spirituality as an ontological given that precedes performance (Hay 26). This is the stumbling block for most critical paradigms.

What appear to be performative signs of spirituality might also be physical *responses* to an internal sense. Thinking of the exterior of the physical body as responding to an internal sense complicates conventional readings of spiritualized bodies. The physical actions we see bodies doing (performance) must be interpreted as responses to an ineffable presence within the body, sensed as spirit (such as the rising of kundalini energy through the body). From this stance, *spirituality constructs performance rather than performance constructing spirituality.*

Consider, for example, a mass-produced statue of a meditating Buddha sold in the United States, a predominantly Judeo-Christian religious environment. In a conventional reading, the statue "performs spirituality." The statue is situated in and produced for a Western market, where it becomes a visual trope for a deep meditative state and participates in popular discourses on relaxation, inner peace, and mindfulness, among others. The figure is not associated with the West's own history of contemplation, such as Christianity's St. Ignatius, but with the exoticized traditions of Asia. In this reading, the statue becomes a theatricalized "performance" of a kind of generalized contemplative spirituality. It is easily reproduced, and its constructed meaning as an icon of Othered spirituality is accessible without any knowledge of Theravada, Mahayana, or any other sect within those two major traditions of Buddhism.

In a conventional reading familiar to performance studies scholars, the statue is understood to be performing a vast range of political, ideological, and identity formations. Its meaning is in play. People who buy this statue participate in the consumption of culture. People might integrate such a statue into their performance of everyday life, without knowledge of Buddhist meditative traditions or awareness of the statue's cultural specificity to China, Japan, Tibet, India, or Thailand. The statue might be placed in a home as a focus for mindfulness meditation (a practice developed by American Jon Kabat-Zinn) and next to books by popular spiritual self-help and longevity guru Deepak Chopra (rather than Buddhist Pali sutras). The statue might be placed in a spot where a person does relaxation exercises or yoga postures to "de-stress" (Carrette and King 100).[85] Other consumers might take such a statue as a piece of multicultural decorative kitsch added to a modern home decor, where it might have no more significance than to perform the owner's open-mindedness, liberal ambitions for Tibet, or an ecotourism trip to Thailand. The statue becomes a material sign of religious pluralism nested in a free-market consumption of religious signs (Possamai, *Religion and Popular Culture* 48). Any of these placements and uses of the statue can be interpreted as the performance of a person's identity, usually with an implicit or explicit critique (of class privilege, appropriation of non-Western spirituality, solipsism, etc.).

The statue also performs in a religious, spiritual, or meditative tradition. As the statue sits with legs crossed and hands in its plaster lap, the surface of the represented body also participates in a network of much more specific cultural signifiers. The figure's physique might be corpulent or slight of build, depending on the cultural conventions, while the dress might identify its culture of origin as Japan, Tibet, Thailand, China, Japan, or India. The position of its hands might identify a particular sect or meditative tradition, perhaps Theravada or Zen Buddhism; the hand positions might be symbolic, perhaps as mudras in the religious traditions of India. The statue might invoke liberatory or soteriological practices leading toward nirvana, samadhi, or moksha, and identify a particular understanding of an internal state of enlightenment or higher consciousness. Depending on the meditative tradition, the figure's eyes might be half-closed or completely closed, its head slightly bowed or lifted upward, or the shoulders up and open or slightly bent forward. The critique inherent in this reading might interpret the statue as an example of a cultural appropriation of non-Western spirituality, or conversely as the incursion of capitalism into spirituality, with marketers, producers, and importers ready to profit on spirituality as an easy sell in a highly materialist culture.

If spirituality enters the picture, there is more going on than what a conventional reading focused on the statue's representational and performative functions shows. However removed from its specific cultural or religious referents and however generalized in its details, the plaster body shows physiological responses to an internal condition of meditation. Beginning with the interior of the body, rather than the visible surface of the statue, the sense cultivated in meditation informs the shape of the statue. The posture and facial expression show how a human body responds to a physical and mental practice of sitting in a specific contemplative practice. The statue's half-closed eyelids show a response to focused mental attention. The upper body shows a response to disciplined breathing. The taut musculature in the bowl of the pelvis shows a body acclimated to sustained stillness. The composed face responds to a conscious effort to free the body-mind from sensory stimulation, while the posture itself is the result of an internal effort to align bones and muscles. The facial expression and alignment of a body also respond to where the breath is directed: between the eyebrows, into the belly, up and down the spine, and so on, depending on the meditation tradition.

Physical responses to spiritual practices such as this might be read as representational and performative. They can certainly be reproduced irrespective of any internal sense whatsoever. However, without those internal sensations having given rise to the representational or performative imagery, the statue does not make sense or carry meaning in relation to any human experience. The statue's power as an object is not in its social and cultural referents, but in the internal spiritual sense it evokes.

As noted above, people associate the sense of spiritual presence with any number perceptual conditions: just a few examples are heightened awareness, sensing a sacred or numinous quality to the world, a sheering away of identity to expose an essential self, visions of spiritual beings, connection with a deity, inner peace, nondualistic thinking, thought that is not linguistic, a radical confrontation with death or eternity, access to truth not otherwise accessible by conventional methods of observation, and union with a universal consciousness. The sense of spiritual presence might also be associated with physiological conditions, such as changes in muscle tension, blood redistribution, breathing patterns, or rushes of sensation within the body. To accommodate spirituality in the paradigm of performance, internal perceptual and physiological conditions such as these need to be balanced with the discourses, practices, visual imagery, and objects that constitute performance.

The experience of spirituality is not stable across individuals in the same practice or across iterations of a practice experienced by the same individual; neurological research cannot fully account for how subjects experience internal sensations as spiritual without recourse to cultural influences. To position ourselves on the issue of internal experience in performance, we need a willingness to attend to how people's internal sense of spirit combines with the social forces shaping our shared material reality. How, then, do we consider the relationship between people's internal sense of spirit and material culture through a paradigm that insists people are always performing?

BODY-MIND AND SPIRIT WITHIN PERFORMANCE

The tripartite formulation "mind-body-spirit" is ubiquitous in the language of contemporary spirituality (Heelas, *Spiritualities of Life* 61). There is still no fourth term in English that synthesizes mind-body-spirit into one concept. "Somatics" probably comes closest but, like phenomenology, does not give ontological status to spirituality. Ironically, the popular tripartite hyphenation mind-body-spirit itself stays within the parameters of the Western tradition, as discussed above, even as vernacular practices (such as those discussed in the next chapter) seek to integrate mental, physical, and spiritual capacities at the level of experience. The hyphenated term mind-body-spirit reinscribes an intellectual tradition that is skeptical of spirit and privileges mind over body. The split is not between mind and body but between mind-body and spirit.

Vernacular practices, such as those discussed in chapter 2, seek to recognize and equalize mental, physical, and spiritual aspects of a holistic self. The hyphenated formulation mind-body-spirit adapts the conventions of the Western tradition to describe an *internal sense*. The two texts discussed in the next chapter, *Skin of Glass* and *Music as Medicine*, describe the experiential collapse of mind, body, and spirit in detail. This language of spirit refuses to distinguish between what is inside the body and what is outside, what is cognitive and what is corporeal, what is spiritual and what is material. The sense of a holistic self persists despite a dominant mode of critical and analytical thinking that brackets spirit and the body as sources of knowledge. The practices of dance meditation and neoshamanic drumming discussed in chapter 2 are examples of vernacular practices that rearrange the conventions of knowledge production governing the social performance worldview.

The conventional hierarchy of mental processes for critical paradigms privileges cognition, ideation, symbolic logic, reasoning, analysis, empirical observation, and explanation. These are the mental mechanisms most valued in the production of knowledge and that produce critical analyses of performance. They are, in effect, the tools of observation and writing. Embodied spiritual practices may privilege different mental processes, and in ways that put them at odds with conventional thinking. In vernacular practice, "mind-body-spirit" suggests a synthesis of corporeality, cognition, and a sense of the numinous that aligns with the kind of interdisciplinary methods discussed above, which seek more holistic interpretations of human social interaction and biological functioning.

Getting at the relationship between interiority and the observable surface of performance may require circuitous pathways through the mental and physical sensations composing people's experiences of a self that is corporeal, mental, and spiritual. In practice, people may transform culturally valued mental processes (e.g., processing sensory input, creating symbols or images, rationalizing insights or awareness, communicating meaning) into a more holistic consciousness of internal sensations (e.g., physical feelings: the sense of a heartbeat or breath, twitching, tears, sweat, pain, blood pulsing, the feeling of thinking). While we can read a body responding to these internal sensations as *performing* spirituality, when a practice values an internal sense of spirit, there is more to bring into the conversation about performance.

Writings such as *Skin of Glass* and *Music as Medicine* evince sincerity of expression grounded in a sensed experience of spirit. Interpretive and analytical methods oblige us to distrust such direct expressions to see what mediates or constructs that experience.[86] This is the architecture of performance as a critical paradigm. However, the paradigm hides as well as reveals: even as practitioners' performing bodies and language are caught in the interplay of culturally determined signs for spirituality, their actions and words emerge from a sense of spirit that can neither be confirmed nor denied by an outside observer.

How might a paradigm that reads culture and behavior as performative adapt to spiritual practices like Collective Awakening and Dancemeditation? How does spirituality inform performance? What if spirituality governs performance? How can methods of inquiry defined by a mind and body divide recognize spirit? How can paradigms in which spirit has no credibility interpret spirituality as an aspect of people's minds and bodies? Spiritual practices shift knowledge from the mind's symbol-making capacity to an internal sense of spirit. If language is the sine qua non for critical and interpretive work, what methods of inquiry are appropriate for knowledge that does not rely on language? If a social practice values internal embodied sensations over what the body does or looks like to an observer, how can those sensations be included in performance analysis? If people's sense of a numinous, ineffable presence does not rely on matter or representation to confirm its reality, how can a mode of critical inquiry that relies on matter and representation interpret that presence?

III. Performance as a Membrane

Spirituality's place in the intellectual conventions construing the social world as performative has been at stake throughout this chapter. Section I examined the epistemological credibility of what people sense as spirit. A discussion of myth and ritual showed how analysis and interpretation of symbolic expressions, whether linguistic or embodied, mitigate dealing intellectually with the ontological status of spirit. Section II addressed the status of the body as the nexus between the sense of spirit and mental processes (an ambiguous relationship). The performance paradigm has been constructed from the materials of an intellectual tradition that marginalizes spirituality. Questions posed in the previous sections have opened space for considering people's sense of spiritual presence within a paradigm committed to the visible materiality of performance. Taking spirit seriously in the performance paradigm requires vocabularies that can work with how people's sense of ephemerality, ineffability, and spirit influences their actions in the material world.

Vernacular spiritual practices, such as those described in chapter 2, transgress analytical taboos against unmediated experience and revealed knowledge. This puts practitioners' claims to a numinous reality, universal human values, fundamental truths, and unverifiable and unobservable knowledge at odds with analytical strategies designed to reveal how people's actions, texts, and bodies perform localized social relations, cultural norms, and ideologies. The authority of an internal sense of spirit resists arguments reducing it to historically situated, culturally constructed, neurologically phantom phenomena.[87] However, interiority is a conundrum for the performance paradigm only as long as "inner" and "outer" are delimited by the presence of a physical body. Practices grounded in a sense of spirit do not merely turn internal sensations outward in expressive forms that can be analyzed (e.g., choreography, musical composition, poetry, drama, painting, concerts). There may be as much or more to be gained by asking what an internal sense of spirit contributes to performance as materiality as there is in dismissing spirituality as a problematic category of human experience.[88]

Understanding how an inner life might be performative requires destabilizing a theoretical approach that interprets inner life as fiction and bodies as identities acting out social and cultural norms. Analytical and interpretive methods must be able to see spirituality as performance and at the same time recognize that whatever people sense as spirit has probably slipped outside the paradigm's borders. There is, however, space in the performance paradigm for granting spirit ontological and epistemological status in individual practices without inhibiting the critical distance required for analysis and interpretation.

TOWARD A HOLISTIC MODEL OF PERFORMANCE

A holistic model for performance would approach internal experience as an exchange between the interior workings of the body and the expressive forms that constitute performance. This model is consistent with current theories of enactive perception and cognition. Approaches to cognition that put mental processes in a dynamic relationship with culture observe that the human capacity for consciousness and experiences of spirit are physiologically interdependent. Language (or, more broadly, symbolic representation) emerges from the mental processes that also register the ephemeral and ambiguous sense of spirit. That language is embodied and bound to internal sensations offers insight into the spiritual practitioners' written texts and spoken words, which I interpret as spirituality through performance:

> People's subjective, felt experiences of their bodies in action provide part of the fundamental grounding for language and thought. Cogni-

> tion is what occurs when the body engages the physical, cultural world and must be studied in terms of the dynamical interactions between people and the environment. . . . We must not assume cognition to be purely internal, symbolic, computational, and disembodied, but seek out the gross and detailed ways that language and thought are inextricably shaped by embodied action. (Gibbs 9)

This dynamic model dissolves the long-standing (and, for critical analysis, safer) distinction between the computational functions of mind, which process and represent external stimuli, and the internal sensations of spiritual knowledge, which people articulate in language.

Reciprocity between embodied internal sensibilities and embodied actions in culture can help reconfigure the referentiality of performance. Cultural conventions might distinguish mental activities, such as formulating propositional statements, from spiritual experiences, such as nonlinguistic communication with a divine power or experiencing one's body as a vibrating field of energy. Internally, however, both are part of an integrated network of neurological processes. This idea is a starting point for thinking about expressive forms as constructed by people's internal sense of spirituality in collaboration with cultural idioms, rather than spirituality as an idea represented in an exclusively material performance or constructed by discourses. Acknowledging how bodies produce the culture and symbolic systems in which they operate expands interpretive options and gives the biological body status in knowledge production.

Attention to conditions under which the human mind does not work like a theater that accesses and represents an objective world, or accesses knowledge only through language—the distinction between mind, body, spirit, and performative actions—shifts the conceptual foundations of the performance paradigm. Over a decade ago, neurologist and philosopher Antonio Damasio observed a gap in the study of consciousness: "We do not know all the intermediate steps between neural patterns and mental patterns" (159). The process of neural activity becoming the re-cognition of internal sensation as spiritual experience may not be a linear progression of neurological activity to cultural context to forming spiritual ideas. Rather than "steps between," a more appropriate image might be "pathways among" neurological activity, internal sensations, material culture, and language. For spiritual practitioners, what we take to be performance might more accurately be viewed as the mechanism enabling internal processes to interact with culture, draw culture into the body, and articulate spirituality in whatever cultural codes and discourses are available.

The space between neural activity and culture in the constitution of an inner, spiritual life is only beginning to be explored. In this space, the circuitous neural pathways through which people experience and identify spirituality meander, intersect, double back, overlap, and split into the expressive forms we have come to recognize. This space is important not only for humanities inquiries seeking a better understanding of humans as simultaneously biological and social beings: an approach to analyzing and interpreting spirituality as performative that takes internal biological processes into account may yield richer ideas about how people negotiate their internal lives and material culture. Performance, as an object of study and a strategy for inquiry, may provide a way to think about how culture influences neurological activity and how internal sensations make their way into culture as formulations of spirituality.

By expanding beyond culture as materiality toward the epistemological viability of people's inner sensations, performance studies can contribute this higher-level expertise that Anne Taves and Edward Slingerland call for from humanities disciplines. We fall short of understanding the processes that give rise to physical expression when we rely too heavily on culture and symbolic systems to define bodies as representational, encoded, and always performing. People's claims of experiencing the numinous challenge performance studies to interpret the observable surfaces representational practices produce with a softer gaze. Studying spirituality reorients the aporia that preoccupied late twentieth-century performance theory—the gap between representations and their slippery referents. Within this reorientation, research can legitimately ask "how we gain access to experience (our own and that of others) and how it acquires meaning as it arises in the body and through interaction with others" (Taves, *Religious Experience* 12). Turning away from representation as a critical concern and toward the effort to better understand human experience has the potential to open inquiries into how an "inner life" of sensations is related to material culture and how material culture is related to people's internal experience.

At some spiritually oriented events I visited, a discernable but ambiguous presence seemed to move within the performative frame. Acts of performance—dancing, drumming, writing, speaking, narrative—seemed to be a conduit for this presence. What we might otherwise call performance was not an end in itself but a means through which people cultivated a sense of this presence. For practitioners, spirit is no less real than the cars they drive to a workshop, the CDs and DVDs they sell, the hands beating drums, or the shoulders moving in a shimmy. Despite performance theory's take on performance or discourse making things real (or making real things), the presence of spirit did not require the symbolic abstraction of language and the physical action of drumming or dancing to call it into being. The status of this sense of spirit in the modern world presents us with the critical problem discussed at length above.

Replacing "critical problem" with "compelling ambiguity" opens possibilities for engaging critically with spirituality rather than rejecting or bracketing what people claim to sense. We do not know the processes by which people sense spirit. Nor do we know how performances informed by spirituality—events, workshops, CDs and DVDs, writings, paintings, and concerts—in turn produce the internal sense of spirit (see chapters 3 and 4). However, we can seek a language that connects people's sense of spirit to the visual codes, performative frames, objects, and embodied actions we read as performing.

New questions emerge when performance is construed as the connective tissue between matter and the sense of spirit. How do people engage their bodies in spiritual experience? What are the physiological processes governing the formulation of sensation as spiritual experience *and* their performative expression? What is the relationship between the cognitive processes that formulate beliefs about spirituality and the sense of spirit? What is the role of culture in the physiological processes involved in the sense of spirit? Do cultural triggers activate neurological pathways that are specific to spiritual experiences? Conversely, do specific combinations of neurological activities generate sensations that prompt people to perceive certain experiences as spiritual? How do people distinguish certain internal sensations from others and mark them as "spiritual"? Can a critical analysis accommodate the possibility that performance might convey spiritual knowledge? If not, how do we account for what we are leaving out? What recognizable performance conventions operate in spiritually oriented performances? Does a spiritually oriented performance represent the sense of spirit, articulate an otherwise inexpressible cognizance—or is the performance itself a physical response to an internal sense? How do spiritual sensibilities inhabit performance practices? What do we do with performance practices and discourses that assume the body's noetic potential? How do we deal with performance practices and discourses that conceive the self as authentic or essential?

We can think of performativity as a double helix: internal sensibilities and cultural idioms twisting around each other. In that twisting, people negotiate complex relationships between the conventional categories organizing knowledge: mind-body and spirit; experience and symbolic representation; individual awareness and social communication; presence as matter and spirit. How people twist internal sensations around the materiality of their bodies, the discourses through which they articulate knowledge, and their expressive forms becomes the interpretive or analytical project.

We can also think of performance as a membrane between people's inner lives and the materiality of the social world. Across that membrane people's sense of mystery, the sacred and the numinous and the cultural idioms that shape sense into form flow back and forth. Performance becomes the medium for that flow, the mechanism dissolving the boundary of internal experience and its external representation. We can then interrogate what spiritually informed performances do to cultivate a sense of a numinous or sacred presence. We can examine how that sense *becomes* performative in language, events, and other expressive forms, rather than how performance produces or structures feeling, emotion, or thought.

Shifting analysis to the relationship between internal sensibilities and expressive forms requires expanding the borders of performativity so that consciously performative acts—framed performances, the performance of everyday life, texts, and speech—can be interpreted as a permeable boundary between people's sense of an inner, spiritual life and the bodies acting in the materiality of culture. The act of performing then becomes a process of negotiation between the visible and the invisible.

Reimagined as a membrane or helix, performance is not only a site upon which to read the play of social forces and identity formation but also a means by which people put the ineffability of their spiritual experiences into dynamic play with the materiality of discourses and material culture. Embodied practices and language can be thought of as conduits through which the sense of spirit moves.

In an intellectual tradition that mistrusts interiority, the body, subjective experience, and the possibility of a numinous reality, these questions must take people's experience of spirituality on their terms. Chapter 2 describes how the spiritual sensibilities in two examples of vernacular spiritual practices, Collective Awakening and Dancemeditation, rethink performance from a sense of spirit. The method could be used to reckon with spirits in other practices, including those of religious traditions outside the contemporary West, and more violent or transgressive practices. The next chapter works from these premises: (1) the sense of spirit is embodied, (2) internal experience is physiological and experiential, (3) an inner life is always in a dynamic relationship with culture, and (4) we can investigate performance as a medium through which people's internal sensibilities collaborate with material culture.

CHAPTER 2

Spirituality in Practice and Performance

> There is pretty much no better story than that—remembering who you are.
>
> —DUNYA DIANNE MCPHERSON, BLOG POST, JUNE 29, 2012

> Today, many are beginning to awaken and remember who we are, where we come from, and where we are going.
>
> —MARTIN KLABUNDE, BLOG POST, MARCH 28, 2010

KNOWING SPIRIT AS PERFORMANCE

Chapter 1 asked how performativity, an analytical paradigm constructed in part by a skepticism of spirituality, can accommodate people's sense of spirit without defining that sense in the terms of matter and discourse. In response to that question, performativity emerged as a membranous exchange between the internal sensations people associate with spirituality and the materiality of bodies, language, and culture. Chapter 1 posited that framed events, practices, objects, bodies, texts, and spoken language are sites at which we can observe that exchange.

Reading through the performance paradigm, the above statements by Dunya McPherson and Martin Klabunde appear to perform a discourse on an essentialized self and a desired memory of authenticity. In the context of the spiritual practices from which the writers speak, however, these statements are knowledge claims based in a sense of spiritual presence. McPherson and Klabunde cultivate that sense in embodied practices of dance and music. Their practices, Dancemeditation[1] and Collective Awakening,[2] hold the possibility of knowing an ineffable, numinous reality of spirit and organizing everyday life *around* that knowledge. They understand meditative dance and ceremonial music to orient people's bodies and minds toward a spiritual epistemology, even as the practices actively engage the materiality of commerce, material culture, and performance.

These practices are but two examples of contemporary Western vernacular spirituality. Such practices have many intersecting lineages: early twentieth-century movements such as theosophy and New Thought, the legacies of figures such as Aleister Crowley and Madame Blavatsky, the New Age movement in the 1960s and 1970s, the human potential movement in the 1970s, and innumerable psychology-based techniques for self-help, personal growth, relaxation, well-being, psychic and somatic healing, expanded creativity, and self-expression.

There are many ways to read the cultural politics of vernacular spiritual practices as performative. From one perspective, they perform gender, social class, consumerism, discourses on the self, and discourses on ethnicity in ways that warrant scrutiny. From another, the physiological and mental states cultivated as spiritual experiences can be explained as biological processes having nothing to do with a domain of spirits, gods, or supernatural forces (see chapter 3). Cultural hybridity, which is characteristic of "not religious" spiritualities, leaves practitioners such as these open to rigorous critiques of cultural appropriation and exoticization (see chapter 4). Those inquiries belong to a different critical project than the one undertaken in this book.

My query here begins in a question posed by the founder of Dancemeditation: "I began asking myself what and where did I think, or feel, spirit was?" (McPherson 49). The project is neither critique of nor advocacy for a domain of spirit but rather asks this question in relation to performance. The project thus describes the cultivation of spirituality as lived knowledge. If the paradigm of performance advocates knowledge gained via observing the material world, lived knowledge derived from spiritual practices offers an opportunity to critique and question performance as a paradigm.[3] As Paul Heelas reminds us, "we don't have to believe the *ontological truth* of what [practitioners] report, but it is appropriate to take their *word*" (*Spiritualities of Life* 93).

Martin Klabunde, founder of Collective Awakening, defines spirituality in his book *Music as Medicine* this way: "Spirituality is an active pursuit of the spirit and the connection to the Divinity inside each of us. Spirituality is a sincere desire to serve the Divine with passion, devotion, and dedication" (12). Following Heelas, such propositional claims are not a performative discourse *on* spirituality but evidence of an orientation to the world, which I suggest reorients performance. Klabunde's definition above invokes phenomena for which practitioners' intellectual orientations, educational training, and cultural backgrounds may have no other language than spirituality—spirituality is not reducible to other terms (including those of material culture, performance, or biology).

The premise that spiritual practitioners access knowledge of or from a spiritual dimension of reality (with which many readers will take issue) raises the question of perennialism discussed in chapter 1. Deciding whether the two practices discussed here access the same spiritual dimension through different means, use different means to access different spiritual dimensions, interpret the same sensations as spiritual experience, or construct spiritual fictions out of corporeal and cultural matter is well beyond the goals of this study. Chapters 3 and 4 address them broadly. Chapter 3 looks into the human body for the physiological connections between the internal sensations practitioners cultivate as spiritual and their expression in language. Part of the discussion of physical interiority in chapter 3 notes the artificiality of some analytical and interpretive conventions familiar to the study of performance, among them the myth-ritual dichotomy, language as discourse, and representation. Chapter 4 looks outside the body for how spiritually oriented practices are situated in culture and draw on cultural idioms to shape spiritual sensibilities, including the ways such practices engage consumerism, the individualism inherent in the constitution of the Western self, and cultural appropriation. This chapter is concerned with how the sense of spirit these practices cultivate alters a perspective on material culture as performative and performance as material.

Dancemeditation and Collective Awakening are examples of how people might come to and cultivate a sense of spirit as the fundamental, ontological ground for expressive forms. Those expressive forms include a wide range of performative registers: pedagogy, everyday life, discursive formulations, media representations, framed events, and so on. Taking the ways these practices articulate the divine or sacred as an experiential condition assumes that practitioners' sense of the numinous shapes the materiality of performance in all of those registers. Beyond the observable objects, bodies, events, texts, and matter out of which we construct and perceive the world as performative, in cases such as these performance functions as a membrane between practitioners' sense of a nonmaterial reality and the material reality we share.

HABITS OF PERCEIVING PERFORMANCE AND THEIR UNDOING

"Reading" spirituality as performance suggests that spirituality is a product of cultural forces and social communication. The Dancemeditation and Collective Awakening websites, through that lens, immerse spiritual seekers and popular culture critics alike in virtual presentations of these spiritualized orientations to Sufi-inspired dance and music inspired by African shamanism. McPherson keeps a regular blog accessible from her Dancemeditation site, where she chronicles her observations on and sensations of her body as a spiritual entity. One blog theme, for example, is "Embodied Spirituality."[4] Her YouTube channel, "Dancemeditation," shows a range of participatory events and performances of Dancemeditation improvisations.[5] Klabunde's website, *Music Is Medicine*, offers a video archive of his performances and a YouTube channel of his reflections on living a spiritual life.[6] Both sites invite readers to receive regular updates, schedules of workshops and events, and information by subscribing to electronic newsletters. Both sites offer practitioners CDs, DVDs, books, and handmade instruments or veils for purchase. The design of the photographs, colors, and organization of these virtual environments suggests a calm stillness, reflecting the inward-focused qualities of body-mind the practices cultivate.

Close readings of Dancemeditation and Collective Awakening websites, video archives, written blogs, DVDs, and CDs as performative texts could easily generate analyses of these practitioners as "performing spirituality." Such readings might, for example, focus on the ways these practitioners participate in signifying systems that link nonreligious spirituality to discourses on self-help psychology or alternative healing, interpreting practitioners' unhurried behavior and gestures, use of eye contact or gently closed eyes, relaxed body postures, and undulating vocal tones and inflections as rhetorical presentations of ideas and information that emphasize achieving a calm, relaxed state.

Further on in a critical close reading, the calm, laconic cadences these practitioners use on their CDs or DVDs might be read as characteristic of New Agey self-help gurus. Their sartorial choices, combining traditional Western jeans with dashiki-style shirts or wrapping the body in layers of silk veils over loose-fitting harem-style leggings, could easily be read as performing cultural Otherness. Such conventional readings might assess how these elements provoke conditioned aesthetic or emotional affects or play into fantasies of exotic cultures and esoteric knowledge. Critical readings might focus on practitioners' self-presentation as gurus, the appropriation of objects and images from non-Western traditions, the construction of individual spiritual utopias that dismiss responsibility to a collective, the illusion of an essential self or ultimate meaning, or the manipulation of people's emotions in order to sell products.

The framed events offered by Collective Awakening and Dancemeditation could also be subject to conventional critical readings assessing how these practitioners perform spirituality. Collective Awakening offers concerts of drumming, singing, and melodic music performed on indigenous instruments. The Dunyati Alembic, the performance wing of McPherson's Dervish Society of America, offers eclectic presentations of individual dancers' choreographic expressions. These framed events use familiar Western performance conventions, such as set start times, performers facing audiences, a raised dais for performers, applause, costuming or special dress, admission charges, and so on.

Readings these events as framed performances (activities set apart from everyday life) would immediately expose a familiar subject-object dynamic in which artists perform for audience members who observe and appreciate the aesthetics and enjoy personal affective responses. Readings of these events might yield analyses of dance and musical styles; the cultural origins (or appropriations) of the rhythms, instruments, and dance movements; facial expressions that convey tropes for mystical ecstasy or deep trance; staging choices; performer-audience interaction; the narrative tropes or myths used to frame the spiritual qualities of pieces; the performers' skill, and so on.

Similarly, the writings these two practitioners produce participate in existing discourses on popular nonreligious spirituality. Their words enter the discursive spaces that English translations of Rumi's poetry and John G. Neihardt's poetic Black Elk narrative created in vernacular culture, as well as more diffuse discourses that reference, in various ways, the metaphysical strands of American nature philosophy and spiritualism, the human potential movement, abundance and manifestation, self-realization, Buddhism-inflected virtues of detachment and compassion, religious transcendence rooted in Christian theology, and the social utopianism of consciousness transformation in the New Age movement.

Collective Awakening and Dancemeditation are consistent with contemporary vernacular discourses on nonreligious spirituality in their conflation of spiritual insights with health, well-being, and attention to the holistic functioning of a discrete self while using the expressive forms of the culture around them. Reading their work as performative thus immediately invokes a critical discourse on the representation of beliefs, myths and rituals constructing spirituality, and the coercive power of popular idioms. Performativity, as a critical paradigm, focuses on performers' expressions as symbolic systems: practitioners' expressions become symbolic, reflexive, "twice-behaved behaviors" without ontological content or origin. Spirituality thus becomes a referent that can be deferred or displaced in the act of production or reproduction. In this paradigm, performance calls spirituality into being (Schechner, *Between Theatre and Anthropology* 36).

Any view of the world, including that of performativity, is itself a matter of practiced habit. Klabunde writes that "the mind will reproduce and project whatever it constructs" (27). McPherson writes that "vision can only project forth from what we've learned" (38). The habit of reading spirituality as performance yields questions that make spirituality material. How do performers give the illusion that a spiritual experience is happening? How do performers represent spirituality? How are observers expected to respond to visual and aural images of spirituality? What emotions or sensations are images and words intended to evoke in an observer? Is the observer's role to appreciate artistry itself or artistry's purportedly spiritual meaning? These questions make sense in a paradigm that constructs knowledge by observing human actions acted upon by cultural forces and bound into systems of social communication. These questions make less sense, however, from the orientation of people for whom a spiritual dimension is accepted, accessible, and real.

Reading these expressions of inner, spiritual experience *only* as discursive or cultural constructions forecloses the ways these practitioners might be challenging paradigms that otherwise bind performance to the physical presence of bodies, images, words, and objects. Reading these expressive forms as performative without attention to how and why practitioners cultivate spirituality risks reducing people's spiritual orientations to cultural idioms, discourses, or affects. The case can be made that these and similar practices offer an engagement with the material world that is very different from the view produced by the performance paradigm. That engagement requires questions that interrogate spirituality as lived practice.

SPIRITUALITY CALLING PERFORMANCE INTO BEING

Familiar formulations such as "spirituality in performance," "spirituality as performance," or "performance of spirituality" treat performance as the structuring paradigm for spirituality—suggesting that performance produces spirituality. "Performance" might remain a useful term for what is observable, but these practices require not that spectators and auditors perceive a performance as we conventionally define it but rather that they sense what moves the performer to move, speak, or play music. Indeed, the name McPherson gives to her performance events is a term from Arabic alchemy for the container in which elements are transformed: *alembic*. She defines an alembic performance of improvisatory Dancemeditation as a "vessel that refines or transmutes."[7]

Both of these practices require that we understand performance as a subtler sensibility working within the codes we are accustomed to reading from a critical distance. Even as practitioners engage familiar performance conventions, it is not the showing, or even the doing, but the being that matters. As Klabunde commented during a performance of traditional and original music and drumming in 2011, "We exist in spirit. Spirit is the reason for the performance" (Collective Awakening Concert, Tucson, AZ, December 16, 2011). This is a challenging statement for a theoretical paradigm that begins in the materiality of the social world.

The spiritual orientations of Dancemeditation and Collective Awakening *make spirituality the structuring principle for what appears as performance*. Even in events these practitioners frame as performance, they emphasize relinquishing the need to be seen or heard, reflected and refracted by the eyes and ears of others, and allowing the presence of something other than themselves. McPherson wrote of that something as an "infinite essence":

> I used to tug at my audience, wanting their good opinion, earned with smart actions and craft, like a fifteen-year-old wants sex. But people resonate with the performer's motivation. All audiences know a manipulation on the gut level. I know the audience there as well. . . . I enter a performance as I enter my practice, beginning the Sisyphean task of releasing myself to the Moment. . . . I release my small, separate self and accept an infinite essence. (Newsletter, February 1999)[8]

Relinquishing the communicative identity or ego of a performing self to the internal sensations of sound vibrations and the body moving yields a distinctly different kind of engagement with the body and material cultural than performativity acknowledges.[9] What audiences, spectators, or scholars might otherwise construe as a dance, music, media, textual, or identity performance is infused with a presence that fundamentally alters the engagement of the dancer's body with space, objects, audience, language, and visual imagery.

What might be perceived as performative (e.g., websites, events framed as performances, practitioners' self-presentation in workshops, textual or spoken language) is for these spiritual practices the membrane across which people engage internal sensations with cultural idioms (e.g., African drums, veils, the form of a memoir, the structure of a workshop, the visual images in a DVD, the engineering of a CD). Like the shifting surfaces glimmering in the play of appearance and disappearance in postmodern performance theories, the membrane of performance has a discoverable richness.[10] However, what is available to be seen, heard, touched, or read as performance does not, for these spiritual practices, begin in cultural or social conditions. Taking these practices on their own terms, what we might see, hear, and read as performative is evidence of spirits working through language, objects, actions, and bodies.

These spiritual practices suggest a significant shift in thinking about performance. In the paradigm of performativity, what appears as real is performance, not spirituality. For these spiritual practices, spirituality is what is real, which gives rise to performance. The activity of performance becomes the condition that makes sensory access to spirituality possible, rather than codes to be read. The issue, then, is less about showing how people perform spirituality and more about how people's spiritual sensibilities inform what we take to be performative.

SPIRITUAL KNOWLEDGE

These practices' spirituality moves into material culture using familiar mechanisms and developing expressive forms and knowledge formulations that match (to the extent possible) sensations of spirituality with culturally recognizable idioms. Spirituality emerges through these practices with a complex of characteristics:

1. Connection with a spiritual domain, the spiritual aspect of one's self, other people, and a common humanity emanates from the sensation of a broad and all-encompassing love.
2. A self is experienced as mental, physical, and spiritual. The mind is not limited to rational thought and observation, and the body's capacity for perception is not limited to the five senses. The sensation of the numinous or ineffable, which is both mental and physical, is understood as spirit. A spiritual self is privileged over social identities.

3. The practices Klabunde and McPherson have developed make spirituality accessible as experience and as a kind of knowledge. Spirituality is associated with personal transformation leading to social transformation, healing emotional wounds, relief from stress attributed to modern life, freedom from limiting thoughts and behavioral patterns, freedom from impediments to contentment, well-being, peace, love, and a deep sense of happiness. Cultivating one's own human spirit is coextensive with openness to spiritual presences or a spiritual realm.
4. Language, which (in modern, Western cultures) is conventionally associated with rational processes and the capacity to represent observable reality, is considered a limitation on a person's ability to access the sacred or the divine (variously formulated as one's own spirit, a universal Great Spirit, the Beloved, individual spirit entities, love, etc.). Language, in the context of these practices, is not bound to the cultural value placed on rational thought, logos, or the psychological life of the mind. Spirituality requires releasing thinking (cognition, logic, language) in favor of nonanalytical awareness.
5. Spiritual knowledge is located in one's inner self, not in authorities outside the body (including texts and social identities). Part of spiritual practices such as these is remembering the self as essentially spiritual.
6. Spirituality is not revealed. Spirits are not posited as controlling forces or even as shared reference points for practitioners. Nor do the practices deal directly with or ritualize major life events (death, birth, marriage/coupling, etc.) as religious systems do. A spiritual dimension to the self and world are present and accessible by means of music or dance. Spirituality is practical, experiential, and directed toward living a more integrated, holistically healthy individual life that extends to the positive development of human society. The sensations of the numinous or ineffable practitioners identify as sacred or divine is experienced as simultaneously personal and universal, immanent and transcendent, the self and beyond the self.
7. Authenticity, in the terms of these practices, is not about reproducing texts or imagery, reconstructing an originary experience, or performing an authentically spiritual culture. Authenticity is a quality of the self: a person senses a connection with something numinous or ineffable that is simultaneously in and outside the self. The internal sensation of that connection without dissonance is experienced as a spiritual self.

8. The sense of the self as a spiritual being organizes mental and physical activities. The mind and the body respond to an energy understood to be spiritual in essence; they do not construct and represent spirituality as an abstraction.
9. Spirituality is simultaneously immanent and transcendent, physical and ephemeral and reliant on cultural resources while simultaneously independent of human culture.
10. The practices cultivate physical and mental relaxation that can lead to a mystical or meditative state. In that state, attachment to a physical, material world and one's identity as an individual softens, transforms, or drops away entirely to make other modes of knowing and new knowledge available. That knowledge is accepted as ultimately ineffable, but described in vocabularies of the divine, the sacred, and spirit. It cannot be directly documented, fixed, or empirically verified in the modes of representation and symbolic logic practitioners perceive as dominant in their home culture. Spiritual knowledge comes out of experience, and can be lived through actions in the material, social world as life praxis.

Many of these characteristics are consistent across a wide range of contemporary, vernacular spiritualities. Dancemeditation and Collective Awakening could be read as constructing these characteristics by replicating existing discourses on spirituality based on an imagined, originary experiences or by conjuring fantasies of authentic spirituality taken from the cultural idioms of Sufism and African shamanism. I want to suggest, however, that these characteristics of spirituality evince a sensitivity to life praxis that has been undervalued in systems of knowledge production that privilege performance (see chapter 4).

Spirituality, as experiential knowledge, moves into and in material culture through the work of practitioners like McPherson and Klabunde. The question for the next section is, what is moving? The next section describes in detail how these two practitioners cultivate spirituality as both an individual and a community experience through their workshops and framed performance events, as well as how their writings formulate spirituality as a specific kind of circulating knowledge.

The material selected for the following sections is drawn from years of following these practitioners' work on-site, online, and, most recently, in print. This is not an ethnographic project but an effort to situate these practitioners' spiritual sensations within the registers we otherwise assume are performative. The immediacy and primacy of spiritual presence to their bodies and minds seem, as I have suggested, orthogonal to the aims of performance theory's orientation in the social. The following descriptions tease out the ways in which perception, in these practices, is less a function of the five senses processing data from the external world (the domain of the performative), and more a kind of internal sensation practitioners understand as a priori knowledge.

The sensations these practices identify as spiritual differ from each other, as do the means by which they cultivate those sensations. These practices are categorically similar, however, in that they both posit a numinous dimension to the self and the world. That dimension distinguishes their engagement with the material world from the trained organization of sensory perception defining bodies and culture as performative and the trained disbelief of a critical perspective. The inner-directed spiritualities of Dancemeditation and Collective Awakening undo the performativity paradigm by positing something outside the performative. That undoing, however, is an opening.

THE PRACTICE OF SPIRITUAL BEING AND OF BEING SPIRITUAL

Klabunde and McPherson are two of innumerable practitioners in the modern West whose life praxis evolves from and revolves around sensitivity to spiritual presence.[11] They are not casual spiritual seekers or shoppers[12] and have crafted lives and livelihoods out of their sense of the numinous, often in resistance to the norms of a materialist culture. In the professionalization of their spiritual practices, McPherson and Klabunde take on cultural roles as teachers of spiritual knowledge. According to the internal logic of these practices, knowledge comes from accepting and engaging an ineffable, numinous dimension to the self and world, and basing an approach to life praxis on that sensibility. In Klabunde's shamanist language, spiritual reality is the Great Spirit; in McPherson's Sufi language, it is the Beloved. In Dancemeditation, an intense, meditative awareness of highly nuanced somatic sensations in improvisational movement yields knowledge of the mind and body as spirit. The traditions of Sufi mystics shape Dancemeditation's interpretations of the body in motion as a manifestation of the divine through mystical union with the Beloved. In Collective Awakening, entering into a different mode of consciousness through drumming and indigenous music yields a direct connection with spirits and spiritual worlds. African shamanism informs drumming and playing music as a way to travel in a dimension inhabited by spirits.

Klabunde is a certified instructor with Mamady Keita's Tam Tam Mandingue International School of the Djembe, a 501(c)(3) nonprofit organization, which runs an international network of schools founded by Mamady Keita in 1991. The organization's mission fosters "interest and participation in traditional West African drumming, dance, and cultural art forms, as well as to preserve and transmit Mandingue musical tradition as a tool to promote tolerance, understanding, equality, and international peace."[13] In the same spirit, Klabunde founded the Dambe Project, a Tucson-based nonprofit organization inspired by a year spent teaching West African drumming to students in East Africa in 2002. *Dambe* is a Mali word loosely translated as "integrity." By 2005, the Dambe Project was able to offer as many as six yearlong classes in East and West African drumming in Tucson-area schools, with the goal of encouraging a more holistic kind of learning. Klabunde taught music in seventy-five schools and offered dance and concert events with an adult professional ensemble, the Dambe Drum ensemble. Klabunde developed a spiritual component of his drumming and teaching called Kalumba: Path of Light.

Collective Awakening has used performances and its website to help other local nonprofits, such as Tucson's Engobe Art Studio (an "art self-help studio") that raises money to send educational supplies to high schools in Uganda.[14] More directly, Collective Awakening encourages donations through its website for African aid, with a particular focus on education. For special projects, Collective Awakening takes donations at its public concerts. Donations taken at a 2010 café performance at Borders Books in Tucson, for example, went to support a family in Uganda, as did proceeds from CDs (which were slim as the now bankrupt Borders required a percentage of CD sales). The cultural priorities visible in the juxtaposition of the donation basket, the negligible profit margin on Collective Awakening's CDs, and the $4.50 soy latte I purchased point to the very problems Klabunde seeks to rectify through a collective spiritual awakening. Service remains a strong component of Collective Awakening's mission and identity: the homepage of the website lists nearly a dozen types of organizations Collective Awakening serves. The list speaks to Klabunde's orientation to spiritual practice as cultural work that serves others, rather than himself.

Dunya Dianne McPherson studied dance professionally in New York

City during the 1970s and 1980s, completing a BFA in dance at the Julliard School. In New York, she directed two dance companies, Dianne McPherson & Dancers and Workwith Dancers Company, as well as developing a substantial profile as a choreographer. Through the 1990s, her work included stage choreography, commissioned pieces for dance companies, and choreography at numerous colleges and universities in the northeast including Princeton University and the Mark Morris Dance Center. She has held a National Endowment for the Arts choreography fellowship, as well. Her studies in Sufism began when she met Adnan Sarhan, Sufi master and founder of the Sufi Foundation of America, in 1980. That meeting initiated what would become seventeen consecutive summers (1,001 days) at Sarhan's Sufi camp complex south of Albuquerque, New Mexico. Sufism, including practice of the *zaar* (Sufi whirling for purification practiced by the Mevlevi Order) and spiritual belly dance, became the overarching language for her evolving somatic spirituality. The Sufi name, Dunya, given to her by Adnan Sarhan, associates her with finding spirituality in the substance of the body and the material world. During this seventeen-year period, she also studied classical yoga at the Dharma Yoga Center in New York with Sri Dharma Mittra, whose teaching reconnects yogic asanas (the Western narrow definition of "yoga") to healing, self-knowledge, and relaxation. She oversaw the training of professional dancers in an academic context as chair of the BFA in dance at the Victorian College of the Arts in Melbourne, Australia, during which she recognized the limitations of dance as performance. A series of physical injuries led her to an interrogation of her body's ways of moving, reconceiving dance as a spiritual practice.

In 1990, McPherson founded the nonprofit Dervish Society of America (DSA). She developed and trademarked Dancemeditation as a unique practice of embodied mysticism in 1995, then started the Alembic in 2005, which frames the meditative dance of her students as performance. She has been faculty or artist in residence teaching Dancemeditation at numerous arts institutions, colleges, and spiritual centers, including the Kripalu Center for Yoga in Massachusetts. The Dervish Society of America is "dedicated to the path of evolutionary Sufism. DSA provides programs and opportunities for personal development, exploratory inquiry into embodied spirituality, and community connection through practice, service, and performance." The society is based in New York and has a permanent home at the Ravenrock retreat center in northeastern New Mexico. Donations to the Dervish Society of America are tax-deductible.[15]

In different ways, both practitioners acknowledge that cultural forces, social conventions, and discourses (including those of popular science) mediate their spiritual knowledge. They are also keenly aware of how the social worlds they inhabit have shaped their bodies, thinking, and assumptions about what constitutes knowledge. The sensibilities they cultivate reorient them within this *habitus*.[16] Even as their strategies for developing practices make explicit use of a contemporary, technologically advanced culture, the perspectives and sensibilities they bring to that culture are distinct from those usually considered in analyses of culture as performative or performance as culture. In practice, the objects, images, discourses, sartorial choices, vocal inflections, and gestures mediating their practices do not substitute the experience of spirituality, nor do they represent or symbolize spiritual realities. They are instead the means by which these practitioners engage their spiritual sensibilities and move their sense of spirituality into material culture.

SPIRIT IN MATERIAL CULTURE

The ways contemporary Western vernacular spirituality circulates in material culture suggest active engagement with, rather than estrangement from, the domain of the wholly human. McPherson and Klabunde bring managerial and fundraising skills to the process of expanding and promoting their work through contemporary media and social structures. They also bring what by any standard would be considered more than reputable artistic skill. Familiar electronic media (websites, electronic mailing lists, social networking) and social structures (conferences, workshops, framed performances, lectures, presentations in schools) move nonreligious spirituality into the broader culture without foregrounding its cultural or intellectual alterity.

Collective Awakening developed from offering shamanic drumming workshops, trance dances with live music, meditation sessions with live music, and sacred drumming ceremonies in the desert Southwest to expansive explorations of personal and community spirituality across the United States.[17] Collective Awakening's offerings take diverse forms, from meditation sessions and drumming classes to public lectures, and appear in a wide range of venues, including schools, universities, yoga studios, arts festivals, camps, and community centers. Together, Klabunde, a former public school teacher, and his wife, Wing Man Law, who holds a PhD in psychology, offer a range of workshops nationally throughout the year. In addition to sacred drumming ceremonies, their workshop topics include "Expanding the Self," "Rejoice in a Loving Heart," and "The Power of Gratitude." Klabunde has produced six CDs of original songs, drumming for meditation, music for yoga, and guided meditation, which are for sale during events. He also sells African hand drums (*djembe*), five-stringed harps (*adungu*), and thumb pianos (*akogo*) imported from Uganda or handcrafted by Klabunde from materials imported from Africa.

Longer retreats synthesize and vary the presentation of Klabunde's work to match the needs of the venue and participants.[18] In August 2012, for example, a ten-day Hawaiian retreat, "Music Is Medicine: Heal and Thrive in the Magical Lands of Hamakua Coast," included guided meditations, sacred dance and drumming sessions, lessons on indigenous instruments (adungu, akogo, djembe), and sacred music concerts. The promotional web flyer for the retreat gives a list of goals, among them to "remember that we are pure and sacred beings capable of creating a life of abundance and profound meaning," "work together to create the change we would like to see on this planet, in this lifetime," and "have a deep conviction that, together, we can transform the world into a more compassionate place!"

A July 2011 Norwegian Cruise Lines cruise from Miami to Jamaica, with stops in Cozumel and Grand Cayman, offered sacred drumming ceremonies, sacred trance dancing and meditation, performances of original music played on indigenous instruments, and presentations on "sound, healing, paradox, perception and the ancient technology of music." Participants on the cruise "experience the traditional music, song and dance of the Maroon people in Ocho Rios, Jamaica" and "travel back in time through the ancient music of the Mayan, Incas, Aztec, and Zapotec people of Mexico in the only spiritual/cultural music museum in the area."

Dunya Dianne McPherson teaches and performs in New York City and across the United States. Her Dervish Society of America is a nonprofit organization "dedicated to the path of evolutionary Sufism providing development and exploratory inquiry into embodied spirituality and community connection through service, performance and practice opportunities"[19] and "the Path of embodied mysticism."[20] Under its auspices, McPherson teaches Dancemeditation, spiritual belly dance, and Sufi dance meditation.[21] In all three permutations, the practice uses improvisational physical movement, informed but not structured by dance vocabularies, to move participants into a meditative state. She offers daylong and weekend workshops, seminars, an annual two-week Summer Movement Monastery, an eighty-day teaching training program with two certification levels, and performances. Spiritual belly dance emphasizes a reorientation to the body (male and female) as sensual, curvilinear, expressive, and mystical (often in direct contrast to contemporary concepts of sexuality), and the use of the veil as an aesthetic extension of the physical body. Sufi dance meditation draws on the tradition of whirling in one place combined with chanting, conscious breathing, and meditations with veils to produce a mystical state of consciousness.

Retreats are often held at rural retreat centers with sleeping and dining facilities (sometimes requiring tents or sleeping bags), such as the Margaret Austin Center in Chappell Hill, Texas, the Synergia Ranch in Santa Fe, New Mexico, and the well-known Kripalu Center in Massachusetts. Shorter daylong and weekend workshops may also be held in yoga studios, dance studios, dojos, and converted warehouse spaces across the country. After a winter 2012 fund drive toward the goal of raising $250,000, the DSA was able to purchase Ravenrock, a three-season retreat in northeastern New Mexico, as a permanent site for the annual Movement Monastery. McPherson's teacher training program and two certification levels cultivate "self-evolution through embodiment."[22] She also offers training in spiritual belly dance.[23] At present there are some twenty-seven trained Dancemeditation teachers certified in the United States. In electronic newsletters and flyers announcing workshops, McPherson describes a process of cultivating sensibilities that integrate mental and physical capacities:

> Dancemeditation™ opens the inward-facing doors of consciousness that live in every cell through Slow Movement, breath-based stretching, Healing Rocking, Intuitive Movement Flow, and expansive dancing, to activate and honor the body's feeling sense, enhance your ability to listen and receive embodied messages, and open the Subtle. You'll leave spiritually refreshed and inspired.[24]

McPherson has produced nine practice DVDs designed to help people familiar with Dancemeditation sustain a home meditation practice or to introduce people to ways to move the body into meditation through a fluid dance-like series of yoga postures, the curvilinear motions of belly dance, or abstract sensory explorations. In each DVD, McPherson leads practice sessions after a brief verbal introduction to the practice and intention of the DVD itself. She has also compiled a Sufi cookbook, and offers hand-dyed veils, mystical note cards, and two CDs of *zill* meditation music and Sufi whirling music. All of these as well as her spiritual memoir, *Skin of Glass: Finding Spirit in the Flesh*, are available on her website.

These mechanisms of a modern, technology-rich culture put spirituality in the mainstream without relying on traditionally religious institutions or traditions. Formulations of what constitutes spirituality and practices for cultivating a spiritual life can also circulate beyond the immediate community. Through familiar channels of knowledge distribution—workshops, websites, books, CDs and DVDs, online videos, and blogs—spirituality moves into and through contemporary American culture. Spiritual practices such as these are accessible to a demographic with the financial means to attend events and purchase resources for cultivating and exploring spirituality. These practices are overtly interconnected with and function in the materiality of consumer culture. They also *contribute to* that cultural milieu by asserting an array of sensory options otherwise invisible or undervalued. Through these normalizing mechanisms, practitioners give credibility to cultivating physical and mental capacities that are not readily supported by dominant social mechanisms, such as education, health care, and the corporate job market as spirituality.

FROM PERFORMANCE TO SPIRITUAL PRACTICE

The spiritual practices Klabunde and McPherson have developed began in their work as professional performers; their practices thus offer a critique of performance from an orientation in spirituality. Klabunde started his professional life as a drummer in a successful popular band, which he also managed, on the West Coast in the 1980s. McPherson trained in the elite of Manhattan's ballet and modern dance scene in the 1970s. Both individuals worked within systems that situated drumming and dancing as artistic expression and entertainment; both sought to make a living performing. Performing required the display of learned skills in the competitive environment of professional arts. In the midst of building professional artistic careers, both individuals experienced an epiphany that shifted how they understood music and dance as performance.

Each discovered a less obvious, but no less tangible, dimension of their bodies and minds in dancing and drumming. They identified this presence (in different vocabularies) as a spiritual aspect of the physical and mental self and a spiritual presence in the apparent solidity of nature and culture. What their cultural influences had constructed as performance of an art form offered instead unobservable, invisible sensations of a presence beyond affect and independent of an audience. Both individuals transformed what had been an artistic profession into a spiritual practice, which they describe in detail in their books, *Music as Medicine: Accessing Sacred Wisdom from the Master Within* (Klabunde) and *Skin of Glass: Finding Spirit in the Flesh* (McPherson).

The titles of these books establish telling similes. What the words describe is elusive, not this and not that, one thing becoming another. Klabunde, in *Music as Medicine*, offers a spiritual manual with personal anecdotes to illustrate the life events and mystical experiences shaping his knowledge of spirits. For Klabunde, "Music reveals a path to the divine, a place deep inside us where spoken language cannot enter" (50). Music mediates between the human and the divine, and "demands that we speak in poetry rather than linear words" (Klabunde 52). McPherson's *Skin of Glass* is written in the memoir genre, describing phases in her life through which she developed the sense of embodied spirituality she teaches. "Besides sensation," McPherson writes, "my body surprised me with an arresting narrative—she wanted to tell a story, tell me secrets I'd kept hidden from my mind. This became a tumultuous research, and wording it felt like translation, stretching and tucking syntax, language, and grammar around the sweep and grind of bone and dance" (xi).

McPherson's narrative traces seventeen summers of Sufi training in New Mexico with a popular American Sufi, Adnan Sarhan. Under his authoritative tutelage she developed what she refers to as an "inner view of life" (McPherson 34). Klabunde offers a guide to a spiritual life through music, including seven virtues that will align a person with a universal spirituality. Both books are selective in the biographical information they present. The authors draw heavily on personal experience, but their purpose is not autobiography. Significant parts of their personal histories not included in the books (for example, Klabunde's study with shamanic drummers in remote villages in Uganda and McPherson's shift from modern dance to belly dance) have come out in other mediums (newsletters, discussions in workshops, newspaper articles, conversations, blog posts, etc.). The purpose of both books is an exegesis of lived experience in service of parsing and transmitting spiritual knowledge. That exegetical project offers a critique of the performative from the domain of spirit.[25]

Their transformational process resituated the activities they had studied as music and dance as spiritual, rather than explicitly performative, practices. The shift is significant for both. Engagement with a spiritual dimension required no observer or audience, did not rely on cultural codes for communication, and was not bound by conditioned visual or aural perception.

Out of this shift in perception, Dancemeditation's Dunyati Alembics and Collective Awakening's concert-ceremonies merge the conventions of concert performance with spiritual sensibilities. Their framed events are offered as a means of investing a gathering of people with a spiritual sensibility, evoking the sense of a numinous reality beyond the world of matter and what conventional thinking can access.

In such events, spirituality contextualizes and structures the engagement of bodies with material culture to the extent that these events cannot be analyzed only in the terms of performativity. While they do draw on conventions of performance, such as a seated audience with clear sight lines to the practitioners, these events are not set out as representations of beliefs, symbolic rituals, or other signifying practices. Though they rely on music and dance as familiar artistic genres, the Dunyati Alembics and Collective Awakening concert-ceremonies are not presented as displays of artistic skill or aesthetics, nor are they presented as displays of the practitioners' mystical experiences or spiritual knowledge. They are intended as occasions for engaging with a spiritual dimension.

LANGUAGE FROM THE BODY

Both Klabunde and McPherson use language to address the experiential sense of spiritual presence cultivated through their music and dance practices. The technology of writing allows them to formulate spirituality as knowledge in the most common medium for conventional epistemology. In addition to the verbal narrations and instructions they give in workshops, they transmit the knowledge derived from their spiritual practices via blogs, song lyrics, and instructional DVDs, for example. McPherson's and Klabunde's self-published books provide the most comprehensive syntheses of their insights into and perceptions of a spiritual dimension. As authors of a spiritual memoir (McPherson) and guidebook (Klabunde), these practitioners interpret their internally sensed experiences of spirituality, the development of their practices, the events in their personal histories that shaped their spirituality (such as confrontations with mortality or unexpected encounters with spiritual presences), and the knowledge they have gleaned from their sense of the numinous.

It is important to note that these practitioners do not locate knowledge in language. These are not doctrinal or proscriptive practices. Spirituality here resides in the mental-corporeal sense of the self as an essentially spiritual being connected to a spiritual reality ultimately exceeding the self. The multiple and overlapping discourses in which McPherson's and Klabunde's texts participate may in part construct the autobiographical hermeneutics of spiritual experience and spiritual selves their books "perform." However, taking these practitioners on their own terms forces an examination of exactly what kinds of knowledge they are extending into contemporary American culture.

Their language is anchored in the process of cultivating embodied, spiritually oriented life praxis. Their descriptions of spiritual experience and practice in their books, websites, brochures, CDs, and DVDs open the possibility that spirituality is a viable basis upon which to ground people's active engagement with material culture, communities, and the human body. These formulations of an inner spiritual life, as Mark C. Taylor suggests, "provide models *of* the world that serve as models *for* activity in the world" (*After God* 17). They offer an active language of the body and mind as spirit: humans having spiritual experiences and spirits having human experiences—embodied spirits and enspirited bodies.

Both practitioners juxtapose traditional Western modes of knowledge (logocentric and symbolic) with a mental-corporeal experience of the world as infused with the numinous. In *Music as Medicine,* Klabunde writes that a spiritual path is by definition experiential: spirituality is "not an intellectual or academic venture" that can be accessed in language or by analysis (13). McPherson's spiritual memoir opens with a critique of the primacy of language in Western culture: "In our culture, a subject becomes real once it is written" (xi). "I knew from experience," she writes, "that dance *was* a spiritual path" (xi). The effort in *Skin of Glass* to give spiritual sensations a discursive voice is, in effect, an accommodation to a culture that recognizes performative language as a carrier of knowledge and disregards the experience of one's body and mind sensing a spiritual presence.

The orientation away from the representational conventions of the culture in which their work is situated raises a different set of questions for Dancemeditation and Collective Awakening than those the performance paradigm produces: How do the spiritual sensations move from people's bodies and minds into material culture? How are those sensations present in the language, visual images, gestures, pedagogies, framed events, and media generated by spiritual practitioners? How does the way we access seemingly familiar expressive forms, such as concerts, narratives, or personal identities, change when we acknowledge that they come from or invoke the sense of a spiritual presence?

MOVING THROUGH THOUGHT AND EXPERIENCE TO THE SENSE OF SPIRIT

Collective Awakening cultivates the sense of spirit in a variety of ways. Communicating with spirits, particularly spirits who have migrated from Africa to the United States, remains the center of shamanic practice (as Klabunde expanded Collective Awakening's services and venues prior to 2013, however, the emphasis on spirit contact has receded). Drumming and music played on indigenous instruments are, for Klabunde, "technologies" that facilitate communication with a spiritual domain. The sense of being in communication with spirits, understood to have identifiable and distinct energetic personalities, can be described as shifting to an altered state of consciousness (the responsibility of a participant's body-mind) and experiencing metaphysical dimensions of the material world (a reality not available to our five data-gathering senses). This sensibility is cultivated by giving over one's social identity, ego, and perception of self to the "technology" of sacred music.

For a trance dance event, Klabunde will assemble musicians and drummers for improvisational dance and music sessions lasting two to three hours (for example, the Shaman's Trance Dance, Yoga Oasis Downtown, Tucson, AZ, February 26, 2011). Participants pay a nominal fee of $12 to $15 to cover the costs of renting space (in this case, an urban yoga studio) and transporting instruments. Musicians play a range of instruments, from Tibetan bowls and Native American flutes to East and West African drums and the Australian didgeridoo. The use of electronic amplification, which at first seems incongruous, functions in this context as another technology that serves people's ability to sense spiritual presence. Within the practice there is no contradiction between the purported authenticity of the premodern past and the mediating effects of contemporary mass-produced electronics. Spirits move through electrified machines as easily as the goatskin head of a djembe. For Klabunde, the suggestion that the sense of spirits present in the trance dance might be an illusion of the senses or a false belief is simply irrelevant. From his perspective, and from that of the shamans who mentored him, it is "arrogance" to think that one is imagining or making up the experience of other worlds (comment after meditation session in Tucson, AZ, July 20, 2010). However, he recognizes that communicating with spirits requires an orientation to drumming, dancing, and meditation that is unfamiliar in the modern West.

"The drum," Klabunde remarked in a two-day shamanic healing workshop, "requires us not to think" (January 24, 2009, Tucson, AZ). Experiencing the spirit world requires releasing linguistic and cognitive formulations of knowledge, with a willingness to access wholly different knowledge than is available in normative Western culture. Framed events and workshops thus presume that fundamental truths start in a spiritual dimension of energy and work their way into and through the physical world of human bodies and societies. Klabunde's vocabulary also expresses his awareness that people's attachment to socially imposed identities interferes with that sense of truth or self. He says, for example, that the spiritual practice of meditative drumming allows us to "be the people we were meant to be" (concert, December 16, 2011, Yoga Tree, Tucson, AZ). Though these ideas resonate with the modern narrative of discovering an authentic or essential self, the practice's commitment is to accessing a spiritual dimension rather than achieving psychological well-being.

Though each workshop is different, "Meditative Drumming for Inner Transformation"[26] illustrates consistent qualities and characteristics of Collective Awakening's spiritual orientation to the world. Klabunde uses many of the anecdotes and ideas in other workshops as well, though they are not presented as doctrine. This "playshop," the term Klabunde prefers to workshop, took place in the afternoon after a sacred music concert and community drumming ceremony the night before in the same space. The large, windowless yoga studio was rearranged from the previous evening's concert event, for which folding chairs had been arranged in a semicircle around a performance area. For the playshop, the entire room was open and available. A circle of chairs had been set up in the center; a display table along one wall held CDs, copies of *Music as Medicine*, imported instruments, note cards, and cloth for sale. A row of Klabunde's hand-made drums lined the wall next to the table. A variety of instruments (didgeridoo, djembe and *dunun*, Tibetan bells, akogos, and a handmade adungu) and electronics used in the previous night's performance were clustered in what had been the performance area.

The playshop began with participants in a circle, each with a djembe (some participants bring their own drums; others use drums provided by Collective Awakening). Klabunde sat next to Wing Man Law. Together, they led the group in a single beat, in the tempo of a heartbeat (about one beat per second), played in unison. The steady, synchronized sound and motion gave the group a sense of cohesion and purpose. Klabunde then asked that each person talk about an aspect of his or her experience or life he or she would like to transform, and the group is asked to respond to each with "*aho*," a word he described as used by some Native American tribes to close a prayer.

Klabunde asked that participants listen without judgment and speak without fear. After each person had taken or passed on the option to speak, Klabunde began to describe spirituality as a practice and the presence of a particular kind of energy. He described the practice of drumming or playing music as a technology for bringing spirits into the physical world by opening a portal to the spirit world. In the practice of drumming, he continued, people cultivate the ability to "go deep" into somatic and conscious capacities for sensing the spirit dimension, and to open to the truth that dimension offers. Spiritual truth is not cerebral or separate from action; in practice, one senses truth and finds in one's self the ability to act on that truth. Bringing spirituality into the physical world is a matter of *doing, informed by spirit.*

In this workshop, Klabunde spoke of the drum, specifically the djembe, as a way people connect with the spiritual dimension. Based on his years in East and West African countries and cultures, he offered a narrative of cultural transformation in which Western incursions have eroded the spiritual connection people indigenous to Africa once had. African spirits, as well as people, have been dislocated and dispersed by disruptions caused by the insensitivities of Western colonialism and capitalist agendas. As a result, African drummers such as those with whom he studied in Africa, who now teach in Western cultures, are exporting drumming to the West. The purpose is to reintroduce spirituality to the West and in so doing heal Western cultures in order to reduce its damaging effects on indigenous and colonized peoples.

In this practice, cultural capital is spiritual capital, and money is an unproblematic conduit for the circulation of spirituality and healing in a culture that needs both. Klabunde spoke of Western colonization as having profoundly altered indigenous spiritualities. Precolonial music, he said, was ceremonial, communal, and commemorative. Spirituality is inherent in such indigenous music when people's intention is to open to a spiritual dimension.[27]

Precolonial societies, unlike the modern West, supported that intention. Postcolonial music, on the other hand, he described as overtly performative. Such music is skillful and communicative and it creates affect. It is not spiritual in intent or origin because, following Klabunde, Western cultures do not recognize the spirituality inherent in the instruments upon which ceremonial music was played. Nor do Western cultures value the African societies that supported openness to a spiritual dimension and indigenous drummers' capacity to connect with spiritual dimensions. Klabunde's narrative identified a transformative shift occurring in Western cultural values, literally a collective awakening to spirituality. People are beginning to seek out and pay money for spiritual experiences such as his workshop, he observed, rather than invest time and money in acquiring objects and status symbols to perform their social identity or displace their inherent spirituality.

Transformation is also individual. In this workshop, Klabunde spoke of his own life trajectory, in which "the drum found me." Letting go of a socially imposed identity in order to connect to one's "inner wisdom," he said, yields the internal sensation that "we are energy." Music allows the self, as an individual entity or physical being, to disappear into an altered, meditative state of consciousness. One's perception and capacities for experience shift as one enters a domain of spirit that is fundamentally different from that which we take as real.

In this context, Klabunde related an anecdote from his studies with a shaman in Guinea. Klabunde expressed to the shaman his concern that his experience of this fundamentally different reality was an illusion, the result of his own mind "playing tricks" (a concern Klabunde recognized as a culturally conditioned assumption about spirituality). His teacher responded that the problem is impossible, that it would not occur to anyone who practices drumming that the experience of a spiritual dimension is not real. "We live," Klabunde asserted, "in a time of transformation," in which this reality is becoming accessible.

The playshop is loosely organized in three phases. The first, after this spoken introduction, is devoted to drumming. In this phase, Klabunde teaches the group a rhythm pattern based on a West African rhythm he learned in Uganda called *kuku*. He explains that the pattern is strongly associated with women. A long drumming session follows, in which he encourages participants to allow themselves to "go deep," meaning to release habitual thought patterns and sense the presence of spirit within themselves as wisdom as well as in other dimensions of reality. In the second phase, music played on an Australian didgeridoo, Native American flute, Tibetan bells, and Native American standing drum accompanies a meditation. With the studio's yoga mats and blankets, participants sit or recline as the lights dim. The steady beat of the drum provides soundscape and focus for about forty minutes of otherwise silent meditation. In the third phase, Klabunde leads a sacred drumming ceremony. For this, participants return to the circle of chairs and their drums.

The ceremony begins with Klabunde asking permission from the four compass directions to open the ceremony. In the center of the circle, he faces each direction and blows a conch shell toward the north, south, east, and west after a short prayer to each direction. He then lights white sage and moves around the circle cleansing each person with its light smoke. Participants recite two prayers, "Of Course it Was Not I" from *Black Elk Speaks*, the 1932 Native American spiritual classic by American writer John Neihardt, and "Walk in Beauty," identified only as a Navajo prayer. Law and Klabunde light candles in the center of the circle to begin the drumming. Klabunde teaches the group three basic patterns, which together create a polyrhythmic, synchronized soundscape for trance and access to spirits. Over the group's drumming, Klabunde improvises more intricate rhythms. His virtuosic improvisations, the result of years of training, lead the group. Most participants play with their eyes closed, allowing for a short, focused journey inward to access a spiritual dimension of consciousness. In the context of this practice, that dimension is as tangible and real as the one in which you are reading this description.

Klabunde remarked in this playshop that "you can hear the words, but until you have the experience you don't really know." For this practice, the experience of the spiritual confirms its reality, not the words written or spoken about it. Symbols, Klabunde says, are portals to a nonphysical realm: that is, they do not signify, stand in for, or represent concepts and ideas. In the sacred drumming ceremony, the candles, prayer words, sage, and sound of the conch shell shaping the group's drumming as a ceremony are not texts—they are understood as openings to a nonphysical aspect of physical reality. Klabunde acknowledges communication in the physical world, the level at which academic analysis operates; however, he advises that we look not at the candle (the physical) but what is around the candle (the light). "We connect with people in the physical world," with gestures and words, "but also in ways that are not observable—the spirit. At the end of our lives—at 100 or 110—spirit is what we take with us."

McPherson's Dancemeditation workshops and retreats can last from one to ten days, depending on the venue. Workshop or retreat days are organized around sessions of improvisational movement, which can last from one to three hours. Participants might be arranged in an inward-facing circle or semicircle around McPherson (or one of the certified Dancemeditation teachers she has trained), or they might be scattered randomly about the room so that each individual can move in his or her own space. Movement sessions alternate with silent meditation periods, time for private reflection and writing, and communal meals or rest breaks. Participants begin by following McPherson's movements as she verbally guides them through movement sequences and breathing patterns. Movements are slow and fluid to encourage relaxation and open the possibility for sinking deeply into meditation.

Sessions allow for stillness and shared solitude in silence as well as physical movement. There is little explanatory discussion. McPherson does very little talking in order to allow students to move into meditation without the distraction of language. She offers minimal instruction: for example, she will arrange people into pairs or small groups for exercises such as mirroring movement or sensing others' movements with closed eyes. Depending on the workshop, she might develop sequences from a seated or standing position or organize sequences around movements characteristic of belly dance, Dervish whirling, and hatha yoga or free-form improvisation.

In workshop sessions, participants begin to follow a Dancemeditation leader's movements reflexively, as if connecting to the leader's physical energy. McPherson describes starting sequenced movement as an opening to the spiritual dimensions of the body: "In my training in Sufism, the beginning is a threshold to enter the room, and what is the room? The room is the presence, being in the present, being in the presence of what is essential in the universe."[28] There is no technical dance instruction; instead, McPherson's minimal guidance relies on precise nouns and verbs that focus attention on the body. She illustrates verbally how legs, arms, feet, hands, head, fingers, sacrum, sternum, spine, shoulders, belly, hips, and back will curve, curl, stretch, touch, bend, rock, push, pull, contract, and expand in contact with the floor, the space, or a veil. Her verbal guidance draws attention to how individual bones, joints, organs, and muscles feel within the body. This pedagogical method, in which participants mirror her movements as they enter meditation, "facilitates the quieting of intellect. It is easier to stop random, chaotic, non-functional thinking if the training method de-emphasizes analytical processes."[29]

As sessions progress, participants begin to sense and respond to the internal sensations that move their own bodies, rather than imitate McPherson. In some sessions people may move freely in their own physical (as well as mental) space, exploring the movement patterns to which their bodies are habituated, including injuries or any physical, athletic, or dance training their bodies might have normalized. It is not uncommon for the movements to release emotions, and for participants to pull away from the collective movement when emotions are strong.

McPherson's own background in ballet, modern dance, Middle Eastern belly dance, and yoga is evident in her improvisations. However, the movements themselves seem to emanate from the center of her body and move outward through combinations of dance languages her body mastered over years of training.[30] In sessions, her eyes usually remain half-open or closed as her concentration moves into her body and her voice takes on a calm, rhythmic, almost chant-like quality. The practice seeks to engage an ephemeral, inner impulse that moves the physical aspect of the body. The practice cultivates somatic sensitivity that leads to spiritual awareness. She encourages participants and students to "let sensation be your guide" in avoiding pain and allowing the body-spirit to heal. Participants invest attention, for example, on how muscles engage and release as the body moves and how the breath moves through the body until consciousness and the body are indistinguishable. The goal of any given session is complete immersion in the body, rather than awareness of its form or capabilities. The practice involves constant, attentive physical movement to the point at which one senses the self in movement without a structuring symbol system or consciousness of being watched.

A workshop given in 2011 by one of McPherson's trained and certified Dervish Constellation teachers offers a particularly strong example of sensing presence evoked by the Dancemeditation practice. This daylong workshop (10:00 a.m. to 6:00 p.m.) allows time for discussion among participants, as well as individual reflection.[31] A converted single-story house located in a thickly wooded area in central Texas (seven miles from the nearest town center) serves as the studio. Yoga mats, blankets, and hip scarves are arranged along one wall. Participants take a space in the open floor plan facing a wall of windows looking out into the woods, each setting out a mat, blanket, and veil. During the afternoon session, participants clear the floor for a solid hour of free-form improvisational movement.

The workshop's morning session begins with participants seated on mats and a Sufi invocation recited in Arabic by the teacher. Participants are invited to "bring divine energy into the space" by opening their hearts to forces beyond normal perception. Participants are given the opportunity to share what drew them to the practice. Most participants speak of healing, accessing a higher spiritual knowledge, or reconciling some aspect of their emotional or intellectual lives. Some speak openly of personal trauma or difficulties. The teacher responds to each with assessments that seem to go directly but gently to the essence of each participant's self-reflection, sometimes revealing what the reflection might be hiding. To a participant who spoke of wanting to give to the world, the teacher responds simply, "You need to learn to receive."

This workshop's morning session is organized around exploring seven "energy centers" in the body, known from Indian Tantric philosophy as the chakras. Movements initiated by the teacher focus on each chakra individually, with explanations of each chakra's metaphoric and physical associations (for example, the second chakra corresponds to the element water and the capacity for creativity). The workshop allows participants to contemplate and write out their responses to sensations they might experience in each area of the body—pelvic floor, pelvis, solar plexus, chest, throat, forehead, and above the crown of the head—and the thoughts or emotions that moving each region of the body brought to consciousness.

This particular workshop develops Dancemeditation's characteristic mirroring pedagogy with instructions for actively listening to the body. "Let what is in the hips begin to speak," the instructor encourages. "We hold a lot in our hips." "Don't think about what you are doing" is a quiet mantra throughout this workshop, a way of encouraging an integrated intelligence that synthesizes consciousness, thought, and corporeality. This particular instructor's ability to sense a wholly integrated body and mind-body affected her linguistic expressions in ways that go well beyond bodily metaphors. She asks, for example, that participants "let the mind go beneath the heart" and spoke of "opening the mind in an embodied way." She also speaks of "an inner sense" and of "the inner ear hearing" the voice of the body.

The afternoon session juxtaposes a silent meditation in a supine or seated position with free-form improvisational movement accompanied by a variety of musical styles, from belly dance to samba. The workshop closes as it began, coming full circle, by "calling in the Holy" with a Sufi prayer read in Arabic and a chanted vocalization to "call in the vibrations" of the divine and to sense those vibrations in the body.

Collective Awakening and Dancemeditation workshops such as those described above are pedagogical insofar as they introduce participants to experiential possibilities not always associated with dance or music. The cultural alterity of the sounds and movements, their association with non-Western cultures and premodern spiritual traditions, provides a referential shift for many participants. The cultural breach might itself constitute a "spiritual" experience for some, a sudden rush of the new, the foreign. My observation of numerous Dancemeditation and Collective Awakening events suggested a range of responses, from boredom to skepticism to altered consciousness. It is certainly possible to read the apparent sincerity of the practitioners as a performance that is either naive or manipulative. Suspending the critical impulse that ends in critical cynicism, however, allows different interpretive possibilities for encounters with framed events like those of Dancemeditation and Collective Awakening.

WHEN SPIRIT PERFORMS

Collective Awakening presents concerts in a variety of settings, both formal and informal, including playing for trance dances.[32] Regardless of the setting, the context for each concert is that music creates a connection between humans and spirits, and the purpose is making that connection possible. Ritual efficacy is not the issue. Collective Awakening's concerts are meant to open a portal for spirits who are already present. Ceremonies are a way to "access energies that can transform and rearrange this physical world" (Klabunde 37). Nor is affect an issue. The musicians call attention to the sound, not to themselves as performers. A spiritual musician "is no longer considered to be an individual" but "part of the universal cosmic message that music carries" (Klabunde 62). As Klabunde said in his introduction to an indoor concert in December 2011, quoted above, "We exist in spirit. Spirit is the reason for the performance."[33]

Some Collective Awakening performances are accompanied by workshops, sacred drumming ceremonies, or meditations, contextualizing the framed event within the spiritual practice. Other events framed as performances do not. Collective Awakening (then under the auspices of the Dambe Project and billed as "African drumming") played at Tucson's annual arts and community event, the HoCo Festival. Klabunde was introduced as a community activist and introduced his set as bringing "precolonial" music to the modern West in service of "well-being" and "mind-body work." At this civic festival devoted to "Celebrating Diversity in Arizona," djembes and akogos were not out of place among the variety of indigenous instruments and musical styles on the festival's main stage. Performers included Odaiko Sonora (a local *taiko* drumming group) and Batucaxe (a local ensemble and school devoted to Brazilian drum and dance traditions). The stage was surrounded by some twenty-one booths representing local nonprofit arts and cultural organizations, including the Symphony Women's Association, the Pascua Yaqui Tribe's "Tucson Meet Yourself," the Bicycle Inter-Community Arts and Salvage, the Tucson Circus Arts, the ZUZI! Dance Company, and the Dambe Project as well. No religious groups were listed on the festival roster. The event was held on a downtown plaza and side street near a major historic hotel. Here the musical invocation of spirits went out through a celebration (and performance) of the material, and entirely human, world of artistic and ethnic culture, social organizations, and civic resources. A passing train swallowed the sound of the song "The Master Within." Yet, for Klabunde and Law, the spirits are always present if one is willing to "listen with inner eyes, hear with inner ears, from the heart."[34]

An example of this inner listening, from Klabunde's perspective, occurred in 2010. Klabunde was one of six performers scheduled to perform hour-long sets at a large open-air craft fair and market. The market was set up on the grounds and parking lot of a well-established Christian church known for its social outreach to the local community and its commitment to the arts. The church was situated on a well-traveled highway overlooking an urban expanse. Its external religious symbols had a distinctly multicultural valence: to the side of the stage area, a tall modernist statue of St. Francis of Assisi rose in parallel with a cylindrical Buddhist temple gong. With religious symbols on one side and commerce on the other, the music of local guitarists, jazz singers, and keyboard players continued throughout the day, providing an eclectic aural background as people bought and sold goods ranging from apple butter to tooled leather holsters.

The day's performers were surrounded by amplifiers, microphones, mixing boards, chairs, music stands, wires, and instrument cases. Their music blended into the white noise of conversations, distant traffic, and the calls of doves and cactus wrens. Around the circular stage area, children learned how to bead friendship bracelets at a long crafts table. Another table held homemade baked goods for a local charity; another displayed artwork donated by local artists to be raffled off at the end of the day. Performers took their turns on a circular stage area set up at the edge of the market, Collective Awakening was another activity for consumption and socializing within the larger cultural performance of a craft fair.

People wandered past the stage area. Some stopped to listen or support known performers; others paused to talk or rest with refreshments for sale near the stage area. There was no formal audience seating, and the area around the space marked off for performers was the only tree-shaded place available. In the midday heat, Klabunde and Wing Man Law, dressed in white, loose-fitting cotton tops and trousers, unpacked their instruments and stepped to the microphones. Without introduction, they began a series of haunting songs in English simply accompanied by hand drums (djembe), five-stringed harps (adungu), and thumb piano (akogo). The lyrics, sometimes barely audible, alluded to awakening, a great being, a spiritual master within all of us, and tranquility. The songs are recorded on a CD, titled *From the Heart: Music for Awakening*, which was available for sale at the festival.

Between songs, Klabunde softly explained the origins and construction of the instruments and the meaning of the rhythms within their local African contexts. Only briefly did he comment on the way he understands music to work as a conduit for the sacred. "Melt," he said without an effort to command anyone's attention, "allow these notes to become part of you." His job is to "let the music speak." Echoing words from his workshops, he told whoever might be listening that the music comes from somewhere else and goes through him, that to be a vehicle for healing sometimes means sacrificing whatever aspects of one's self need to drop away. Some passersby barely took notice of this comparatively quiet performance; others let it be background for their conversations as they found relief from the heat. One woman slowed her pace. She stopped directly in front of Klabunde and Law, facing them. She remained there, unmoving and silent, standing in the path as other people passed around her until Klabunde and Law concluded their set and began packing their instruments.

After the performance, Klabunde and I talked about what it means to shift the sounds and rhythms he knows to be imbued with spiritual power from the intimacy of a ceremonial or meditation space to a public place, thus adding a performative frame (signaling entertainment) rather than a spiritual one. Klabunde asked if I had seen the woman who stopped to listen. I told him I had. He commented, "The woman who stopped—she got it."

The "it," for Klabunde, is some sense of a spiritual aspect to the world. In that moment, Klabunde felt that someone who was not expecting to hear spiritual music, and would likely not associate the unusual instruments and songs with any familiar religious tradition, experienced the energy in the music as spiritual. He did not perceive the person's response as appreciation or affect, but a connection with the same spirits he himself senses when playing. For attendees who, in Klabunde's words "get it," a sense of spirit is palpable, real, and unarguably present, clearly distinct from emotion, thinking, feeling, or other affective responses associated with performance.

The Dunyati Alembic is the performing component of the Dervish Society of America and has a core group of dancers, some of whom also appear in McPherson's DVDs.[35] The core group has offered dances as artists-in-residence at the Kripalu Center, as part of the Monday Evening Art Salon in New York's Metropolitan Building, and by invitation to festivals and conferences such as the Theatrical Bellydance Conference and the Dramarama Festival in New Orleans. Within the overtly performative frame these venues suggest and in more informal settings such as yoga or dance studios and found spaces, Alembic performances involve a series of dances. Individual dancers or dancers in pairs or groups may vary widely in style and skill level, and McPherson always offers a dance as part of Alembic evenings. Choreography may involve poetry, finger cymbals, veils and other costumes, music, or silence; it may invite participation from people in attendance or allow people to witness as the dancers enter into a state of dancing meditation. The variations in presentation allow for movement of spirit as well as physical bodies in the spaces.

The purpose of any given Alembic event is an inquiry into inner sensations. The electronic flyer for a 2010 Alembic evening event, "Mystic Body Alembic Performance," described the way the presentation of spiritual experience has the intention to transform matter:

> Core Alembic explores questions and themes germane to spiritual seeking that can be viewed in theatrical venues as well as unusual settings—cemeteries, gardens, ballrooms, etc. The dancers share Dancemeditation™ as a dominant influence in their self-understanding as well as professional dance backgrounds. Performative presentations include composed dances as well as framing of group and personal practices, with a vision of absorption into Beauty and Mystery.[36]

This particular Alembic performance was held in a fitness and dance studio in Houston, Texas. A single door opened into a small entryway, with a changing room to the right and cubbyholes for shoes on the left. Dancers mingled with people as they entered the studio and paid the $25 fee at a desk set up in the entrance. The six dancers greeted friends or participants from the previous day's Dancemeditation workshop. Beyond the desk, the studio itself had no formal seating. People took yoga bolsters and blankets to sit on, and set them facing a wall draped with veils framing a performance area. There was no clear division between the performance area and where people sat to experience the dancers; the dancers themselves sat in the same general area as the people who had come to witness their meditations, though most of them clustered off to one side near the sound system that would provide music for the event. The series of dances included a finger cymbal dialogue between two dancers, an elegantly expressive belly dance by the only man in the ensemble, a long flamenco-inspired solo, and a seated veil dance. Two individual dances offered a striking contrast in the interplay between framed performance and the internal sensations of spirituality.

McPherson entered from the back of the room and began her dance in the upper right corner of the performance space. Elements of her attire were incongruous: a layer of pink net skirting over loose leggings, a dark colored jacket, a silk veil. During her improvisation she removed the net skirt, as if dropping an identity, and left it on the floor. Her body's vocabulary was as eclectic as her attire: the pointed toes of ballet, contractions and twists of modern dance, angled arms and legs of American jazz, fluid undulations of belly dance, butoh-like contortions, dervish whirls (though not sustained) knitted together then fragmented her body. Sudden contortions and exuberant stretches seemed to tear her body out of her costumed self, perhaps allowing a sense of her own essence to move without hindrance. Her eyes remained closed, her focus inward even as her movements pressed energy outward.

This "mystic body" is electric, very much of this postmodern world. Its spirit finds multiple, layered expressions hiding as much as they show and seems overtly performative in the conventional sense—an invitation to hunt for complex signification, to read the performance for its symbolic meaning or internal logic. McPherson's own perspective resists that reading.

In an interview from 1999, McPherson spoke of the accessories of belly dancing (costume, makeup, jewelry, veils) as a distraction for most audiences. She explained that whatever props, costume pieces, or other accessories she might put on become extensions of her body's internal sensations. Accessories, such as the bright pink net skirt in this Alembic performance, become part of a corporeal language that does not signify but rather *is* the sense of spiritual experience. Costuming, like her body, is not an iconography of spirit but part of the spirit's movement. To someone observing the performance, McPherson's face and gestures might seem to express emotions, from anger to anguish to love. In the context of the Dancemeditation, however, her body movements are not intended as communicative gestures (as much as they invite reading as such) but responses to her internal impulses. Movements of muscles, tendons, sinews, bones in limbs, torso, hips, face, back, hands, and feet respond to some energetic force. Whatever physical forms her body takes, and clothing with it, are the shapes of that energy.[37]

OBSERVATION FROM WITHIN

These expressions or experiences of spirituality happen in an explicitly performative frame, which, by convention, invites interpretation of whatever is within it. The frame sets what it contains apart from life praxis. As the examples in chapter 1 illustrated, a performative frame intensifies the complexity of assessing or accessing spirituality as a kind of inner sensation. Framing devices—a designated performance area, special dress, hesitation before applause, artistic skill—make people present as performers. Performance asks to be observed and to be heard. In these spiritually oriented performances, the frame that signifies performance is a convention. It holds the potential for its own undoing, the possibility of a different presence emanating from a particular kind of engagement with sound and movement. At the same time, the threat of representation forces that possibility into the shadows, making what is not audible and not visible not real, limiting bodies and words to their materiality. This is, of course, the conundrum. How can we know spirituality when we cannot see it, or see spirituality when we cannot know it? With a bit of irony, the question brings us from sensation and experience back to reading texts and material culture, but with the sensibility cultivated in the practices: with the "inner eyes" of experience.

Klabunde and McPherson identify a cultural disposition toward seeing and hearing that creates spectators and audiences habituated to constructing meaning when light hits the retina and sound vibrates the eardrum. Their practices, however, suggest different modes of encountering the spiritual in the materiality of the body and musical instruments. Through practice, spirituality as formulated by these practitioners redirects seeing and hearing inward rather than out into the material world: what is available to be sensed are less objects in an external environment than conditions of physical, mental, and spiritual being. Those conditions are available to "inner eyes" and "inner ears," which the practices cultivate. *Skin of Glass* and *Music as Medicine* both articulate the ways "inner" eyes and ears perceive differently from spectatorship. A spiritual orientation literally reconfigures capacities for perception (see chapter 4):

> Music is a manifestation of an inner sound, a cosmic sound, that exists inside each of us. . . . All people can hear audible sounds, whereas cosmic sound can be heard by those who practice deep levels of detachment and transform their perceptions of the mundane world—by those who can see and hear beyond the veil of the material, those who see with inner eyes and hear with inner ears. (Klabunde 45)

> The drum surged, charging and stamping around inside my guts. It shoved aside my interest in a sense of displacement. Night vision opened. Inner eyes began to see. (McPherson 37)

> Our spiritual eyes allow [us] to "see" through the veil of the physical realm and perceive the magic of the spiritual realms. Our spiritual eyes are connected to our intuition and imagination. We need to remember how to use these eyes in a deep and meaningful way. We can use music to help us see with our spiritual eyes. (Klabunde 189)

> Roped together, seeing and sensation alchemized into one—a felt-seeing, a sensory-sight. I was, paradoxically, more located and interrelated with my world than when my eyes were open. Dancing with an inward gaze was freeing. (McPherson 38)

Whether or not a critical view of these practices can accept the authority of "inner" eyes and ears, or the spirituality they access, the performative expressions these spiritual practitioners make available are invested with these sensibilities. Seeing and hearing "beyond the veil of the material" suggests that what is available to the critical paradigm of performance requires, for such performances, at minimum a willingness to engage what these sensibilities might suggest for a more rigorous critical perspective.

In addition to shifting familiar modes of perception, both practitioners also identify a broadly accepted emphasis on materiality in American or Western culture being an impediment to spirituality. At the same time, they rely on technology, travel, commerce, and an infrastructure of venues from conferences to cruise ships, as well as workshop fees and the sale of CDs and DVDs. This apparent contradiction seems at first problematic (see chapter 4); however, the contradiction contains a critique of the social and commercial systems in which spiritual practitioners operate. From within these practices, a lens trained outward on the broader culture sees spirituality set against materiality, and spirituality as anathema to conventional modes of thinking. In practice, spirituality and materiality are integrated. McPherson wonders about the effects of Western culture on the sense of a spiritual self. Her language evokes Pierre Bourdieu's habitus:

> I can remember that, before Sufism brought them to me, I felt only a faint keening in my cells. I wonder, had *stam'ba'li* or *zaar* been in my culture, would I have become a dancer or gone to therapy or even been an artist? So many of my needs are met by a community trance dance. Not a nightclub, which is our sexually based bacchanal of smoking, drinking, and hunting. A *zaar*'s scope is bigger and wider. I grew up in a world where dance, like Latin, was a dead language known to a handful of scholars and theologians. To think of a culture where dance is spoken freely relaxes me and, even if I do not live among them, I wrap the remote sisterhoods around my shoulders like a lavish stole that warms me while I clear rooms and initiate Dancemeditations amidst America's sport-pocked, gym-flayed body-dearth. (McPherson 213)

Likewise for Klabunde, spirituality as life praxis is anathema to a cultural impulse that locates meaning in objects of perception and activity rather than the sensations available to consciousness and the body:

> It seems almost impossible to develop these spiritual practices and virtues within a culture that denies them and bombards us with messages to continually look outside ourselves for answers. Ironically, we see this happening in spiritual circles as well. So many people are searching outside themselves for spiritual enlightenment. So many are traveling to exotic places in search of what is already inside them. (233)

Performance, too, is outside.

THE DISAPPEARANCE OF PERFORMANCE

Performance studies has adapted a stance, derived in large part from Judith Butler's theory of performativity and identity, that social performance constructs what we take to be natural and that indeed there is no "natural" body other than that which performance naturalizes. McPherson moves in opposition to this ubiquitous academic stance. For McPherson, social and artistic performances do not naturalize the body but *obscure* its naturalness: "My dance teachers had scrutinized me as I scrutinized myself in the mirror. Our eyes smothered my frame in corrections and adjustments, carving my nervous system, molding my clay calves and thighs into stainless steel. This mutual gaze buried physical naturalness" (33). McPherson's narrative is one of transformation, leaving behind this culturally determined obsession with performing her body's appearance in the mirror and the ingrained, habitual need to perform that idealized body in her own mind. At the end of *Skin of Glass*, she is simultaneously the observed and observer. Writing of her experience leading a group of people into meditation through dance, she observes,

> As sensation leaks parts of me together, I feel, beneath the cacophony of their emotions, the quietude of their essential selves swimming in my bloodstream. No longer distracted from what is, I open my eyes to see the firm floor, the chair's crisp edge, and through the window, the afternoon's wide-eyed gaze fixed on me. I watch them close their eyes and face a different sort of mirror, one that refracts the naked glimmer of self. (McPherson 204)

McPherson is, however, keenly aware of how embodied cultural codes construct and perform identity. She writes about the performance of identity in ways any performance theorist would recognize as deconstructions of ethnicity, religion, class, and gender. Yet for her this performed identity is an illusion, not a site of meaningful inquiry; the performance of identity is worth parsing in passing but only to expose it as a veil. She describes, for example, finding herself using a railing as a ballet barre for stretching on Pier 17 of the South Street Seaport in New York City, and contemplating the ways bodies and clothing signify. The detail of her analysis warrants full quotation as a conventional reading of material culture, which, in the context of *Skin of Glass*, McPherson deconstructs:

I'd charged outdoors through windy Wall Street canyons in red cotton pants and a designer T-shirt made of high-tech moisture-wicking fabric, which now tugged on my damp skin, sweaty from vigorous walking on a warm spring day. A woman sat on the nearby steps, her legs crossed at the knee; black leather spike-heeled boots disappeared under her black skirt. A man's bare forearms wrapped around her, holding her close against his chest as his head curled adoringly into the neck folds of her black *chador.* The breeze danced over his arms and mine, pushed his hair and mine. Hers were hidden away.

I'd thought hard that day, as I did every day, about what to wear for my workout walk—a hip outfit, attracting, but neither too sexual nor too dowdy. All my choices had subtexts that must be weighted within context. In the first decade of 2000, jeans and T-shirts worked everywhere across America. But the exact shape, snugness, and color varied from region to region and fashion season to fashion season like passwords on a computer. Lately, exercise gear had become couture. How I covered my body was prescribed, a veiling within my culture's rules. My neighbor in the *chador* was draped from head to toe in black, no questions there. In public, she was a moving cloud of mystery. My empty stomach and full closet of thin clothes were my *hijab*. We both dressed to conform.

On Pier 17, I contemplated what made stretching my body in public an acceptable exercise and not provocation. Part of it was my outfit and part how I draped, angled, and displayed the actual position of my limbs and torso. If I stuck out my rump (a word that can't help but conjure the idea [of] an animal for slaughter and roasting) with legs at a half-way angle, I looked, by someone's definition, like a slut; if, however, I extended my legs into a superhuman split, the startled viewer asked "How can she do that?" and lost, if only for a moment, a sense of dominance. My capabilities lifted me from call-girl availability into an unattainably sexless superiority. (McPherson 175–76)

The previous passage demonstrates an awareness of one's self as always performing, which emerges in both McPherson's and Klabunde's books as an imperative in contemporary Western culture. In different ways, both practitioners identify three perceptual habits encouraged by modern, Western culture that are at odds with spirituality: representational thinking, the ocular orientation of an externally focused gaze, and the epistemological primacy of rational thinking over intuition or more subtle sensibilities. These are the habits of thinking that, to varying degrees, govern the paradigm of performativity. Klabunde writes,

> We have allowed our minds to run the show. . . . The mind has created an elaborate system of layers designed to keep what it perceives to be "outside forces"—anything originating outside itself—from taking over. Ironically, this means that our innate desire to seek out an inner meaning and define the purpose of life and our existence as human is carried out by looking to the outside world, the physical world and anything and everything outside ourselves. Walking a spiritual path requires us to recognize the affliction that the mind can produce; it requires that we begin to look inward and develop a relationship with our inner being. (185)

The impediment to spirituality, from the perspective of a spiritual reality, is the organization of mental capacities into syllogistic thinking based on analysis and observation. McPherson writes,

> On childhood Sunday mornings, I heard the minister say, "The peace of God which passeth all understanding . . . [k]eep our hearts and minds in the knowledge of Him who is in Heaven." And I wondered, as children do when they grasp a deepness floating by in a world of inconsequential detritus, if something passes all understanding, how can you understand it? In the stillness following *Shams*, I experienced that Divine Peace did not pass all understanding—it passed all *cognitive* understanding and all *articulation*. I slid across the portals of my frontal lobes, past the juices of the amygdala, into Essence, and entered Divine Peace. As we sat chanting Koran, my entire being completely understood peace. I was at one with peace. I *was* peace. (71–72)

In this anecdote, McPherson dismantles the theater of the mind from the depth of a sensing body. Mental processes trained to see and represent an external world (e.g., René Descartes's theater of the mind and Antonio Damasio's "movie in the brain") inhibit the capacity for refining an ability to sense beyond what the eyes can access and, at the level of experience, split the mind from the body (the gap these and many other practices try to bridge) and the mind-body from spirit. McPherson writes critically of the ocular obsession that drives performance and casts inner sensation into the chasm of invisibility:

> I don't know exactly when or why my eyes ceased to be part of my body, but at some early point they became spies belonging to a world of intelligence detached from my body, relaying instructions about what it was or should become. I gazed out from inside my skull. . . . I lived the way one sits in the theatre looking at a brightly lit stage. Beyond the proscenium arch, dancers or actors display the philosophy of human life. Perhaps I was drawn to performing because I imagined it could place me in the light of action where the people speak to one another, touch one another, lift one another, or perhaps I hoped I could step out of my skull. Yet fantasy and reality are seldom the same. (34)

SPIRITUAL EPISTEMOLOGIES

As noted above, McPherson and Klabunde both achieved considerable success as professional performers. Turning away from the careers into which they had been socialized came at some psychological, emotional, and financial cost.[38] Klabunde writes,

> Initially, I had to undo some training I had developed around the drum. I came from a background of being trained to play specific parts in a specific way. My mind was deeply involved in making sure I was playing "correctly" and abiding by the rules I had learned regarding playing technique, posture, rhythmic sensibility and timing. I came to realize that these were all assets if I could learn to let go of the mind and further develop my faculties if intuition and intention. . . . I began a process of no thinking and no judgment about what came through my being, into my hands and out the drum. I found that I was able to utilize all the training I had gotten from initiated masters of the djembe, and I did not have to think about any of that. I had learned the language of the djembe well enough that I could allow my inner being to speak an ancient language of music and lead the way to the spirit realms. (56)

Reflecting on her early dance training, McPherson critiques the tyranny of the dance studio mirror. "Perfecting my reflection soon became the truest part of dancing," she writes, and "what floats most clearly in my mind's eye is worry over being thin enough" (McPherson 9). She recounts a sexualized encounter from her childhood that drew a sharp line between her sense of being in her body and the awareness of her body being watched. In her adult life, performing in daily life and on stage thus became

> a way of *hiding* what worked with open eyes in a world where life is visual. I adopted this persona [of performance], this Body Guard self, as my protector. There was one small sacrifice: sensation. With open eyes, I was numb. My glassy flow of movement reflected in a mirror was empty as dust. (McPherson 99, italics added)

Her struggle is to *not perform* because performance cannot commit to presence; instead, it empties out content, testifying to lack, loss, and displacement of the real. What contemporary performance criticism celebrates in the aftermath of postmodern theorizing, this performer critiques as destructive and damaging. Commitment to a spiritual sensibility, as defined by these two practices, turns away from the performative imperatives of American culture, which are now so well theorized.

The spiritual epistemology these practices produce suggests that the moment when sensing a spiritual presence transforms the physical body and material environment is the moment when performance becomes an irrelevant, if not impossible, category of perception. The sensations of spirituality begin to inform thought, including the thought that shapes the actions and products we take as performative. After one particular *zaar* (whirling dance), McPherson writes of the sense of spiritual presence in relation to thinking:

> I was able to speak about *Al Hathra*—the Presence. I rarely speak of this unless the state embraces everyone at once. In fact, I am unable to articulate it from thought alone. Words about this state form themselves from beyond my mind and deliver themselves across my tongue almost without my knowledge. Someone did tell me that I'd described the state as having the sensation of being in a spacious, soft, subtle, vast, still center of a perfect sphere, and because you are in center, wherever you are is perfect. There is clarity. (153)

These spiritually oriented epistemologies shift emphasis away from culturally supported mental activities (such as computational thinking and rationality) that rely on processing sensory data. They cultivate, instead, a kind of consciousness that attends to inner sensations, from which they formulate knowledge.

Klabunde, for example, writes, "The mind is relentless at wanting to create some kind of separation between itself and what it considers to be outside itself" (97). Music resolves that restlessness; it is "the action of the heart; it informs our thoughts" (Klabunde 52) and "slowly dismantles the mind" (Klabunde 55). "Spiritual music," Klabunde writes, "is a stream of consciousness that reflects the inner state of the spiritual musician" (61). Thus, "We cannot listen to our spirit and think at the same time. We need to stop thinking for just a moment and allow the voice of our spirit to be heard" (Klabunde 13). The ways Western culture trains people to use their minds, following the spiritual logic of Collective Awakening, is severely limited. "Until we remember the power of our Spirit," Klabunde writes, "the mind will lead us. When the Spirit leads the way, the mind will follow" (33). Music played or experienced with the intention to make a spiritual connection

> opens doors to other dimensions and offers us access to the knowledge and wisdom contained there. Music is also our interpreter when we travel to these dimensions. Our mind is not equipped to translate the message waiting for us there, but music is a language that is bidirectional. We can use it to communicate and receive the messages the mind cannot perceive. Music opens pathways to and from our spirit center, or our inner being. Our inner being does not use the mind, rather it uses energy to gain knowledge and information. (Klabunde 44)

In McPherson's Sufi language, this experiential synthesis of thinking with action, self with other, body with mind, and knowledge with experience is the totality of the Beloved. She depicts the experience of the Beloved rendered simultaneously as thought and sensation:

> *There is no beloved but the Beloved.* The Beloved is everything. The Beloved is me and not me. Everything is me, and everything that is not me, is me, and everything, including me, is not me. I've thought this thought a million times but suddenly I am inside the thought and the thought, although a paradox is simple. I liquefy and reconstitute. This epiphany emanates from blood moving through openings and closings. Thought is not isolated from flesh. Thought and flesh, though not the same, are one. Are cells thought? (McPherson 209)

Despite efforts to theorize beyond them, the familiar binaries of subject-object and observed-observer still undergird the study of vernacular culture as performative. Yet, for these practitioners, what might otherwise be observed as spirituality is a condition of sensible awareness that affects the physical world:

> For many, the goal of a spiritual path is to reach a state of awareness where the mind no longer places judgment on anything outside itself and accepts everything as belonging to itself. If we want to take this deeper we could say that this state of awareness is beyond the mind altogether, a place of no mind where the mind no longer identifies with anything other than the realization of complete oneness with everything visible and invisible, physical and spiritual. (Klabunde 87)

If the sensations of "oneness" or that "the Beloved is everything" described in the two paragraphs above is the fundamental condition of performance, then the modes of analysis we currently use apply binaries that limit (if not invalidate) what these people are doing as they cultivate very specific sensibilities and what it means when they engage resources available to express those sensibilities. If, in the spirit of cultural criticism, we take these practices as "performing spirituality," we are Flatlanders unaware of a dimension that is unquestionably real for these practices and formulated as knowledge.[39] McPherson describes a class where the external gaze and consciousness of performance disappears, and spirit infuses matter:

> Now the eye-less women ooze, their countenances morphing. At the outset, when the motion image, not yet felt, is still devoid of kinesthetic connection, the flesh of their faces remains opaque. Then the skin's patina softens, a signal that self-consciousness has been eclipsed by sleepy, sensual pleasure. Finally comes quietude. The descent into Absorption. The whole body is a silky skein. (216)

Klabunde describes the integration of spirituality and materiality, what is visible and what is invisible, as a moment of completion, fullness, and undivided presence:

> Making and maintaining our connection to the invisible is a powerful way to exist in the physical. When we participate in the realms of the spirit, we connect to a consciousness that gives meaning to the physical. Our humanness is complete when we access the spirit. (98)

SPIRITUAL SELVES AND SOCIAL IDENTITY

The human self of these spiritual practices is a process, rather than an entity. This is not the decentered self of postmodernism or the fragmented self negotiating multiple social, cultural, or ethnic identities. We often think about bodies as saturated with meaning, overdetermined by culture (as if there is some norm for a determined identity). Essentially spiritual selves are sensed as profoundly *underdetermined*, open to perceptual anomalies and experiential mysteries. This is a self-legislating, self-regulating self in which sensation has ontological status. The *interior* self has ontological status. At the same time, this self is communal, relational, and engaged in the material world.

Both practitioners use gendered pronouns, suggesting gendered cultural identities.[40] McPherson's story is gendered strongly female and heterosexual. Klabunde's pronouns are masculine, but the writing itself is otherwise not gender specific. The ways each writer assumes masculine or feminine gender might well bear scrutiny in relation to the sense of the self as essentially spiritual. Pronoun use and the gendering of spiritual experience, however, also express an important point made in both books: people who cultivate spiritual lives live between worlds. Klabunde writes, "We are humans with one foot in the physical and one foot in the spiritual" (60). McPherson narrates this feeling of living in two worlds after returning to Manhattan from her seventh summer at a Sufi monastery in New Mexico. After weeks immersed in a spiritually focused regimen of dancing, isolation, meditation, and fasting in primitive living conditions, she writes not of the juxtaposition of two radically different environments—the material-cultural and the spiritual-numinous—but the sense of living as a spiritual being:

> I live in New York City's downtown Manhattan early 21st Century America. My neighborhood, Little Italy, is a hub of international chic. The World Trade Center towers no longer preside, but the streets thrive. It should be so simple to traffic in the world of humanity, to open my inner borders, but I'm often imprisoned in my sanctuary of self, jailed in scripts that resist, prohibit, and shelter me from what is. . . . The challenge is to actually have an experience, not the shell of an experience, nor an experience filtered through expectation, not one's dream imperfectly fleshed out, but the full brunt of newness that shimmers everywhere. I

> try every day to leave the monastery. How else can I know that the world is divine, that my body is my soul? (McPherson 49)

In these formulations of spirituality, gender is a viable category at the level of culture. McPherson explores gender explicitly as both culturally constructed and biological, with strong emotional and psychological valences. Gender comes through in these formulations as a culturally significant category of identity that a spiritual sensibility can profoundly transform. McPherson writes,

> I was brought up to be a woman and, after that, a Sufi. In each instance the definition of "woman" and of "Sufi" came from the minds of men, the dominant culture of men. I now chose to do each of these differently. Sufism removed veils enough for me to see my authentic center, and once in center, I saw the way to remove veils in a manner intrinsic to my authentic self. I unlearned and re-learned being a woman, and in the small single shape of one woman Sufi, became a re-definition of both Sufism and woman. (170–71)

These practices ground knowledge in the self. However, the inward focus is not a license for solipsistic whims. There is a rigor to exploring inner sensations that have no traction in the immediate cultural environment and to parsing out their ambiguity. There is an unwillingness to accept a socially constructed identity, even in the acknowledgment that such identities are inescapable. The tension between social construction and agency is at the center of postmodern debates about human-social interaction. Klabunde observes the limitations of a socially constructed identity, using theatrical representation as an appropriate metaphor for social identities:

> We are born in a specific place and time, with roles, rules and regulations we are asked to follow. This "training" forms the foundations of our personality, beliefs, thoughts, and actions. The process of becoming has always been heavily influenced by the culture of the society that surrounds us. If we look around the globe at different cultures, we will see that each one has created a unique but often-similar perception of what it means to be human and what the process of becoming offers us.

> This criterion sets the stage for our training to be productive members of society. We will develop focused ways of thinking, being and behaving within the society, and we will begin a journey of becoming who we are trained to become. (84)

For these practices, agency trumps social construction and is governed by principles that (following the spiritual logic of the practices) would yield a social order more conducive to human flourishing.

The perception articulated in these texts is that social systems limit human potential, while spiritual practices *in any culture or society* release people from socially defined identities into the awareness of existing as an essentially spiritual being. At a point when she "felt nothing" after leaving the harshness of Sufi training, which had itself imposed an identity on her mind and body (74), McPherson describes transforming her apartment's front room into a space for daily, solitary movement practice. In that space, she writes, "I climbed around an increasingly scant rigging of identity, an imprecise Essence Pattern that was not so much a self as a way in which electricity tagged 'Dunya' moved. Corporeal strokes dissolved into a page of space, reefed time's sail, and woke me beyond chronology or locale" (McPherson 80).

Klabunde writes that a spiritual musician "has a responsibility to the highest spiritual Masters to relinquish any desires and completely let go of any identity that he may have carried" (62). McPherson writes of knowing in a Sufi dance "this place of 'I'-less-ness" where there is "no sense of separate identity, no sense of identity at all, just a unified wash of energy" (57). Critical discourses on identity politics can place Klabunde and McPherson, but their sense of spirit has no place in those discourses.

MYTH AND RITUAL AS ENGAGEMENT WITH SPIRIT

Ritual and myth, as noted in chapter 1, are the most common conceptual frames for analyzing spirituality as performance. Analyzing ritual rubrics for symbolic meaning, assessing ritual efficacy, and tracing the ways everyday activities become ritualized as habit or hermeneutics has long been a staple of performance studies. Performance, in a sense, came to define ritual. In the context of these practices, however, ritual emerges out of practitioners' sensations of spirituality and is a means of consciously cultivating those sensations. In practice, ritual is alive and fluid. Its purpose is to transform mental and physical processes rather than display power hierarchies or belief systems. Klabunde's approach to ritual thus has no traction in Adam Seligman's dichotomy between sincerity and ritual.[41] Sincerity, for Klabunde, is essential for ritual. Regardless of a ritual's purpose, the actions require nothing less than the internal sincerity and complete concentration of its participants. Klabunde writes,

> The heart of the ritual may be healing, cleansing, protection, freedom, and liberation. Whatever the intention of the ritual, one thing must be clear: your undivided attention to the task at hand. Ritual is a powerful way of connecting to the Spirit realm to manifest transformation in the physical realm. It is not we humans who dictate the transformation, it is Spirit who ultimately concedes to or denies whatever outcome we desire. We are humble servants to Spirit, and it is our sincerity and our willingness to serve that allow for the dance with Spirit to take place. (207)

Richard Schechner's observations on the experiential properties of dervish whirling that exceed the rubrics of ritual are relevant again here (see chapter 1). McPherson describes whirling as an exercise of purification, suspending the whirler "amidst these forces: the columnar heaven-earth pole, the torqued, diagonal current curving and bending, and the band of infinite circling" (145). She writes:

> I once thought that whirling's curative properties lay in aligning my mind with its cosmic metaphor of planets, solar systems, and galaxies, all rotating and revolving. Such a placebo of fervent intention could easily have activated healing and cleansing, but I've done this practice thousands of times over many years; it has long since erased associated intellectual and emotional structures and I'm left only with a plain well-traveled road devoid of coherent justification. Perhaps one day neuroscience will quantify the beneficence. For now, I have the Mystery and the Beauty. (McPherson 145–46)

Both practitioners narrate mystical experiences and the sensations of being spiritual that transformed their life praxis. These narratives constitute the central mythologies of their practice, describing experiences beyond those of everyday life praxis—journeys that cannot take place in the normal parameters of linear time, geographic space, and matter. These are extraordinary experiential events, meticulous in their detail and illustration of the practices' central themes: the presence of a sacred or divine reality, the presence of spiritual beings, an expansive and comprehensive principle of love governing the universe, and the power of a spiritual connection. As different as these practices are, the narratives of mystical experience end in exactly the same place, ultimately telling the same story of opening the heart.

THE OPEN HEART OF PERFORMANCE

McPherson describes an intense, complicated vision in which she encounters a mysterious visitor in three different settings: a country road, a spaceship, and a city street. The visitor tells her, "You must never forget what we experienced for it is the Real Reality. It will never leave you. I will never leave you" (McPherson 135–36). She describes the vision as pivotal, akin to a shift in consciousness called in Sufism "piercing the veil" (McPherson 137). The vision left her with two gifts of knowledge, which, she writes, "continue to guide my life. The first: my basic nature is dance. The basic nature of the Universe is dance. The path I am on, of dance as a mystical communion, is a unifying, truthful path. The second: all the energies in the body are one energy, and that energy is love" (McPherson 138). Klabunde describes a very different out-of-body experience; however, he draws a remarkably similar conclusion about love as an energetic principle governing human life:

> I felt my heart open so wide that I had to regulate my breathing so I could stay with it. . . . I thought this would be an excellent way to die, to feel such an overwhelming sense of euphoria that I could just go with it. Within seconds of surrendering, I felt and saw myself lift from my body. I was now hovering just above my head, and then I was near the ceiling of my living room. It was then that I noticed a force greater than me pulling me toward the heavens. I began to fly upward, through the ceiling and above the house. I could see everything, the trees, my neighbors' hoes, the lights of the neighborhood. . . . I was now among the stars, the planets and the galaxies. I had left the Milky Way and was on a path to the brightest star, beyond what I could have ever imagined. I soon felt as if I was moving toward the star and then realized that I was being pulled into it. I looked down at my chest and saw it open; there seemed to be a slit in the middle. Two flaps opened and exposed a ball of light inside

> me. I looked toward the bright star I was moving toward. There was a beam of light coming from the star and going directly into my chest. It was giving me life, a kind of energy I had never felt before. It was beautiful, and the feeling it produced in me is beyond any words I can say or write. . . . I was surrounded by hundreds, maybe thousands of other beings, some human, some not human. We are all attached by beams of light and connected to this beautiful source of life-force energy. . . . We remembered how to open our hearts in a way we never thought possible, and we remembered that all things are created from love. (25)[42]

These experiences, narrated and presented as knowledge in *Skin of Glass* and *Music as Medicine*, are understood as truth known through direct encounters with spirit. Neither narrative problematizes love as a discursive construction, suggests that the discovery of the universal principle might be the legacy of monotheism, or explores the culturally bounded assumptions encoded in the word "love." Whereas in critical analysis, the knowledge of love as a universal energy is not a valid claim, from the perspective of spiritual practices, the knowledge produced by such analysis holds no power.

The sensation of the heart opening is one of the most prominent images in both Klabunde's and McPherson's books and is closely related to the mystical experience of love as a universal and all-encompassing force. It is very clear that the physical sensation of an open heart is not a metaphor and the sense of an all-encompassing spiritual love is not a hermeneutic fancy; instead, these are the conditions that define the essence of being spiritual, in which veils are lifted away from habitual perceptions. "We hear about having an open heart," Klabunde writes, "but I think we do not fully comprehend what that means. It is a perception of the world and the universe we live in. What does it feel like? For me, it is a vibration in my heart chakra, or heart center, like a motor running. A burning sensation" (20). As McPherson describes the sensation at the very end of *Skin of Glass*, "A sugar syrup explodes through a small oval in my chest, and now Divinity pries my heart walls wider until I cry, as I always cry, coming home to this feeling I can't remember with my mind, never understanding how it works" (216).

"Never understanding how it works" might be the most salient reason why spirituality sits so uneasily in explanatory or analytical paradigms that posit ways of understanding the world. Perhaps this explains why knowledge derived from spiritual experience, or the experience of being spiritual, remains suspicious territory. These are only two examples of contemporary vernacular spiritual practices. They are described here to serve as a means of working out how people might sense spirit in the interstices between mind and body, and how that sense connects to the material, social world.

Ultimately, however, orientations to a spiritual reality such as these undo familiar interpretations of performance. These practices do not constitute reality in material terms. Knowledge comes from internal sensibilities, not thought processes. The subjectivity at work in these spiritual practices is not based on the same premises from which performativity constructs identity as subjects positioned in and shaped by culture. If performance is understood as a membrane, the ephemerality of people's internal experience can be recognized at the intersection of internal processes and material culture without being reduced to either. Activity inside the body flows into culture and cultural idioms flow back into the body, across the membrane of performance.

Dancemeditation and Collective Awakening differ in how they encounter the sacred or divine, experience the ineffable, and articulate spirituality as knowledge. They developed their practices from different cultural traditions and sense spirit differently. For McPherson, spirituality is sensation deep in the interior of the physical body, experienced as consciousness dispersed in the sinews, tendons, cells, bones, neurons, and viscera. Her conscious body moves into and with the presence of spirit. For Klabunde, spirits move across dimensions of time and space through the vibrations of music in the body. A person's body-mind, too, moves across dimensions as spirit. The striking similarity between the two practices, however, is the sense of knowing a direct, unmediated connection with spirit, where the experience of a profound love constitutes knowing that reality. This sense of spirit, as a kind of knowledge from the liminal space between mind and body, is what undoes the performance paradigm. In that undoing, the sense of spirit opens performance to radical rethinking.[43]

CHAPTER 3

Spirit in Bodies

EMBODIED SPIRITUALITY

Chapter 1 asked how the performance paradigm construes presence as material; from that critical perspective, spirituality is something people can perform, where performance as action is understood as making things present. But performativity cannot fully account for the internal sensations people experience as spiritual. Shifting critical focus from what culture and discourses write *onto* bodies to understanding what is written and performed *from* within bodies allows for a more comprehensive perspective on performance practices informed by knowledge derived from a sense of spirit.

The discussion reoriented ontological questions such as "What is spirituality?" "Can people have an inner life?" and "What is mind?" to questions about how people cultivate spirituality as an internal sense. This reorientation opened a space to ask what such sensibilities bring to the materiality of performance: How does spirituality, as an internal sense of a nonmaterial, numinous presence, inform performance?

Chapter 1 acknowledged that "spirituality" can be performed and written about without that internal sense. The circuit preacher Marjoe, one example given in chapter 1, used the techniques of charismatic Christian delivery he learned as a child to create the powerful affect his followers associated with the presence of God, though he himself felt nothing. Another example, Lincoln Center's White Light Festival, staged spirituality within the secular context of high art, with the implication that audiences might find something transcendent in the aesthetics.

These examples are performative in the theatrical sense: performance is the medium that re-presents spirituality to an audience, with or without any cognitive or experiential commitment from the performers themselves. Performance of spirituality, in these cases, is the material presence that produces aesthetic or religious affect. The critical stance of the performance paradigm accommodates performances such as these well. Performances infused with people's sense of spiritual presence, however, propose a very different orientation to the materiality of performance.

Chapter 2 described how the cultivation of a sense of spirit in two particular spiritual practices takes apart some of the fundamental assumptions that ground the performance paradigm. The sense of spirit described in the previous chapter involves a range of experiential qualities, including mind-body unity, nonrepresentational perception, a self apart from identity, the presence of forces and spirits, and, finally, the sense of one's heart opening. This sense of spirit infusing bodies, language, and matter is radically different from the representational thinking that undergirds the performance paradigm. Further, people know the presence of spirit in these practices through sensation rather than observation. That knowledge infuses the social and cultural domains we recognize as performative.

These practitioners describe what we would otherwise see and read as performance as existing between the physical world and a domain of spirit. Klabunde remarked in a workshop: "When we drum, we have one foot in the physical and one foot in the spiritual."[1] McPherson describes whirling as

> a force field through the body; like a lightning rod, electricity funnels into the up-facing right palm, moves through the body, and exits out of the down-facing left palm. The whirler suspends amidst these forces: the columnar heaven-earth pole, the torqued, diagonal current curving and bending, the band of infinite circling. (145)

For these practitioners, the materiality and embodied action of drumming and dancing are a kind of connective tissue for the sense of spirit. How can this sense of performative embodiment as connecting matter and spirit come through in a paradigm structured by visibility, representation, and matter, and which operates by citation, translation, and decoding? How do capacities for sensing a numinous dimension of the self and world intersect with those for organizing perception around symbolic logic, representation, and referentiality? These are the central questions of this chapter.

Michael S. A. Graziano observes that the distinction between the inner self of private experience and the outer world people perceive around them is in fact an artificial one (58–59). As these spiritual practices reconfigure the boundary between internal sensation and the social world, I have suggested that performance becomes the border, or membrane, across which the sense of spirit migrates. Seeing the interplay between spirit and the materiality of performance expands readings of performing bodies to include the biological body as the substrate for performance.

How do we study selves engaged with the numinous rather than the social through the performance paradigm? Practitioners' claims that spirits or energies work through the self and that selves are spiritual beings need not impede critical analysis. Rather, the questions have to shift to allow performance to begin in people's sense of an ineffable, rather than material, presence. How do performances and texts informed by spiritual practices situate people in the experience of the self as a body, a mind, a spirit, *and* a social agent? How do these practices negotiate the experiential interior of the self and the world outside the physical body through performance?

THE SPIRIT OF THE BIOLOGICAL BODY

One of the ways we now imagine an inner life is through visual images of the brain. Biology, like performance, is a paradigm that sees material forms, in this case the matter of spirit. Neuroscience, with its focus on the brain and mind, thus sometimes serves as an explanatory paradigm for spirituality. Today we can envision an inner life as electrochemical signals lighting up regions in the brain that account for the ephemerality of our mental experience. The brain quite literally becomes the biological matter of spirituality, where we now seek spirit in its embodied activity rather than as a disembodied aspect of the mind (or as Descartes' immortal mind-soul).

Taking people's sense of spirit seriously, however, does not necessarily mean translating the sense of spirit into biological terms, or reducing it to brain events (Schüler 89). Rebecca Sachs Norris and David Cave point out that looking to the brain for people's sense of spirit naturalizes the body as matter in ways that are not always apparent. They point out that conceiving of the body "as electro-chemical processes operating in a bounded locus of matter, the 'naturalized body,' is so deeply embedded in the 21st century

Western worldview, hidden by our own enculturation, that we are often unaware of how much this conceptualization shapes our discourse" (Cave and Sachs Norris 1). Further,

> However much our "secular age" possesses more alternatives to religion than ever before, people still look for that which gives them meaning and hope for tomorrow. The biological and neurological revolutions of today are no different in their contributions to this hope. They offer constructs of meaning and salvific promises not unlike the most transcendent of religions. (Cave and Sachs Norris 4)

If people develop practices that cultivate a sense of spirit as embodied, internal, and culturally engaged, what do studies of the physiology of spiritual experience offer to theorizing embodied spirituality, and what influence might this perspective on the body have for the membrane of performance?

Neurotheology investigates "the relationship between spirituality, spiritual experience(s), and neurological processes" in search of "the neural substrates putatively mediating spiritual experiences" using "brain-stimulation experiments, neuroimaging studies, and evaluation of the neuroanatomy of pathologic conditions" (Giordano and Engebretson 218). Approaching spirituality by observing neural networks, neurotransmitters, neurons, hormones, and brain regions shows and measures activity inside the body as people engage in meditation, prayer, rituals, and reading spiritual texts, or respond to visual and aural stimuli such as religious iconography. Whether these neurological patterns correlate to experiences researchers and practitioners have already identified as spiritual or respond to nonphysical forces as yet unmeasurable (or spirit, as practitioners hold them to be) remains an open question.

Humanities research is often hindered from collaborating with the natural sciences because of methodological commitments to cultural products, resistance to biological determinism, and suspicion of a natural (as well as supernatural) world. Accepting neurological explanations for human behavior wholesale may be as much of a hindrance as the humanities' resistance to collaboration. However, as Taves observes, "A number of self-identified neurotheologians, most of whom lack training in theology or religious studies . . . have enthusiastically embraced the challenges of identifying the neural correlates of religious experience without engaging the critiques of the concept that led many scholars of religion to abandon it" (*Religious Experience Reconsidered* 8). Slingerland also suggests that "cognitive scientists exploring human-level realities need a great deal of help in framing their research questions and interpreting their data and are often hampered by an ignorance of even the most basic history or 'thick' cultural background of the topics they are investigating" (298). Slingerland argues that the cognitive sciences "have much to learn from humanists, and . . . require the higher-level expertise of anthropologists, literary scholars, and historians if they are to avoid reinventing the wheel or committing egregious interpretative errors" (299).

LOOKING WITHIN IN THE PERFORMANCE PARADIGM

Neither neurological correlates to spiritual experiences nor expressive forms performing spirituality give us an ontological explanation for spirit. Both paradigms confront the ambiguity of spiritual experiences across cultures, varieties of spirituality within traditions, the impossibility of accurately documenting the sense of spirit, a material body that can sense a self that is *not* material, the problem of faked spirituality, the confusion between emotional affect and spiritual experience, and what to do with claims of noetic insights or spiritual wisdom such as those presented in chapter 2. The conventional reliance on social, cultural, and intellectual norms to categorize internal sensations and their effects on behavior is especially pronounced in the conflation of spirituality or mystical experiences with emotional affect or mental illness.[2]

People's sense of spirit clearly does not reduce to one identifiable kind of experience. Spirituality requires cultural norms to identify it in practice as well as in neurological studies. Studies of neural activity associated with spiritual experiences, however they are defined, immediately reveal the difficulty of isolating precise patterns, pathways, or brain regions from which people's sense of spirit emerges. Researchers must first define spirituality either as a baseline condition or a special type of experience in order to measure it. If the neurological activity was measured without the researcher's awareness that the subject is engaged in a predetermined spiritual practice (such as moving-meditation or shamanic portal drumming), the neurological activity might appear to link to other mental processes, such as those associated with emotion.

Neurological studies that take SPECT or fMRI images of brains engaged in Christian or Buddhist meditation, for example, do so with the assumption that this activity is inherently religious, spiritual, or extraordinary. In order to know what to measure, internal sensations must have already been identified as spiritual before the first electrode can be usefully applied. Not surprisingly, the variety of cross-brain neural processes that correlate to spirituality turns out to be as varied as the kinds of experiences people identify as spiritual. As Lee A. Kirkpatrick observes, in the search for neurological correlates to spiritual experience, "It appears that brain areas have been identified that are associated with a motley collection of vague feelings and experiences that are sometimes interpreted in spiritual terms—usually by already-religious research subjects" (161).

Patrick McNamara concludes that "there is a network of brain regions that consistently are activated when a person performs a religious act"—the identification of what constitutes a religious or spiritual act must involve cultural conventions that predetermine what constitutes "spiritual" or "religious" (127). He identifies seventeen psychological properties of religious experience (McNamara 15–16);[3] one of most prominent is their long-lasting, transformative potential (McNamara 17). A spiritual orientation affects how people engage with the world, ascribe meaning, understand themselves, and establish connections with other people. However, just as an activity such as hatha yoga might generate a spiritual transformation for one person, the same yoga practice might simply be a relaxation technique for another person and physical exercise for another. The internal sensations one person experiences as spiritual in yoga might be experienced by others as emotional, psychological, or physical, depending on the context, presentation, and personal outlook.

Brains are mutable, and mutability characterizes our neural responses to the world. In physiological fact, "Our ideas and practices configure and reconfigure our own sponsoring brain structures" (Rolston 26). Practices like Dancemeditation and Collective Awakening create sensory and discursive environments for cultivating the neurological capacities that subserve the kinds of experiences described in practitioners' writings: the self as a spirit in a body, the self experienced as a disembodied spirit, a heightened state of noetic awareness, encounters with spirit entities, and so on. In these contexts, drumming and dancing, together with practitioners' language (e.g., the recitation of prayers, narratives, movement instructions), direct neural activity that encourages and reinforces those sensations.

MATERIAL CULTURE AND BIOLOGICAL BODIES

What are the connections among physical expression (performance), a sense of spirit, and the internal workings of the body? In a Dancemeditation workshop, participants watch and follow McPherson's internally motivated movements. Neuroscience might explain that connection by "mirror" neurons. Imitating another person's movements (as opposed to observing one's own reflection in the mirror of a ballet studio or holding a mental image of one's body as a swan, or dancing to communicate with an audience) has the potential to cultivate the capacity for empathy and noninferential attunement, as well as access to the sensations of others (Gibbs 36; Schüler 94; Sachs Norris, "Examining the Structure and Role" 195).[4] Similarly, Collective Awakening's music-meditation and trance dance sessions cultivate people's ability to sense spirits in the physical action of drumming and immersion in sound. The corresponding neurological conditions could easily induce altered states of consciousness by encouraging theta and alpha brain wave production, dissociative states interpreted as spiritual, or the suppression of the superior parietal cortex, which can induce a sensation of the body's boundaries dissolving and leaving one's body (Winkelman "Cross-Cultural Assessments of Shamanism" 150; McClenon 135; Giordano and Engebretson 219; Blanke and Mohr 186–87).[5]

These are physiological explanations for the sense of spirit as an emergent property of neurological activity potentially produced when people dance, drum, play or hear music, or watch other people dance. However, the innumerable ways people cultivate the sense of spirit makes precise neurological correlates for spirituality nearly impossible to define. Still, at the level of experience, the sense of spirit is entwined with the body's internal processes. Rather than seeking neurological explanations for the sense of spirit, we might ask how these neurological conditions become important enough for people to cultivate as spirituality. How might we think about those internal conditions in relation to what we see as embodied performance or texts? Could what cannot be observed become as important as what *can* be observed?

A paradigm that observes and explains the materiality of expressive forms, like a paradigm that observes and explains brain activity, defines people's sense of spirituality by what practitioners insist it is not—matter. The interpretation of performance as expression ("pressing out") of whatever is inside people's minds and bodies looks something like this:

1. The performance of drumming or dancing creates internal sensations.
2. People interpret those sensations as spiritual experiences with the aid of cultural resources such as shamanism and Sufism.
3. People represent those experiences in performative ways, such as concerts or narratives.
4. The materiality of the performance then symbolizes or signifies spirituality in ways that can be imitated and reproduced.

Spirituality experienced as *being present with or in a numinous dimension* falls outside such a schema (see chapter 5). People interpret internal sensations in radically diverse ways compared to the conventions with which explanatory thinking frames spirituality.

In practice, people can deliberately shift away from the normative reliance on conventions that mark identity, legitimate knowledge, and define communication as symbol-making to a reliance on internal sensation. A spiritual self may be experienced as an essence not perceived as an identity, knowledge may be sensed rather than represented, language may not parse difference but reconcile it, and so on. Taken at their word, spiritual practitioners insist on an unseen, sensed aspect of minds and bodies, which informs their concerts, ceremonies, writings, CDs and DVDs, poetry readings, and workshops. Interpreting these material forms as a membrane opens an exchange instead of following a linear trajectory in which ideas must be pressed from the body out into the social world that then assigns their meaning.

THE PARADOX OF SPIRIT IN THE MATTER OF PERFORMANCE

A performing body informed by a sense of spirit is invested in the relationship between internal sensations and cultural resources, including objects (like drums and veils) as well as discursive formations (like spirituality). Performance, I have suggested here, is the observable site of the exchange between the body's interior and material culture. We could think of performance as the sensory organ of a cultural environment that makes possible an ongoing dialogue between bodies caught in matter and their internal sense of mystery, or knowledge beyond sensing matter. For spiritually oriented performances, thinking of performance as a membrane helps ameliorate the opposition between internal experience (whether the Cartesian theater of the mind or the radical interiority of religious mysticism) and the sensual materiality and contingent realities of shared cultural norms.

Performance, to return to the questions posed by Ann Taves and Edward Slingerland (chapter 1), might turn out to be one way to know other people's interiors. In *The Meaning of the Body: Aesthetics of Human Understanding*, Mark Johnson asks, "How can thinking about abstract, nonphysical entities possibly be grounded in the body?" (176). Paradoxically, the workings of the physical brain make it possible for people to conceive of the body's opposite—what is not accessible to the sensory organs, not physical, and not knowable—as an aspect of the body itself. Performance works in a similar way by making what is visible and material stand for what cannot be shown: a domain of spirit.

If what people experience as spirituality can be correlated to physiological processes, we can speculate that what we read as performance might be a body's response to those processes. Getting at this dynamic requires taking the body as the generative site of spirituality, rather than making performance the means by which people construct spirituality. Shifting from understanding an inner life as performative to understanding an inner life as *interactive* allows ephemeral experiences, such as spirituality, into discussions of embodied performances and language.

THE BODY AS THE GENERATIVE SITE OF SPIRITUALITY

Performance has long investigated the biological body as a social construction and critiqued the social constructedness of biology as an explanatory paradigm. Physicalist approaches to spirituality as an adaptive or evolutionary function of the brain,[6] as a function of the mind's perceptual and reflective capacity,[7] or as an epiphenomenon emergent from neurological processes[8] present a host of problems for humanistic inquiries. If people's sense of spirit is a quality of consciousness, then it is independent of human culture as well as an illusion produced by the brain.[9] If the brain produces spirituality, then the sense of spirit is a cross-cultural constant.[10] Positions such as these place natural and biological limits on spirituality, as well as privileging mental processes produced by the brain over how people's subjective sensations of an inner life are situated in cultures and societies. The cognitive bias discussed at length in chapter 1 looms large in the effort to find correlates to spirituality in the workings of the brain.

The determinism implied by physicalism "seems to deny human dignity and value" as well as to ignore the forces of culture on bodies and identity (Albright 174).[11] Conversely, however, if the brain *could* be shown to register a supernatural or metaphysical reality that is independent of both body and culture, humanities research would be driven back to theology, again forced to compromise its commitment to material, human culture. Interpretive strategies in the humanities have gravitated toward analyzing social or cultural conditions as the determinants of human flourishing, rather than accepting biological determinism. A humanities inquiry might well point out that if cultural and intellectual norms construct distinctions between reasoned conclusion and unreasoned faith, between rationality and irrationality, or between mystical states and mental illness, then there is little to be gained by looking at the workings of the biological body. But if performance is defined by embodiment, how can we ignore the human body's inner life?

Scientific study of spirituality has a tradition going back to the nineteenth century. The metaphysical strand in American philosophy, the Romantic fascination with the occult and the supernatural, and the rise of spiritualism all contributed to an interest in finding spirit in the body. The physical body was viewed (literally) as the medium for showing the presence of spirit.[12] In the early history of empirical body-spirit studies, electroscopes and cardiographs sought spirit in the physical body.

Theological premises might still undergird approaches to the biology of an inner life today, as Charlene Burns notes (178–79). However, the positivism that sought empirical proof of spiritual realities in the body differs from current inquiries into the neurobiology of spiritual experience. Current approaches to the biology of spirituality seek the sense of spirit in more conventionally defined neural activity such as information processing and computation, perception, attention, memory, symbolic reasoning, and sensory processing (Spezio 212). In this framework, emotion and religious experience are closely linked through the limbic brain. Emotion is understood as a transitory sensation involving bodily and cognitive processes (fear, sadness, or happiness in response to a situation). Mood or feeling is understood as a sustained emotional response (anxiety, depression, peace, overwhelming love) (Spezio 213).[13] As we have seen, spiritual practices may cultivate neural patterns that render familiar discursive distinctions among mind, body, and spirit, between subject and object, or between internal and external meaningless. The experiential practice is consistent with current thinking in neuroscience, which holds that mental, physical, emotional, and even spiritual sensations are not neat categories of neurological activity but converge in the sense of a holistic self.

The experience of direct perceptual access to an unmediated, unified self, however, is not consistent with what identity politics suggests should be our experience of a self constantly adapting and changing in response to social stimuli. The interior conditions these spiritual practices cultivate, what Heelas calls "holistic spirituality," nudge people's perceptions toward unity even as environmental stimuli demand fragmentation. The ontological status of "mind" and "soul" may be an open question, but as Marilynne Robinson rightly suggests, "They are at least terms that have been found useful for describing aspects of the expression and self-experience of our own very complex nervous system" (xi).

PERFORMATIVITY, THE THEATER OF THE EMBODIED MIND, AND SPIRITUAL SELVES

Current theories of embodied cognition question spiritual experience in ways that allow for interpretive flexibility. The questions start not with theology but with consciousness. Models of embodied consciousness help insofar as they acknowledge the interplay between the mind and body in the sense of spirit, as well as the role of expression and culture in shaping mind-body experiences. The basic framework for these models, which came to prominence in the late 1990s, is the same representational mode of thinking that governs the paradigm of performance.

Lakoff and Johnson provide a foundational model for integrating mind and body, which can be extended to the sense of spirit. This model assumes a familiar logocentric hierarchy that privileges symbolic thinking over corporeal sensation. However, it does shift the philosophical distinction between mind (as processes of cognition, consciousness, and awareness) and the transcendent spiritual domain of theology by locating both in the body. They propose that mental capacities are not independent of bodily capacities" and that the brain, as "the joint locus of reason, perception, and movement," is part of the body even as it makes representing the body possible (Lakoff and Johnson 17, 20).

This reorientation turned neurological, consciousness, and cognition studies to questions of how thought and perception depend on a sense of the body and on how the interior of the body allows for the sense of spirit.[14]

In this model, spirituality becomes a process of "imaginative empathetic projection" that gives rise to sensations people identify as spiritual (such as feeling one's self to be part of a "larger all-encompassing whole," ecstasy, mystery, moral engagement, or revelation) (Lakoff and Johnson 564–65).[15]

Models of embodied consciousness posit spirituality as a mental process or internal state that depends on socially constructed symbolic systems for expression. Consciousness might be embodied, but bodies are still perceived as acting in a social, cultural environment. In this model, thought performs as a body. The sense of spirit becomes real, materially, in the metaphoric language of myths and the enactment of rituals. Though spirituality might be understood as originating in the body (and present in bodily metaphors), the grounding assumption is that words and gestures represent ideas *about* spirituality rather than embodying spirit. Such a model is very useful for the performance paradigm, but does not go far enough to take practices such as those described in chapter 2 on their own terms of spiritual presence.

Performativity, as a paradigm, shares Lakoff and Johnson's emphasis on the primacy of symbol systems and the cognitive processes that produce them. Neural beings, Lakoff and Johnson posit, cannot achieve "purely uncategorized, unconceptualized experience," though this is an experiential goal in some meditative and mystical practices (19). Parsing the interior of the body as mental states does not answer the ontological question of whether spirituality is emergent from the brain and shaped by the mind's capacity for representational thought or whether the brain responds to and records the effects of some substantially different, nonmaterial influence. Social and cultural expression remains the hermeneutic force acting on consciousness or the material out of which people shape consciousness.

Still within the project of finding the bodily basis for consciousness, and remaining within a representational model, Antonio Damasio opened his now iconic study, *The Feeling of What Happens*, with a theatrical metaphor. Theatrical representation illustrates how our minds represent ourselves to ourselves. When we become aware, Damasio proposes, consciousness comes onto the stage, and the self literally comes into light as an entity. The self is known by the mental patterns of sensory modalities—a mental image. From this model, Damasio concludes, "Something like a sense of self was needed to make the signals that constitute the feeling of emotion known to the organism having the emotion" (8). For embodied cognition, the problem with the image of the mind as a theater becomes twofold: "how the movie-in-the-brain is generated, and the problem of how the brain generates the sense that there is an owner and observer for that movie" (Damasio 11).

A foundation in theatrical representation, such as in this example, moves along the same analytical trajectory as the performance paradigm. That trajectory moves toward, but does not quite accept, people's sense of spirit as a radically different kind of mental-physical experience. Damasio makes a familiar distinction between sensory processing (external stimuli) and the sensations of feeling emotion (internal sense). With this line drawn, vision, hearing, touch, taste, and smell trigger nerve activation patterns that correspond to the *external* world of performance, whereas emotions are nerve activation patterns that correspond to the state of the *internal* world. If we experience fear, for example, our brains will record this bodily state in patterns from neural and hormonal feedback; this information may then be used to adapt behavior.

With regard to spirituality, this representational model describes how the embodied sensations people associate with spirituality are represented to the self. For Damasio, consciousness is the process of representing information, which we come to know as our selves (8).[16] What we recognize as representational or symbolic thinking is in physiological fact no less embodied than beating on a drum or swaying to music.

Addressing mind-brain reciprocity, Johnson asserts that "concepts are not inner mental entities that re-present external realities. Rather, concepts are neural activation patterns that can either be 'turned on' by some actual perceptual or motoric event in our bodies, or else activated when we merely think about something, without actually perceiving it or performing a specific action" (157). Johnson describes the kind of mapping brains do as representational only "insofar as a specific neural map is loosely isomorphic with some structure of an organism's environment-as-experienced," which neuroscientists call representations (131). Johnson observes that a representational model, in which the internal workings of the mind create a representation of the exterior world, holds to the extent that "something 'in the brain' appears to correlate structurally with patterns of the 'external environment,' even though the environment is not, strictly speaking, independent of the organism" (131–32).

The theatrical model, in which the mind conceptualizes the body, is giving way to newer models in which the body is an aspect, rather than an object, of the mind—bringing us closer to interpreting people's sense of spirit as a component of body-mind. They provide valuable starting points for reorienting the theory of the social world as performative because they link consciousness to the material world. Enactive approaches to cognition observe brain activity across neural domains, including between biological bodies and the cultural environments they inhabit. This more fluid model of person-world interaction is replacing the theatrical model of consciousness.[17]

Raymond Gibbs clarifies that what is available to consciousness is more complicated than maps of neural activity suggest: "Human brains have clearly evolved to represent body parts," he asserts; embodied perceptual experience "is not simply a matter of mapping stimulations with brain states," nor do internal somatosensory activities explain how people perceive their bodies, minds, and the world (47). This orientation "reject[s] the idea . . . that perception is a process *in the brain* whereby the perceptual system constructs an *internal representation* of the [outside] world" (Noë, *Action in Perception* 2). The mind's operation in this view engages, rather than represents, the body, the self, and the world.

The enactive model of how human minds participate in the material world suggests that the performance paradigm is limited by an attachment to bodies performing as objects and a reliance on observers receiving and processing performances as sensory data (primarily visual, aural).[18] If spiritual practitioners cultivate conditions that generate an experience of mind and body integrated with a sense of spirit, that organization of consciousness—different than that which views the material world as performative—is the foundation for the events and texts they produce.

If the model of mind-brain-world interaction is replacing the representation-based model of the mind, the performance paradigm can release its theatrical model of perception. Spirituality can cease to be a thing performance makes real or constructs via the interpretation of shared cultural codes, and instead can become a dimension or quality of performance that requires a shared sense of what cannot be shown.

Replacing the dualistic metaphor of a mental theater with dynamic and interactive models of sensation, perception, and cognition invites orientations to performativity that can accommodate spirituality. Reconceiving the mind and its processes as embodied, as well as developing models for the reciprocity between the physical brain and the sensation of consciousness, opens space for considering the kinds of embodied spiritual experiences practices such as those described in chapter 2 cultivate.

THE SENSE OF SPIRIT IN AN EMBODIED MIND

As chapter 1 discussed, representational thinking is the cultural norm in the Western thought tradition.[19] Numerous performance theories and theater practitioners have worked against it. Chapter 2 suggested that spiritual practitioners may cultivate and sustain a kind of nonrepresentational consciousness that orients them differently to performance. Representation, as a mode of performance practice, would simply not happen in this condition of consciousness. Neurologically, spiritual experiences such as visions, contact with spirit guides, a holistic self, and an overwhelming feeling of love may overlap with and even recruit these more culturally acceptable capacities for analysis, representation, and critical distance.

Collective Awakening and Dancemeditation do not set out to create an aesthetic affect in an artistic or representational frame around the sense of spirit. Nor do they play on avant-garde tropes, making performance a mechanism for shifting people's perspectives or reinventing spirituality by means of performance. Arguably, these practices begin in a consciousness that may not be organized around the conventions of representational thinking. Rather, they invite participation in a particular condition of being. Though the practitioners are certainly aware of how they present themselves, in practice and framed events, the goal is not to solicit an emotional response from an audience or to represent their spiritual orientation. Their expressive forms do not depend on audience identification with the performers' spirituality or on observers' critical distance.

A Dancemeditation teacher described spirituality as kind of awareness that does not distinguish between the physical activity of dancing and the conceptual processes that structure language. Shifting between improvisational movement and reading poetry, for her, is a matter of operating in what Dancemeditation practitioners refer to as "integrated intelligence." The question for practices like these is not how performance *represents* spirituality as if it were a theological proposition or how performance *references* spirituality in expressive forms such as texts, framed events, rituals, and myths. The issues are how people cultivate internal processes that allow for a sense of spirit and how those internal processes orient them to understand performance. As enactive models of the mind propose, we can seek this integrated intelligence in overlapping neural networks that connect a sense of spirit to what we observe as performance.

Exactly how bodies generate or register the nonmaterial reality or presence that constitutes spiritual experiences is a perennial and open question. Francis Crick, a famously confirmed physicalist, acknowledges that "it is universally agreed that it is not completely obvious how the activity of the brain produces our sensory experiences; more generally, how it produces consciousness" (103). Whereas Western traditions of thought have construed spirit as "nonmaterial substance" (see chapter 1), some neurological investigations characterize spiritual experience as a particular kind of interaction between brain activity and mental processes, rather than as an altered state of mind or the mind's access to a transcendent reality (Peters 139).

Efforts to figure out how the workings of the brain become sensations available to consciousness, including sensations of spiritual experiences, have produced a range of theories. Eugene D'Aquili and Andrew Newberg, the advance guard of neurotheology, posit the mind and brain as "two different ways of looking at the same thing." From this view, the mind is the mechanism of the brain that makes all experience, including spirituality, available:

> We have no method of experiencing the world, which includes the soul, other than through our senses, emotions and thoughts. These are certainly functions of the mind and brain. Thus, even if there is a sensible soul, our cognitive and emotional experiences of it must be mediated ultimately by the brain. Every other aspect of human experience that can be documented in living human beings must also be generated and modulated by the human brain and mind. (D'Aquili and Newberg 22)

Carol Rausch Albright takes a similar approach to the holographic relationship between the physical brain and the ephemeral mind, which allows for the kind of perceptual adaptability at work in spiritual practices. She posits the brain as a noun, a thing, and the mind as a verb, a process: "The mind is what the brain *does* . . . the brain becomes what the mind *is*," and

> the mind is in fact a function of both brain and body, since brain and body are continually interacting and influencing one another. We could say that the brain is the principal organ of the nervous system, and the mind is the action of the entire embodied nervous system. Personality changes, including changes in spiritual organization, are thus correlated with changes in the organization of the nervous system, and particularly of the brain. (Albright 174)

Consciousness, following Albright, encompasses multiple modes of mental activity, including those that sense spirit as an ephemeral and ineffable presence, those that formulate that sense in the symbolic logic of spiritual memoirs (*Skin of Glass*) and spiritual guidebooks (*Music as Medicine*), and those that engage cultural idioms such as shamanic drumming or meditative dancing in the cultivation of that sense.

James Giordano and Joan Engebretson subvert the problem of spiritual experience as unique, ephemeral, and perennial by seeking the neurological processes associated with the sense of spirit and physical healing. Their approach avoids concepts of the sacred or divine altogether, instead suggesting that preexisting mental concepts of spirituality determine what people understand to be "spiritual." Their guiding axiom for neurological research seems entirely applicable to the "spiritual, not religious" demographic, consistent with the scholarly methods of lived religion, and in keeping with the cultural and intellectual condition of postsecularity discussed in chapter 1:

> Spiritual experiences are frequently associated with religious events and/or circumstances. However, the phenomenon itself is definable in secular contexts, and terms such as liminal or transliminal and sublime and/or ecstatic occurrences could be used instead, thereby preventing any overt religious connotations when circumstantially inappropriate. (Giordano and Engebretson 217)

After identifying neurological mechanisms that account for spiritual experiences, "whether epiphenomenal or a direct mental process," Giordano and Engebretson ask how "such [neural] experiences come to be such a fundamental part of the cultural repertoire of diverse social groups" (222). This is the cultural phenomenon evident in the proliferation of spiritual practices and the number of people who identify as "spiritual, not religious."

Giordano and Engebretson take a position somewhere between the brain as a biological constant in spiritual experience, the role of environmental stimuli, and the subjective perception of a metaphysical domain. This physicalist-materialist approach to spiritual experience as active neural pathways shows that the activation might be initiated within the body or externally, and "that actual *subjective (spiritual) experience* is, on some level, necessary for the induction of the subsequent (physiological) effects" (Giordano and Engebretson 221). Giordano and Engebretson argue that neural mechanisms

> may engage a cascade of physiological events that may be both internally perceptible . . . and produce changes in neurochemistry to elicit feelings of reinforcement and reward. The sum of these hierarchical events could be a considerable change in multiple domains of consciousness (e.g., attentional and nonattentional mental states), in which the relation of the conscious state (i.e., the neural events) and its *qualia* to an identifiable object or "other" might be framed within the environmental, sociocultural, and/or circumstantial contexts of the subject. (222)

Responding to the question of whether the brain is stimulated to produce spiritual experience or whether spiritual experience emerges from the physical brain, Giordano and Engebretson suggest that what people sense as spiritual experience is situated in and stimulated by culture and discourse—the raw material of performance. At the same time, it might begin as sensation within the body. Giordano and Engebretson also address the ontological problem with the uniqueness of spiritual experience as a brain event, which is that

> the brain-mind condition(s) induced by experience *itself* appears to represent a distinct "state of" consciousness, as well as an event that we can be "conscious of." Certainly, the spiritual experience fulfills many of the requisite criteria for a conscious event and/or state. It is subjective; it has structure; it is familiar and transparent to the subject as an internal event; it possesses a range of attention; and it has self-situatedness, possesses varying degrees of unified form, and manifests some dimension of pleasure or unpleasantness. (221)

At first glance there seems to be an ontological problem of deciding which comes first, the brain's activity or the stimulation that prompts the activity. But if mind and brain are, as D'Aquili and Newberg suggest, a kind of holograph, what was an ontological problem becomes a matter of reciprocity between the physical body and ephemeral mind, between internal experience and material culture (5).

Philip Hefner, however, takes spirituality more fundamentally as a particular and positive hermeneutic predisposition. Spirituality is "the organization of our consciousness that makes richness of life possible, for individuals and communities" (Hefner 124). Kenneth Pargament similarly defines spirituality as a "search for the sacred" that organizes behavior and thought to serve psychological, social, physical, and material goals (12–13). Based on narrative reports of spiritual experiences—*Music as Medicine* and *Skin of Glass* serve as examples here—McNamara works out a phenomenology of neurological activity that assesses not what people's brains are doing but how they understand the neurological phenomena they experience as spirituality:

> Relative to both happy and ordinary experiences, participants rated their religious experiences as significantly more meaningful, with stronger altered states of awareness, increased inwardness of attention, higher amounts of imagery, more internal dialogue, lower volitional control, and more negative affect. Levels of positive affect in religious experiences fell between levels for ordinary and happy experiences. (150)

These perspectives do not necessarily conclude that people's spiritual experiences must be a cognitive fiction that accounts for otherwise inexplicable sensations, or that neurological activity registers a spiritual reality along with that of the material world accessible to the senses. Rather, these perspectives propose that the practice of cultivating spiritual experiences also cultivates neurological patterns that interact with, and may even organize, other brain functions. If spirituality can be understood as a particular way of engaging with the world that does not rely on the critical distance required for representation but on the extension of a particular kind of internal sensibility into culture, spiritually oriented performances are evidence of that engagement.

SPIRITUAL SELVES IN PERFORMING BODIES

Constituting the self as a culturally produced, performed identity (the critical position of performativity) is consistent with a strand of cognitive neuroscience that posits the self as a functional illusion.[20] Lakoff and Johnson state unequivocally that perception of a self apart from categories of social identity is neurologically implausible. Even within a dynamic model of self-world interaction, Gibbs concludes that one might feel a "self" that transcends the body, with the body as the vehicle for thoughts, but that "this kind of quick introspectionist analysis may be misleading and due as much to one's cultural 'folk beliefs' as it is to veridical phenomenological insight"

(14). So, too, do lines of inquiry in cognitive neuroscience "suggest that the feeling that our conscious will serves as the causal basis for our actions may be illusory" (Gibbs 22).

The study of culture, bodies, and language as performance is a variation of the person-world duality evident in this line of cognitive science. The performance paradigm makes the self a subject position and embeds the possibility of an agential self into a critique of the individual, autonomous Western subject. The paradigm has thus emphasized the ways people embody culturally proscribed identities marked by race, class, gender, (dis) ability, and sexuality in order to read the self as a site of hybrid cultural and social identities operated upon by legislated social norms. In this mode of thinking, there is no concept of the self without a body that is situated in and marked by culture. This paradigm emphasizes that there is no essential or authentic self, despite practitioners' assertions of the opposite.

Spirituality can certainly be read as the performance of identity. An om T-shirt, a lotus blossom tattoo, a miniature Zen garden on an office desk, and a Celtic pentagon necklace all perform spiritual identities. Spiritual identity can be read in rhetorical statements and practices: prominent phrases like "Happiness is our birthright," ethical practices such as not eating meat, claims of religious outsider status in statements of identity such as "I am spiritual but not religious" (McNamara 25). Self-identification with a spiritualized practice—as a shamanic drummer, a hatha yogi, a Vipassana meditator, a spiritual dancer, an energy healer, or a chakra reader, for example—can also be read as the performance of identity in everyday life. Everyday life practices may not be limited to a private, apolitical internal realm of self but rather may be performed in people's connection to spiritually oriented communities, political commitments, websites and newspapers, and businesses. Spiritual identity can be read as derivative "from the internalization of formalistic renderings of the ethic of humanity (as taught at school, for example)" even as practitioners assert the experience of an internal, authorial voice as a unique expression "rather than as a socioculturally laid down 'ought'" (Heelas, *Spiritualities of Life* 31).

According to performance paradigm conventions, these readings situate spirituality amid cultural codes through which people perform social identities. That people might imbue an individual sense of self with universal content, however, disrupts most interpretive and analytical frameworks (McNamara 1).[21] The sense of a *spiritual self* has no place in a paradigm that dismisses (even denies) the self an essential being, essence, or soul. The experience of a unified self that embodies a spiritual essence does not align with the idea that identity is constructed—a view that subsumes the self in debates over cultural identity, agency, and autonomy.

Even as we are compelled to read spirituality as a performed identity, the sense of a spiritual self shows up not as an identity but as a condition of being. McNamara points out that "we can and do experience our Selves as a unity, and there is little doubt that all of the world's religions believe that there is a unified sense of Self and that the Self is central to the religious enterprise," and further argues that "modern cognitive neuroscientific studies of the Self indicate that virtually every higher cognitive function is influenced by the Self" (147; 59). Despite the centrality of the self to human experience, religious or otherwise, "Basic problems concerning the nature, representational properties, and functions of the Self remain understudied and unresolved" (McNamara 59).

The spiritual self described in *Skin of Glass* and *Music as Medicine* is fluid yet authentic, agential yet subject to spiritual forces, simultaneously natural and supernatural.[22] It is experienced directly, yet consciously mediated or enhanced with cultural idioms and cultural references (see chapter 4). In the context of these practices, performing an identity is less important than the sense of a self that is not bound to an identity at all. The sense of spirit is entwined with the sense of self, and the sense of self is vital to the sense of spirit. Spirit may be sensed in many different ways: as a force or energy moving into and through the self, as an experience that overwhelms any sense of self all, or as an encounter with other people as spiritual beings. Regardless, the experience of a self that is not bound to social constructions is taken as both fundamentally real and authoritative—and at odds with the performance paradigm. This generative and creative cultivation of the self in vernacular spiritual practices warrants attention along with the ways people construct and perform identities.

EMBODIED, SPIRITUAL SELVES

The body remains the matter from which people sense their interior selves even as they construct and perform social identities (Gibbs 20). In the examples given here, drumming and dancing make the body the experiential site of a spiritual self, a self that is embodied but not bound to the physical body. Practices like Collective Awakening and Dancemeditation cultivate an experiential synthesis between mental processes and physical activity in the cultivation of a sense of spirit.

In these practices, bodies might move through space with a veil, respond to inner sensations with expressive gestures, hear music as vibrations of spirit, or fall into a trance while beating a hand drum. The practices become sites at which a self is experienced as unified, whole, and healed. Through them the conventional perception of mind and body synthesize into an unconventional sense of a spiritual self. These practices also cultivate techniques for releasing styles of thinking that interfere with this sense of self. The styles of thinking they release are precisely those that govern the critical stance interpretive paradigms bring to them. What might be viewed as "performance" of spirituality is thus more appropriately interpreted as the effect of spiritual experience in and from a body.

A sense of spirit embodied in a self could be understood as the fundamental condition of what we see as performance, rather than the object or referent of performance. As noted above, the framed events and autobiographical writings described in chapter 2 are not antimimetic, nor do they suggest a failure of representation. Taken on their own terms, they propose ways of thinking about performance that can account for ephemeral, internal human experiences without being bound, even in rejection, to representational and referential models.

The writings describe becoming a self and losing a self, a self without another, the self in relation to a spiritual other, and the self as a physical body and a nonphysical entity. Performance thus takes on a different valence when the self that is performing has been cultivated in a practice that recognizes spirituality apart from identity and in which socially constructed identities are already understood to be transient. Neither of these practices purports to critique or challenge the construction of identity along lines of difference (e.g., race, class, gender, sexual difference, etc.). Rather, the sense of a spiritual body subverts those identity categories at the level of experience.

Still, the experience of a spiritual domain, spiritual energies, or a self as spirit cannot be verified by observing the body's physiology or the bodies in performance. Even as they deploy the technologies and techniques of modern marketing and draw inspiration from premodern cultures, practices like Dancemeditation and Collective Awakening take their own critical stance against the devaluation of spirituality in their home culture (see chapter 4). These practices serve as communities that sanction, cultivate, name, and value experiences and ways of knowing that are not otherwise considered legitimate.

Internal sensations one person might experience as spiritual other people might register as emotion, psychological awareness, or insight into a problem. A person's mood, memories, or religious background might impose assumptions about a spiritual reality on the conditions created in a drum circle or an improvisational dance session. The conditions that provoke boredom and eye-rolling in one person might provoke a radical experience in another that is inexplicable except by spirituality. These practices' styles of mental processing and physical activity may be more compatible with some people's neurological constitutions than with others'. Some people will, in Klabunde's words, "get it," while others will remain indifferent, even hostile or resistant. A neurological propensity to sense something beyond the body, mind, and material culture might make spirituality seem "natural" to practitioners.

That spirituality "relies on the same neural capacities as the self" (Hogue 225) is thus not insignificant for the performance paradigm. Interpreting such practices on their own terms requires a way of understanding performance that accommodates an ephemeral aspect of the self along with materiality, corporeality, and affect. The neurological link between the self and spirituality suggests that spiritually oriented practices may balance an internal sense of self with one that performs in the world. While the performance paradigm might understand spiritual practices as constructed by cultural and discursive frameworks, the practices themselves may cultivate neurological conditions that do not subserve a performative identity.

THE COMMUNICATIVE CAPACITY OF EMBODIED, SPIRITUAL SELVES

A sense of spirit engages multiple overlapping brain functions within the body, including those that support the representational and symbolic thinking cultivated in performance theories. Neurologically, a sense of spirit emerges *along with and as part of* the relational capacities associated with the sense of a holistic self, which, as discussed above, distinguishes sensing the self as spirit from the self as a socially constructed identity. The neurological capacity for spirituality thus need not be viewed as a "distinct or unusual human ability" (Hogue 224), but can be recognized as a form of interconnectedness that extends to the divine and also to other people. Further, "sharp distinctions between spirit and self are difficult to maintain" (224). This particular kind of relationality extends to conceptual and experiential abstractions such as spirits, deities, forces, universal knowledge, or ethics, as well as to material objects, living things, sensory stimuli (such as music), or the environment. It also suggests that performance may involve relational dimensions not usually addressed in the effort to theorize the social or discursive construction of people's ideas and actions.

A hemispheric organization of neural functions, for example, reinforces the integration of people's capacity for sensing and observing, and suggests a similar integration might apply to how we interpret performance. The sense of a self involves both brain hemispheres. The right hemisphere supports a holistic sense of self that is "intrinsically, empathetically inseparable from the world in which it stands in relation to others"; the left supports "the objectified self, and the self as an expression of will" (McGilchrist 87). People's linguistic and communicative capacities for expressing the representational awareness of self, upon which the performance paradigm depends, is associated with the brain's left hemisphere. These are also the capacities that can render the world as performance (Giordano and Engebretson 219).[23] This model of the brain supports an interpretive approach to people's social practices that integrates an embodied self, a spiritual self, and action in the social world. Iain McGilchrist notes that in a hemispheric model of the brain "the personal 'interior' sense of the self with a history, and a personal and emotional memory, as well as . . . 'the self-concept'" are supported by the same hemisphere associated with religious experiences (87).[24]

A sensory image of the body is also supported by the capacities of the right hemisphere. The right yields "a living image, intimately linked to activity in the world—an essentially affective experience," as well as volition over the capacities of the left hemisphere (McGilchrist 66).[25] Processes of conceptualization, which make it possible for us to recognize human expression as performative, are thus also bound to the ways the brain organizes perceptions of the body through the sensorimotor systems, the somatosensory cortex, and insula (Lakoff and Johnson 20; Giordano and Engebretson 216). Cultivating the capacities of the right parietal lobe makes it possible for people to imagine the whole body, though not as a representational picture (the purview of the left hemisphere).[26] At the level of the body, then, the kind of focused attention on internal, somatic sensations and subcortical experiences cultivated in these practices produces a sense of self that is not entirely representational.

The point here is that, using a hemispheric model of the brain, spiritual practices might privilege the neurological capacity for spirituality over that of symbolic representation. The sensation of the self as spirit does recruit the cognitive, symbol-making, representational processes that express internal senses symbolically in language. However, as Hogue, drawing on the work of Michael Gazzaniga points out, the left hemisphere constructs coherent narratives even out of conflicting internal sensations or sensory data, but narratives of spirit (such as those discussed in chapter 2) rely on "the contextual framework of the right hemisphere as fully as it does the language centers of the left" (226). Spiritual practices may give this neural aptitude for context greater credibility than an aptitude for symbolic representation; they may attribute authenticity to the sense of a larger, more comprehensive self than can be defined by the social roles or cultural identities the performance paradigm emphasizes.

In practice, releasing volitional control of one's socially situated self allows people to experience of the self as a conduit for divinity, spirits, the sacred, or simply wisdom (usually focused on knowledge of the self by the self). In practices such as Dancemeditation and Collective Awakening, sensing a "true" self is closely associated with losing one's self as an individual identity. The process of losing and literally re-cognizing the self is valued as a veridical experience of unity, harmony, oneness, bliss, and undifferentiated consciousness.

In the heightened physical activity of the two practices described here, releasing the sense of control that allows people to construct a functional social identity—normally identified with the prefrontal cortex—also allows people to sense the self in radically different ways. Practitioners may overcome their aptitude for the rational thinking valued in the modern West and cultivate instead neurological conditions that allow them to sense a self as all-encompassing love, for example.

McNamara identifies this mental process as decentering, or the "temporary decoupling of the Self from its control over executive cognitive functions and a search for some more effective controlling agency over cognitive resources and mechanisms" (5). Approaching spiritual experience as a dynamic process involving multiple brain sites and processes, McNamara proposes beginning with what practitioners would call "letting go" of the ego or the need to control one's self and environment by opening up to energies, spirits, the sacred or divine, or a true self:

> When a religious experience begins with a reduction in intentionality or a turning over of the will to God, this reduction in intentionality is transient in normal religious experiences but is prolonged in entheogenic experiences. After the suspension of intentionality, there comes a flood of images and affects that resolves into a process of attempts at meaning and then finally insight and gratitude/joy. (143)

If spiritual practices diminish or bypass people's neural capacity for self-representation, practitioners' mental orientation makes performance, which arguably defines modern technological societies, less relevant. How does that cultivated release of identity into meaning, insight, and gratitude/joy affect the emphasis on social identity in the performance paradigm? How can we accommodate the internally experienced, spiritual selves these practices cultivate into a critical stance with which their basic conceptual framework and neurological conditioning is incompatible?

THE SENSE OF SPIRIT IN MYTH AND RITUAL

Myth and ritual, as discussed in chapter 1, have become signifiers that allow us to talk around spirituality. In practice, the language of myths and their embodiment in rituals once provided people with a means to explain the natural world. From a critical stance, we now look to the "natural" world of human biology and the social world of human culture to explain why people still rely on myths and rituals. Myth and ritual theories have provided performance studies with a convenient theoretical framework to analyze religious performances. These genres of performance contain spirituality by making it representational.

The extension of spiritual experience to texts and framed performances seems, at first, amenable to analysis as modern mythmaking and recuperation of ritual for modern sensibilities. The performance paradigm frames myths and ritual as forms of social performance. Myths represent spirituality in explanatory narratives, providing the textual basis for exegesis and speculation. Rituals embody myths. By giving myths corporeal and sensory form, rituals are understood to produce or represent spiritual experience either through symbols (such as a cross, mandala, veil, or icon), sensory stimulation (such as incense, music, candles, or flowers), and action (such as dancing to induce trance, ingesting food to commune with a deity, or giving offerings).

In the framework of performativity, however, myth and ritual provide systems for constructing spiritual experience as symbolic representation rather than as experience. Underpinning the distinction between myth and ritual is an assumption that language and embodied performance function differently in relation to the sense of spirit. Carl Seaquist observes rightly that "the symbolic approach to myth and ritual may seem intuitively obvious, because it has such a strong tradition in both scholarly and popular literature, from antiquity to the present, but there are good reasons to be skeptical of it" (206).

Interpretations of the neural activity correlating to spirituality often rely on a conceptual framework that distinguishes the abstractions of concept formation in language and imagery from the materiality of bodily sensation in corporeal expression. This division constitutes the sense of spirit as produced by external cognitive content (a myth, metaphor, or other cognitive medium) prompting inwardly directed attention and constructing spirituality as a kind of experience.

This distinction between myth as cognitive and ritual as corporeal parallels the familiar, though often hidden, distinction between mind and body. The myth-ritual framework for spirituality separates the cognitive functions of the mind, organizing meaning via abstract symbol systems, from the body's physical activity, with its capacity to organize meaning through spatial patterns, gestures, and body positions. With this division in place, the experiential aspect of spirituality can stay comfortably contained within frameworks that reinforce the interpretation of human expression as symbolic representation.

Using myth or ritual as an analytical starting point limits the experiential synthesis of mind, body, and spirit to discourse and reenactment. In the myth-ritual framework, the question of internal, spiritual experience turns on whether the symbolic language of myth or the physical actions of the body construct spirituality. The descriptions in chapter 2 and the discussion of integrated neural processes above suggest richer interpretations, where performance is understood as the integration of body, mind, spirit, and the material, social worlds in which people act. As Mark C. Taylor notes, "The complex nonlinearity of cognitive networks calls into question any theory that associates religion exclusively with thinking (cognition), acting (volition), or feeling (affection)" (*After God* 20).

That integration breaks down the distinction between linguistic and corporeal expression that supports the myth and ritual model. Inside the body, where sensation originates, the neurological processes that produce language and action are much more closely interconnected than the analytical frameworks of myth and ritual allow. *Skin of Glass* and *Music as Medicine* articulate an experiential interconnectedness in which "feeling, thinking, and acting mutually influence each other" to the extent that they may be indistinguishable *except by* the intellectual convention of distinguishing mind, body, and spirit (Taylor, *After God* 20–21).

The trajectory of the discussion thus far moves toward revaluing the interior of the body, which knows no duality between thought and action or between what is real and what is symbolic until normative intellectual frameworks make those distinctions. The neurological processes that generate expressive forms as myths, rituals, or knowledge claims do not separate out neatly into top-down (conceptual, linguistic) and bottom-up (affective, emotional, prelinguistic) schemas.[27] The emphasis here has been on how overlapping physiological processes give rise to both the language of myths and the embodied actions of rituals. In myths, language may not only be embodied in the performative sense; language quite literally comes *from* the body. The repetitive actions of rituals not only activate concepts symbolically and communally—the corporeal and mental investment in the physiological activity of rituals generates internal sensations.[28]

In conventional critical analysis, the distinction between mind and body remains deeply ingrained in the seemingly intuitive division of myth and ritual. Interpretations recognizing the potential that concept formation emerges from a holistically functioning human body are closing the gap between top-down and bottom-up interpretations of spirituality. Studying lived religion, McGuire sees the physicality of ritual as the impetus for internal meaning-making through a linked chain of "embodied practices, each link having the potential to activate deep emotions and a sense of social connectedness, as well as spiritual meanings" (100). Gibbs reinforces this bottom-up trajectory from the vantage point of cognitive neuroscience in his observation that "the regularities in people's kinesthetic-tactile experience not only constitute the core of their self conceptions as persons but form the foundation for higher-order cognition," including language and concept formation (15).

Giordano and Engebretson's interpretation of how overlapping networks of neurological processes give rise to both myth and ritual also corresponds to the ways people cultivate spirituality as internal experience. They suggest that the neural pathways generating spiritual sensations may be initiated within the body *or* externally. That is, some kind of in-body experience may precede the body's observable physical response, and the "actual *subjective (spiritual) experience* is, on some level, necessary for the induction of the subsequent (physiological) effects" (Giordano and Engebretson 221).[29] Their suggestion that the human body responds to spiritual sensations with the concept-formulating capacity of language and the activity of the physical body is significant for a view of myths (texts, language) and ritual (embodied action) as performative. They propose that internal sensations initiate what we take as performative, rather than the reverse. Human biology as the source for the language of myths and the physical expressions of ritual reinforces the embodiedness of performance. It is also a reminder, however, that the ways critical frameworks, such as performativity, parse and assign value to spirituality, rational thought, and corporeality are conventions subject to revision.[30]

THE PLACE OF SPIRITUAL KNOWLEDGE

Conventional organizations of knowledge distinguish the mental capacities of a religious imagination (e.g., spiritual experiences, mystical visions, religious belief, creating myths, faith in divine powers, etc.) from those that process sensory data (e.g., rational thinking, symbolic reasoning, perception, computation, propositional logic, representation, memory, reflection, etc.). The familiar dichotomy of reason and religious faith hinges on the ontological status of two modes of knowledge construction: (1) organizing external sensory stimuli to construct rational systems of abstract ideas and (2) taking internal sensory experience as the basis for knowing (whether or not the resulting perceptions or conclusions can be verified against a shared perceptual reality).

How does the formulation of spiritual experience as knowledge in the autobiographical narratives, spiritual guidebooks, blogs, website texts, and speech acts in workshops extend the internal sensations of spirituality?

Framed events, such as music or dance concerts, allow practitioners to cultivate the mental-physical conditions they know to be spiritual, irrespective of how the performance frame might cast their bodies as representational or symbolic theatricality or as the twice-behaved behavior of ritual-as-performance. The practitioners may also express the internal logic of their spiritual knowledge in language with no tension between spirituality and rationality or between reason and faith.

At the level of their experience, most people distinguish the sensation of rational, linear thinking from that of feeling and emotion (Hurlburt and Schwitzgebel 61, 167). Some people may, however, cultivate much more nuanced and expansive sensitivities to what is normally referred to as "thinking," and hence have much greater tolerance for what might constitute knowledge. A variety of sensations might be construed as thought (Taylor, *After God* 19). Knowledge may not be in the words themselves but in the internal sense that supports the words. "Think" might imply a range of internal senses that yield some kind of knowledge: ideation, an inner voice, translating mental imagery into words, perception of qualia (e.g., luminosity), or some other kind of awareness that has an epistemic quality to it. Thinking might also have a phenomenological aspect, as in observing thoughts that pass through one's mind without meaning attached to them, or simply the sensation of being conscious.

As in the earlier discussion of the self, the hemispheric model of neural interaction provides a valuable model for understanding how myth and ritual function as analytical strategies for managing the elusive qualities of spiritual experience. At first the familiar hemispheric organization of the brain seems to support the conventional divide between logical thought (left hemisphere) and imagination (right hemisphere). Mental processes associated with spiritual experience are associated with networks across the right hemisphere (McGilchrist 93). Spiritual practices can acclimate people to the right hemisphere by subverting the left hemisphere's impulses or by inhibiting the left parietal lobe, which suspends rational thought. McGilchrist argues that the right hemisphere's capacities are undervalued in Western culture (a point made by both Klabunde and McPherson). Referring to Western styles of thought, McGilchrist observes that "when we think of meaning we tend to think of language," and "[the brain's] left hemisphere's great contribution to meaning is language, symbol manipulation" (70). The capacities for nonverbal communication and "whatever is implicit" are given scant credibility in dominant cultural norms (McGilchrist 71). These are precisely the capacities valued by spiritual practitioners, informing their orientation to expressive forms.

Klabunde's suggestion to "take your mind out of [the drumming]" or "take your brain out of [the drumming]" does not mean abandoning rational thinking. "Take your mind out of it" means to cease relying on habitual rationality grounded in empirical observation. Spirituality, so understood, is not irrational: rather, two aspects of what would traditionally be called mind—logical thought and spiritual insight—become a single, embodied mode of awareness. This is the mode of awareness practitioners describe as connection with the self, the material world, and an ineffable spirit. The experience of releasing familiar styles of cognitive thought processing yields the "integrated intelligence" some Dancemeditation practitioners use to describe the internal sensations of their movement meditations.

Though the brain's left hemisphere is strongly associated with the kind of representational thinking the spiritual practices subvert and performativity encourages, the critical distance that its frontal lobes make possible allows, paradoxically, for one of the most coveted internal sensations associated with spiritual experience—"the experience of the peaceful detachment from the material realm and 'emptying out' described by experts in meditation as a mystical experience . . . an elaboration of what the left hemisphere affords" (McGilchrist 92). The contributions of right-brain activity become the material out of which practitioners formulate spirituality as a kind of knowledge. The cultivation of the right hemisphere's aptitude for making nonlinear connections combined with the left's for peaceful detachment may make spiritual practices such as these alternative in more ways than the "spiritual, not religious" label suggests.

The repeated resistance to relying on "our logical minds" in these practices and the invitation to "release thought patterns" associated with rational cognitive processing and analysis suggest a desire to cultivate a nonrepresentational, experiential mode of thinking. The practices emphasize suppressing mental processes associated with logical thought and representational symbols in favor of the alternative—mystical or spiritual thinking. That style of thinking is untroubled by contradictions and need not be referenced to empirical observation to make sense. It is a mistake, however, as Sachs Norris points out, to dissociate spiritual experience from logical thinking or writing. Sachs Norris explains:

> To say that transcendent or religious experience is grounded in the body does not mean that logic or verbal cognition is entirely absent from the larger experiential context. Zen practitioners in the monastery consult daily with the Zen master to assess their development, and those engaging in practices such as Christian contemplative prayer have traditionally had a spiritual advisor whose role is in part to ascertain the reality and value of spiritual experience. These experiences are primarily bodily states in the sense that they cannot be learned through merely thinking, reading, or reflection. Interpretation, evaluation, and contextualization of transcendent experience are necessarily culturally specific, as are all religious/emotional states. ("Examining the Structure and Role of Emotion" 183)

The construction and conveyance of meaning (the relationship between internal sensation and language) is specific to the individual practices. There are, however, points of convergence in the experiences Klabunde and McPherson describe, such as encountering spiritual beings. But the experiences are contextualized differently in keeping with the ways each practice cultivates and shapes spirituality as an experience of the self: out-of-body travel (Klabunde) and a trance-like vision (McPherson).

The sense of the self as spiritual is the authority in these practices, not spirituality *as* performance (as it is conventionally theorized). Practitioners' writings require the symbol-making, representational capacities of the left hemisphere as they articulate these distinctive interior sensations of spirituality and move those experiences into material culture via the expressive forms we recognize as performative (e.g., DVDs, CDs, website texts, blogs, books, workshops, and concerts). *Skin of Glass* and *Music as Medicine* both work from the sensations cultivated through practices as they formulate spiritual experience in knowledge claims and offer narrations that follow a logic. The left hemisphere's capacity for symbolic language makes sense of internal sensations as spiritual experiences.

"Taking the brain out of it" in order to enhance less familiar (and culturally sanctioned) neural pathways is thus not an anti-intellectual stance but a willingness to suspend conditioned thought processes and allow for other types of awareness. Practitioners obviously rely on thought processes that communicate in language, construct narratives of self, analyze their experiences, and formulate the sense of spirit as knowledge. However, the mental qualities cultivated in practices such as drumming and dancing support the contextual, nuanced, nonlinguistic, and nonanalytic style of thinking associated with right hemispheric activity. This cultivation results in alternative modes of sensing, experiencing, and knowing, which ground their texts and framed events and make conventions based on a mechanistic body and a representational mind inappropriate interpretive paradigms.

Both Klabunde and McPherson, as described in chapter 2, identify Western culture as logocentric. From within their cultural context, they subvert styles of thinking associated with Western constructions of knowledge, which they negatively describe as linear, rational, and grounded in empirical observation. Performance theory has sought to counter that same logocentricity with theoretical approaches to embodiment, whereas practices posit spirituality as its foil. They work against a cultural preference for the analytical and representational capacities of the left hemisphere and find alternative modes of thinking in their embrace of cultural idioms from outside the West (see chapter 4).

ENSPIRITING THE MATTER OF PERFORMANCE

Biology and culture are the matter of spirit. Questions about the status of spirituality in performance—is he *really* in a trance or is he *performing* being in a trance? is she *really* experiencing a sense of profound bliss? or is she *performing* a discourse on bliss in the familiar cadences of a New Age guru?—can be reoriented around an exploration of how the internal conditions cultivated in a spiritual practice engage material culture. In practices cultivating inner conditions that people sense as spirit, awareness *of* spirit can be just as easily described as awareness *in* spirit.

Drumming and dancing as spiritual practice cultivate the inner life of the body as a dwelling place for the sense of spirit, as well as mental capacities that simultaneously experience and articulate perceptions of that sense. At the level of the individual, cultivating spiritual experience may be a way of establishing internal homeostasis (note the emphasis on relaxation in both practices) and also equilibrium between internal states and the external world. Culture and discourse give people common referents and symbolic systems for articulating the sense of spirit. In practice, however, internal experience offers no such consensual stability. The question for performance, then, is how culture interacts with the sensations generated by internal physiological processes. What we recognize as performative is not embodied because bodies perform, but because embodied processes of consciousness make cultural performance possible. There is an ongoing exchange between internal physiological activity and one's environment in the way people experience sensations. What we by convention recognize as performance in these examples works like a regulating membrane to balance the experiential release of cognitive control with the demands of symbolic communication in a contemporary Western cultural environment.

Reading framed bodies as performative or taking narratives of spirituality as discursive fictions rather than assuming continuity with the interior of the body limits the possibilities for the study of performance. Performance, including writing and speech acts, cannot be separated from the body's internal sensations and the ways people experience them. Analyzing spirituality as performance is not only a matter of identifying neurological correlates to the phenomenon of theatrical watching[31] or even finding parallel models of internal preparations for theatrical performance.[32] Such readings may occlude or dismiss spirituality as the sensibility that informs a text or performance and, in so doing, inhibit the potential for cautiously reintroducing a discussion of ineffable qualities into materialist readings of performances. At the extreme, such readings foreclose on the potential for people to resist dominant critical paradigms.

Though knowledge of and from inner sensations is always approximate, because no two bodies can share sensation, we need not deny interiority even when the aim is analyses of ethnicity, gender, social class, or sexuality (Andrieu 138). People's sense of an enspirited self and body might be as important as the external, observable actions we recognize as performance. Reflecting on her internal sensations, McPherson writes, "Perhaps one day neuroscience will quantify the beneficence. For now, I have the Mystery and the Beauty" (146). Performance may be the membrane between matter and the mystery.

CHAPTER 4

Spirit in Culture

> It is not only that (post)modernity's secularism renders the Sacred as tradition, but it is also that tradition, understood as an extreme alterity, is always made to reside elsewhere and denied entry into the modern.
>
> —M. JACQUI ALEXANDER, *PEDAGOGIES OF CROSSING* 296

REVISITING CULTURE

The orientation toward vision and materiality that supports the performance paradigm does not easily validate spirituality, though it readily exposes the complexity of cultural practices. Chapter 1 situated the relationship between matter and spirit in the conventions of the Western thought tradition and in performativity as a critical paradigm. In these conventions, representation and symbolism point to transcendent spirituality, such as deities or people's sense of spirit, but do accept a dimension of spirit in the formation of knowledge. The focus stays on the representations, or performances of spirituality. Chapter 2 described two examples of contemporary, vernacular practices in which the sense of spirituality, the materiality of performance, and the intelligibility of language are experienced as overlapping, and the sense of spirit privileged as a kind of knowledge. Chapter 3 looked into the human body for the physiological matter of spirit. Inside the body, the nuanced, impressionistic qualities that people associate with spirituality overlap with neural processes associated with more prominent (and culturally validated) kinds of knowledge, such as concept formation, syllogistic thinking, symbol-making, abstract reasoning, and representation (including that of self-representation and identity formation).

The sense of spirit and self people cultivate in the practices described in chapter 2 goes against the general preference for observation and representation, rather than sensing, as a foundation for knowledge. The question of how to capture people's internal sense of spirit in a paradigm that does not readily accept spirituality shifted to questions of how the paradigm might expand to include such sensibilities. Doing so allows for the complexity of what cannot be seen in vernacular spiritual practices but is (for practitioners) nonetheless present.

While these practitioners appear to "perform spirituality," in the conventions of Western performativity, the interconnectedness of physiological processes suggests that a sense of spirit literally infuses practitioners' expressive forms, including writing, framed events, workshops, media, and so on. The interconnectedness within the body-mind suggests that we consider people's internal sense of spirit is as important as signs, discourses, representation, and the material presence of performance. We can consider the inside as continuous with the observable outside of people's bodies.

The materiality of performance, however, is also inextricably bound to the materiality of culture. How does the experiential presence of a sense of spirit meet the shared presence of material culture? How can interpretive and analytical strategies account for the sense of spirit as present in the materiality of performance? This chapter takes up that question.

SPIRITUAL EPISTEMOLOGIES IN WESTERN CULTURE

A person sits cross-legged on the floor in an urban yoga studio. Performativity, as a critical framework, makes this body in its act of sitting a richly encoded, culturally situated text. The eyes are half closed and fingers arranged in a triangle in the lap. To an observer, the material presence of this body reads as the performance of a meditation posture. The body becomes a sign of mental concentration, focused attention, or perhaps a mystical state. The posture can also be read as performing cultural identities. Those identities might be associated with a religious tradition, a geographic region, an ethnicity, or a monastic lineage, even if the physical features of the body's clothing, gender, or ethnicity contradict those identities. The person sits on a round cushion. The cushion is a commodity, available online from any number of vendors selling meditation products to a modern, Western market. In the present-day West, however, the cross-legged lotus position—like the drum and the veil—signify the Otherness of spirituality to the Western cultural traditions.

The suspicion of spirituality in a contemporary Western context leaves little epistemological space for whatever knowledge might inform or be produced from such a practice. Spiritual practices today negotiate that suspicion in a wired, interconnected world in more subtle ways than their predecessors from the countercultural resistance of the 1960s or the intercultural synthesis of the 1970s. Meditation and yoga may be mainstream and stripped of their religious origins, yet the sense of spirituality such practices imply remains a significant marker of intellectual and cultural difference. That marking is especially obvious when the logic of cultural criticism comes up against epistemologies originating in people's subjective sense of a spiritual dimension.

The sense people like Klabunde and McPherson cultivate suggests a fundamentally different claim on subjectivity than that offered by Western modernity and postmodernity's critique of subject positions. Presence, in these spiritual practices, becomes a kind of embodied awareness. This is a condition of being present *in*, rather than present *to*, one's self. One of the challenges to performativity is their reliance on idioms from cultures of difference, from Othered cultures. The logic of performativity sees and critiques material culture, interrogating identity formations and subject positions. Arguably these spiritual practices do seek a cultural Other and reconstruct that Otherness as a desired difference within their home culture, against its intellectual framework of modernity and religious roots in Judeo-Christian monotheism.

Dominant critical approaches to contemporary Western spiritualities paint concerns about cultural difference in primary colors, focusing on how cultural appropriation and consumer capitalism structure people's desire for spirituality (see chapter 1). Without dismissing this line of criticism, Courtney Bender advocates a comprehensive, nuanced approach to contemporary metaphysicals like McPherson and Klabunde. "Contemporary Americans," Bender acknowledges, do "latch onto a seemingly unending number of imagined primitive, ancient, or foreign cultures where they locate true religion, authentic practice, and unending wisdom" (154). But rather than rehearsing "well-known critiques that point out the dangers of the spiritual marketplace," Bender advocates more holistic methods for investigating spiritual practices. She advocates methods that can

> articulate a place for mystics within the world; a place that allows them to participate in what seems like predatory cultural borrowings in good conscience. While criticisms of spiritual appropriation ring true in many respects, the recent focus on contemporary spirituality's connection to

> consumerism (in the "spiritual marketplace") as the engine of appropriation gets us only so far toward understanding the logic of spiritual borrowing. (Bender 154)

Indeed, the case can be made that cultural borrowing in service of a spiritual life is unavoidable in the West, where secular and sacred, physical and metaphysical, natural and supernatural, and self and other are binaries rather than interdependencies. Spirituality sits not only at the margins of an intellectual tradition privileging secularity but *outside* the cultural norms the intellectual tradition supports. Spirituality emerges, as Heelas observes, "with the inner realm of life serving as *the* source of significance and authority" (*Spiritualities of Life* 28).

Though their practitioners may be firmly rooted in European privilege, these vernacular spiritual practices cannot readily be defined as belonging entirely to the global North-West. This is the critical problem of spirituality migrating across cultural borders, and who "owns" particular spiritual or religious traditions. The knowledge they cultivate has a different foundation than the theistic, transcendent religious orientation of the modern West, though the traces of that orientation may be evident.

At the same time, these spiritual practices are not wholly Other to modernity and the West. They are active, sophisticated participants in the mechanisms of contemporary social living: technology, media, education, commerce, the arts, and expository writing. This participation creates significant discomfort for a critical stance that celebrates cultural difference but assumes imperialism in cultural borrowing. Along the axis of spirituality, critiquing cultural borrowing preserves the West's characteristic privileging of knowledge from observation, constructing symbol systems, and transcendent knowledge, keeping spiritual knowledge at a distance.

Spiritual practitioners may operate in the space between the conventions of their home culture and the alterity of the cultural idioms they adopt, whether African shamanic drumming, dervish whirling, Indian yoga, medieval European mysticism, Mayan rites, Buddhist-derived Vipassana meditation, spiritualized Middle Eastern dance, Native American sweat lodges, Celtic pagan ceremonies, Vedic mantras, and so on. Cultural liminality in itself becomes a mechanism for knowing the numinous. This liminality allows vocabularies and practices that both make sense to people and allow them to cultivate a sense of spirit that seems, for whatever reasons, unavailable through other religious means (including secular humanism).

The ambiguous position of such spiritual practices in the contemporary West makes them richly challenging but also fundamentally intolerable, from a critical viewpoint. "Richly challenging" does not invite an apologia for the often facile and uncritical cultural hybridity that characterizes "alternative" spiritualities, nor advocacy for "authentic" spirituality. The point here is that people's sense of the numinous need not be limited to or excluded from cultural criticism.

Contemporary vernacular spiritualities' adapting other cultures' rituals and myths as authentic and folding them into a Western ethos of individualism and visibility has rightly been a long-standing concern for critics of contemporary spirituality, including investigations into the cultural politics of expressive forms. A practitioner performing spiritual practices with historical roots outside the West appears to be evidence of a desire to replace Abrahamic monotheism's promise of transcendence through institutions and doctrines. However, cultural appropriation of spirituality being framed as a problem reveals just how closely spirituality is tied to culture.

Any effort to recognize spirituality comes up against the Western intellectual tradition's structuring power (Orsi 195). How does a critical stance that privileges cultural difference deal with spirituality? How can we take spiritual practices on their own terms when critical discourses relegate spirituality to Othered cultures, bracketing or denying spirituality in the modern West and global North (Alexander 296)? How do categories of analysis, systems of representation, models of comparison, and criteria that do not include spirituality affect interpretations of such practices (Smith, *Decolonizing* 43)? In the Western critique of vernacular spiritualities as essentializing, romanticizing, or exoticizing other cultures, the dominant critical stance accepts spirituality in other cultures but treats spirituality in the West with skepticism. Spirituality becomes a marker of Otherness that cannot be reconciled with Western knowledge paradigms.

SPIRITUALITY, AUTHENTICITY, AND THE PROBLEM OF CULTURAL APPROPRIATION

Wade Clark Roof points out that in contemporary Western cultures, the numinous wanders a meandering course through labyrinths of cultural hybridity and consumer capitalism:

> Meditation techniques imported from India are repackaged in the United States; Native American teachings extracted from their indigenous contexts pop up in other settings. A global world offers an expanded religious menu: images, rituals, symbols, meditation techniques, healing practices, all of which may be borrowed eclectically, from a variety of sources such as Eastern spirituality, Theosophy and New Age, Witchcraft, Paganism, the ecology movement, nature religions, the occult traditions, psychotherapy, feminism, the human potential movement, science, and of course, all the great world religious traditions. (73)[1]

Vernacular practices such as spirit drumming or trance dancing would seem to be examples of this dispersion of spirituality, where their performance is a naive longing for authentic experience rather than a veridical experience of spirit. Circles of African drums and the swirling silk veils of an Orientalist fantasy would seem to spiral around an empty center, filled only by an imagined real called "spirit."

Critical perspectives raise significant concerns about how people use the mechanisms available in materially developed countries to merchandize, personalize, professionalize, and perform spiritual practices from indigenous, non-Western, or ancient traditions. The critical concern focuses on the degree to which economically and socially privileged people betray these cultures in service of their own needs without adjusting or evaluating their dependence on that privilege. Adam Possamai points to the observation that the "quest for cultural inclusiveness" in vernacular spiritualities "erases all difference and often reduces indigenous practices to shallow therapeutic devises, the appropriation being effected through a process in which meanings are transformed within specific hierarchical structures of power" ("Alternative Spiritualities" 33). As Possamai points out in his review of the literature, the consumption of culture "'invades' the space of indigenous people, is neo-colonialist and is a romantic 'expropriation' of indigenous culture that avoids, even undermines, issues such as land rights and self-determination" ("Alternative Spiritualities" 33).

The Othering of non-Western or indigenous cultures along the axis of spirituality also seems to fall into an old Freudian anthropology of religious difference: belief in spirits marks primitive cultures that have not evolved into a materialist orientation to society and social relations, which manifests in the colonial suspicion of indigenous practices as dangerous and unfit for modern society. Postcolonial studies emphasized subaltern voices that resist oppression to overturn the imperialist hierarchies that viewed nonindustrial, nonscientific cultures as subordinate to the West. The resistance of the postcolonial project challenged the universalizing and unifying tendencies of liberal humanism, founded upon transcendent monotheism, which seems to permeate vernacular spiritualities in the emphasis on universal knowledge.

Still, spirituality, with its valences of premodern backwardness, remains on the margins of dominant discourses on knowledge. Vernacular spiritual practices can be interpreted as reconstructing European monotheism in the sunny guise of easy multiculturalism and spiritual perennialism. Practitioners adapt culturally specific myths, rituals, and beliefs to serve their own psychological needs, and in the process incorporate culturally specific practices into discourses of universal spirituality and cultural inclusiveness based on a Western model of liberal humanism.[2] People may be drawn to unfamiliar objects (such as *zills* or djembes), exotic ways of thinking (e.g., a "Great Spirit" rather than God), and new ways of conceptualizing themselves as selves (e.g., bodies moved to dance or drum by spiritual forces). The shamanic journeying in a practice such as Collective Awakening could be seen as a return to superstition, and the feminization of Sufism in Dancemeditation can be read as a self-serving distortion of a traditional belief system.

Practitioners might conceptualize spirituality as premodern by definition, and locate authentic spirituality outside Western religious and cultural traditions. The idea of spirituality being preserved in ancient traditions, excluded from modernity, and waiting to be discovered, however, becomes a form of resistance against a contemporary devaluation of spirituality. Vernacular spiritual practitioners in the West might imagine other cultures to be immune to the materialism and secularity of modernity, even as they are deploying its mechanisms. In practice, however, the qualities that distinguish spirituality as non-Western, indigenous, and premodern can become, for them, a corrective to modernity. Spirituality within the practices may be understood as a means of healing Western selves corrupted by modernity, even as Othered cultures embrace modernity.

Ontologies of difference in discourses suspicious of spirituality more comfortably reduce religion to its function in power relations, political ideologies, the capitalist marketplace, and symbolic performances, without attending to how a sense of spiritual presence might create very different models for interpreting cultural practices. Thus, what appears, from a conventional critical stance, to be a kind of violence committed in ignorance may in practice resist what practitioners might view as the West's arrogance, self-interest, and destructive imperialism.

Vernacular practices reimagine premodern, non-Western, or indigenous cultures positively as "in touch with nature, themselves, each other and the sacred" as a contrast to modernity (Partridge 1:77), moving premodern culture to the top of the evolutionary ladder. With that move, experiential spirituality is no longer the bottom rung of an evolutionary climb toward the textual, institutionally structured doctrinal religions of the West—spirituality is the arrival point. As Christopher Partridge rightly observes, within vernacular spiritual practices,

> It still seems to be the case that the "ancient wisdom" of these [Othered] cultures is understood to be the uncorrupted wisdom of a humanity unrepressed by the external dogma, rationalism and authority of later institutionalized religion and culture. They are therefore treated as spiritual and cultural paradigms. This, of course, is equally true of contemporary indigenous cultures which, it is believed, still retain their ancient wisdom and live in a symbiotic relationship with the environment. (1:77)

Borrowing from Othered cultures allows people to reconstruct spiritualized selves as authentic in a home culture that treats selves as performed identities (Roof 73). How these expressions of spiritual sensibilities synthesize borrowed cultural idioms to reinforce claims of universalized knowledge (for example, that love is a universal force) produces critical tensions.

The problem for the project here is the degree to which the alterity of spirituality in the contemporary Western intellectual tradition makes it difficult for critical analysis to engage practices such as Collective Awakening and Dancemeditation other than along an axis of difference relegating spirituality to somewhere (anywhere) else. Spiritually oriented perspectives may in fact be critically reflexive when appropriating Othered cultures. In that reflection and engagement with their own constructions of spirituality, some practices may productively challenge fundamental assumptions about spirituality structuring its reduction to consumerism (in the West) and cultural traditions (outside the West).

REREADING THE CULTURAL POLITICS OF SPIRITUALITY

The tendency of vernacular spiritualities to lift idioms from non-Western, ancient, or indigenous cultures does demand critique to expose facile appropriations and distortions in cross-cultural borrowings. Participants in spiritual practices like Collective Awakening and Dancemeditation should not be exempt from critical examinations of how they adapt cultural idioms. Appropriating surface characteristics from Othered cultures in service of spirituality suggests a variety of motivations: response to religious alienation, the appeal of the exotic, the privilege and pleasure of spiritual tourism, the desperation to relieve psychological distress, and so on. The 2013 documentary *Kumare: A True Film about a False Guru*, in which American filmmaker Vikram Gandhi creates the persona of an exotic Indian guru and develops a following of sincere devotees, is an excellent analysis of how this process works. As the film illustrates the ambiguity of people's purportedly spiritual experiences in response even to a false guru, it critiques its own assumptions about contemporary spirituality (see chapter 1).

Spiritual tourists can and do appropriate surface characteristics from Othered cultures, then invent practices and beliefs to fill voids in their own intellectual, social, religious, or cultural worlds. Collective Awakening and Dancemeditation present spiritual wisdom as universally accessible to experience, even as they ground their practices in cultural idioms from the localized traditions of Eastern and Western African societies and the religious mysticism of the Arabic Middle East. Klabunde's effort to put middle-class Americans into contact with African spirits through the drumming he learned from shamans in Africa and McPherson's exploration of Sufi mysticism at a summer ashram in New Mexico can indeed be read as cultural appropriations, while their public work can be taken as performances onto which people project their longings.[3]

Collective Awakening and Dancemeditation can thus be viewed as taking a "developed country" approach to professionalizing and performing spirituality as authentic experience while masking their own cultural privilege. Their practices might have little to do with the way the drumming or dance functions socially, aesthetically, religiously, or institutionally in African or Middle Eastern contexts. At the same time, the vernacular narrative of recovering a perennial, universal spirituality for the modern world has little affinity with the older anthropological model in which naive belief in spirit worlds evolves into text-based monotheism or is abandoned for a secular perspective. Rather, spirituality is considered an advancement over modernity. This narrative of recovery, though it has the valence of colonialism and appropriation, also constitutes a form of reverse critique of the ways the Western intellectual tradition marginalizes spirituality. Both dynamics are in play when we look at vernacular spirituality as performative.

The critical issue may be less *that* people construct spirituality from cultural idioms to fill some lack in Western culture than *how* those idioms migrate and transform across cultures in service of spiritual sensibilities. McPherson reflects on how a culture of alterity influenced the development of her spiritual practice. She writes, "I came to Middle Eastern culture through the back door of Sufism. As my teacher was Iraqi, I necessarily absorbed cultural information along with the spiritual nurture for which my being was so thirsty" (McPherson 193). Given the variety of spiritualities circulating in the global marketplace, it is worth considering that the internal sense of a spiritual "self," spirits, or a spiritual dimension propels people to seek narratives, images, practices, and formulations of knowledge that align with that sense of spiritual presence.

Klabunde and McPherson both redefined their careers in professional dance and music as spiritual practices in their encounters with experiential excess. Internal sensations, which they came to recognize as spiritual in origin and nature, exceeded available forms of expression. That excess forced a fundamental shift in their orientation to their work and the culture around them. As they relate in their narratives, that shift was not facile or for show; it involved a reorientation away from performance, from perception as representation. Such reorientations changed their relationship to their immediate culture. In that shift, working with previously unfamiliar cultural idioms (drums, veils, sacred circles, meditation) became appropriate and logical.

In critical practice, the conventional critique of vernacular spiritualities as borrowing or appropriating from already Othered cultures serves to keep spirituality where the intellectual tradition says it belongs: somewhere else, in some other culture, in some other time. Spirituality can then remain cordoned off in the safe domain of "folk belief," exposed as complicit in the insidious domain of consumer and cultural capitalism.

It is possible that in practice vernacular spiritualities may be trying to reconcile the Western tradition's historical vexation with spirituality and religion by looking elsewhere, to Othered cultures and imagined historical times. Yet the very borrowings and appropriations from non-Western, indigenous, and premodern cultures that might make that reconciliation possible instead prompt critiques of spirituality's cultural politics. That critique is necessary, but not comprehensive.

SPIRITUALITY AS AN AXIS OF CULTURAL DIFFERENCE

Religion and spirituality sometimes operate differently in analyses of the cultural politics of expressive forms. Religion, construed as the institutional and doctrinal organization of belief, more easily serves a critical agenda privileging cultural difference. Religion marks people's identities with histories and common beliefs. People might identify as Jewish, Hindu, Muslim, Christian, Coptic, or Jain or set themselves apart from religious belief by identifying as atheist, agnostic, or nonpracticing. Religion is marked on people's bodies with behavior and dress, in people's minds with beliefs, in geography with buildings and territorial borders, and in behavior with ethical codes.[4] Religion lends a regulation to cultural differences in ways the fluidity and ambiguity of spirituality does not.

Religion can more easily define identities (e.g., Catholic Christians), national identity (e.g., Rome, Italy), beliefs (e.g., transubstantiation), institutions (e.g., the Vatican), texts (e.g., Augustine's *Confessions*, the New Testament), truth-claims (e.g., the Nicene Creed), and historical events that to outsiders appear as myths (e.g., the birth, death, and resurrection of Christ). For purposes of cultural analysis, religion can limit people's sense the numinous to the analysis of religious texts, rituals, institutions, and other observable performances of belief (e.g., pilgrimages to sacred shrines). In this way, religion, as a critical category, keeps people's sense of spirituality manageable as religiosity (the performance of religious belief, faith, or feeling). What, then, of my neighbor, a newspaper columnist and home health care worker whose shrine to the Virgin Mary "performs" Catholicism on her front lawn as she leads a home study group she calls "The Pontifical Biblical Institute of the Holy Hippie Sisterhood"? From the stance of trained disbelief discussed in chapter 1, whatever sense of spirit this "performance" encodes can be fitted to paradigms that occlude spirituality while accounting for its persistence in modernity as religious belief, without ever asking how the "performance" fits this sense of spirit.

Spirituality in Othered cultures, outside the institutions and doctrines that have conventionally identified spirituality as religious, receives less scrutiny than spirituality among educated, economically privileged people of the modern West. In the latter context, a critical stance and reason are privileged ways for constructing knowledge and distinguished from a religious or spiritual orientation. In the effort to tease out incursions of Western thinking and values, postcolonial discourses effectively inoculate indigenous and non-Western spiritualities from critiques of spirituality as naive folk beliefs, as well as scientific explanations.

Music as Medicine and *Skin of Glass* describe encounters with spiritual beings, a sense of the self as participating in a spiritual dimension, and an insight into love as the fundamental human condition. These practices put the Otheredness of spirituality into direct contact with the culture shaped by the Western intellectual tradition. Observed outside the West, such sensibilities might easily be viewed as interesting aspects of local cultures. Thus the spiritual traditions of Othered cultures (shamanism and Sufism) simultaneously validate a spiritual orientation to the self and world even as they its Otheredness.

Spiritual practices such as Dancemeditation and Collective Awakening absorb the most profound markers of cultural and intellectual difference into Western secularism and religion. Vernacular practices in the West that adapt spirituality from other cultures thus present a problem. The sense of spirit they cultivate (whether attached to religion or not) is already fundamentally Other to contemporary Western epistemologies. It does not fit into modernity. Thus ideas, practices, and artifacts *must* be imported, with the cultural imperialism that implies. At the same time, spirituality *identifies* cultures as Other to the modern West. Critical discourses that preserve or protect spirituality in non-Western cultures reinforce its foreignness to Western modernity and ensure its cultural value elsewhere. The problem of moving spiritual traditions from Othered cultures into the West is thus a serious critical issue. That movement need not preclude, however, asking how a critical investment in the effects the sense of spirit people cultivate might have an influence on the home culture of people like Klabunde and McPherson or my neighbor. For critical purposes, the *presumption* of spirituality's foreignness opens the conceptual space in which to rethink the sense of spirit apart from reliance on the symbolic abstractions of representation and performance that have come to define modernity.[5]

By constructing spiritual epistemologies out of non-Western cultural idioms, vernacular spiritualities cross a major fault line of cultural difference. However, in imagining indigenous or non-Western cultures as uncompromised by modernity's materialism and secularism, and therefore assumed to preserve an authentic spirituality, it may not be cultural alterity that constructs practitioners' spiritual experience but rather the recognition that, in their home culture, spirituality has been devalued. Practices like Dancemeditation and Collective Awakening may be sensitive to the cultures they draw on in ways that most analytical lenses do not see. They may be resituating spirituality as a structuring discourse in contemporary Western culture against the cultural imperative to perform.

CULTURE, AUTHENTICITY, AND THE CONSTITUTION OF SPIRITUAL SELVES

Authenticity raises another set of critical concerns with contemporary vernacular spiritualities. These concerns are shaped by suspicions of subjective sensations and an essentialized Western subject. Cultivation of spirituality as internal and personal yields what Stef Aupers and Dick Houtman critique as the "binding doctrine" of contemporary spiritualities: "the belief that in the deeper layers of the self, one finds a true, authentic, and sacred kernel, 'unpolluted' by culture, history or society, which informs evaluation of what is good, true, and meaningful. Such evaluation, it is held, cannot be made by relying on external authorities or experts, but only by listening to one's 'inner voice'" (204). The sincerity of that "inner voice" goes against prominent discourses on the impossibility of authenticity.

The argument can be made that authenticity is always imagined and thus always performative. The potential for people to exoticize spirituality as inherent, pure, traditional, and authentic when they find it (or think they find it) in Othered cultures is probably the most problematic issue for postcolonial discourses. Cultural appropriation in service of authentic spirituality is immediately recognizable as performative. As Philip Vannini and J. Patrick Williams assert, authenticity "is not so much a state of being as it is the objectification of a process of representation, that is, it refers to a set of qualities that people in a particular time and place have come to agree represent an ideal or exemplar" (3). Authenticity is "strategically invoked as a marker of status"; it is a "moving target" as what constitutes authenticity shifts with changes in "tastes, beliefs, values, and practices" (Vannini and Williams 3).

The assumption that claims of authentic experience such as those expressed in *Skin of Glass* and *Music as Medicine* constitute a perceptual deception is a fairly recent, twentieth-century development in Western thought. A critical framework that is dependent on performance as representation to produce and reproduce endless images of selves reinforces inauthenticity as the norm.[6] Reality television shows such as *Desperate Housewives*, to give just one example, register the degree to which vernacular culture has adapted the critical stance of performative irony, once the privileged purview of academic critical theory. An "authentic self" appears in scare quotes to mark it as the performance of emotional or sensory affect intended to elicit some response from observing audiences.[7] In this cultural context, authenticity becomes just another product. E. Doyle McCarthy points out how the perception of one's self as an authentically spiritual being is in fact constructed by today's "therapeutic culture of self-aggrandizement," which holds out the false promise that one can know one's true self through systematic processes like psychotherapy (or Dancemeditation or Collective Awakening).[8] McCarthy holds that

> whether authenticity is viewed as an escape from the confines of a material civilization or as a kind of selling-out or material entrapment, the discourse of authenticity throughout its relatively brief history takes as its problem the pursuit of inner truth and meaningfulness in a social world of lies, deceits, and fabrications. Authenticity is always a type of self-knowledge, especially a self-knowledge that allows us to disentangle the true from the false self. (243)[9]

Statements such as, "Our cosmic memory is the realization of the self, the true identity of who we are and the recognition of one's own spirit," (Klabunde 188) and "I am a body of knowledge" (McPherson 138) can be read, in this view, as discursive performances constructing self-knowledge as authentic. The sacred drumming ceremonies and Alembic concerts, dance DVDs, and music CDs these practices produce are then understood as performative gestures that reproduce or represent a desire for some kind of authentically spiritual experience. That the sense of an authentic spiritual self cultivated in these practices might have some cultural value and that their concerts, writings, and products might offer a dissent from the cultural habit of irony disappears in a discourse on authenticity.

RESITUATING SPIRITUALITY

As the discussion above shows, vernacular spiritual practices such as Collective Awakening and Dancemeditation are solidly positioned in nearly every paradigmatic problem zone of cultural and intellectual criticism. However problematic it might seem to accept that people continue to constitute a numinous dimension to their experience, spiritual practices do shape people's engagement with public, social worlds. While practitioners might mythologize Othered cultures as holding ancient wisdom, the specific myths, rituals, or practices *within* those cultures do somehow reverberate in and destabilize their sensibilities. Another perspective on these practices might see them as confronting familiar knowledge in unfamiliar ways. The myths, rituals, and practices they engage with might offer possibilities for different perceptions of, and relationships with, the cultures they live in. Even as we can observe spirituality in non-Western and indigenous cultures as a mark of cultural difference, people's sense of spirit in Western vernacular culture pushes back against the bracketing and irony that have marked performance theory. Can these perspectives become part of, rather than separate from, critical inquiry? The emerging focus on indigenousness in postcolonial studies offers possibilities for reflecting on critical perspectives that have avoided spirituality and assesses the costs of doing so.

Spirituality has, as discussed above, functioned as an axis of difference dividing contemporary Western cultures from ancient, indigenous, and non-Western cultures. That axis of difference, however, is itself problematic. As this next section suggests, writing spirituality out of modernity has effectively erased multiple ways of knowing in unacknowledged forms of intellectual imperialism. Linda Tuhuwai Smith has asserted the need for indigenous or colonized peoples to revisit the histories "western eyes" have written for them. She examines the failure of Western historical writing to recognize knowledge from other cultures that does not fit into Western epistemological systems (34). The ways "western eyes" see the world are not the ways people might sense spirit with what the practitioners described in chapter 2 also describe as "inner eyes."

From Smith's perspective, spirituality outside the West is afforded legitimacy because from the safety of critical distance. Spirituality need not be dealt with as a way of knowing. Rather, the critical paradigm produces knowledge about spirituality (e.g., performance structures the spirituality of a shamanic ritual). In Dancemeditation and Collective Awakening, for example, what appear to be performative distortions of culturally Othered traditions serve a desire for authentic spiritual experience. These same expressions could also be interpreted as evidence of the human capacity for sensing the sacred even in modern, technologically advanced cultures. Awareness of how critical paradigms occlude the sense of spirit that might underpin myths, rituals, and other expressive forms in any cultural context opens critical possibilities for expanded theories of presence beyond the material to include the sensible.

THE MANAGERIAL FUNCTION OF THE PERFORMANCE PARADIGM

The imperative to perform and the habit of seeing the world as performative are as much cultural constructions as spirituality. That performance as materiality produces reality around a sense of lack, loss, and erasure is a familiar theoretical premise. Based on this premise, performance is the visible, embodied materiality upon which multiple meanings are inscribed and contested, and thus displaces any authentic presence. The familiar formulations "x as performance" and "performing x," which render people's practices performative, comes at the expense of engaging in a dialogue with modes of knowing that do not depend on visibility or materiality. The new investigation becomes how expressive forms (which are always situated in culture) and people's sense of the numinous (once given equal status with material culture) inform each other.

Practices like Dancemeditation and Collective Awakening in the West can easily be read as "performing" spirituality by deploying cultural codes, or as "spiritualizing" dance and music. However, when people's sense of spirit orients them to a condition of being, not to the materiality of representing, showing, and observing, the performance construct collapses. The sense of unseen, nonmaterial presence in effect deconstructs performance as we know it.

Malidoma Patrice Somé offers insight into the representational mentality of Western thinking from his perspective as a medicine man of the West African Dagara tribe who holds advanced degrees from French and American universities. Somé perceives the cultural investment in what Richard Schechner calls "showing doing" combined with the idea that performance marks absence as evidence of a seriously misguided culture. In stark contrast to this perspective, Somé writes that

> the *problem* with Western culture is that it is a show-off culture that intimidates. This is why it is *generating so much death, loss and displacement.* To perform ritual for show is to generate some kind of death or loss. Concealment of ritual is an act of life preservation because it is only in its concealment that needs are met that cannot be met in any other way. (39–40, italics added)

For Somé, the process of "explaining showing doing" that structures the performance paradigm gives credibility to ways of engaging with the world that are damaging rather than celebratory or liberating (see Schechner, *Performance Studies* 22). Seeing the material world and people in it as performing, with the consequent investment in the visible surfaces of objects and bodies as sites of meaning, is for Somé a very dangerous view.[10] Representational thinking, along with the demand for visibility prominent in Western culture, is also antithetical to the sense of spirit cultivated by people like Klabunde and McPherson.

Performativity's gaze actually becomes repressive when turned on spiritual practices. In an environment that makes spirituality an axis of cultural and intellectual alterity, people whose social identity marks them as privileged are subject to criticism for adopting "weird" spiritual practices, and people whose spiritual practices are already marked as culturally Other may be compelled to repress or hide their practices. Somé understands the value placed on "showing" in the West as not the critical stance that exposes the condition of lack but as the very *source* of lack.

A mode of thinking that sees the world as performing and performative, Somé suggests, produces and exports "death, loss and destruction" because of its focus on what is absent, missing, or displaced by what is shown. Practices like Dancemeditation and Collective Awakening work against the emphasis on showing and an orientation to performance that accepts lack, loss, and erasure as the conditions of performance.[11] In their insistence on spiritual presence, the practices undo the theoretical construct of performance.

What if what we see as "performative" in these practices—drums, veils, amplifiers, costumes, gestures, a concert frame—is the effect of spirit? What if people's sense of spirit is as significant as a mentality organized by representational thinking? What if spirit enters the discussion as a kind of presence along with the materiality of bodies, texts, and objects? What if critical strategies included spirituality as a legitimate component of cultural practice and performance? What if methodologies engaged what the visibility and materiality of the performative cannot contain—that which becomes present in different ways?

How do we engage these particular "what ifs." If critical discourses force knowledge into conformity with the epistemological rules governing scientific, critical, and interpretive paradigms (including the performance) insights such as Somé's and the knowledge of spirit cultivated in Collective Awakening and Dancemeditation have no status on their own. They must be managed in the terms of representation, material presence, and observation.

Linda Tuhuwai Smith uses feminism as an example of how the rules of critical discourse force conformity. She observes that feminism works under the Marxist and psychoanalytic paradigms, thereby "conforming to some very fundamental Western European world views, value systems and attitudes towards the [feminine] Other" (43). In the conforming process, these epistemological systems either reject or fail to recognize ways people access and construe knowledge. They are either invisible or Other.

Spirituality, even when it is vitally important for the survival of a people or culture, does not fit into the legacies of empiricism, visibility, materialism, and language as knowledge. In this mode of thinking, spirituality simply cannot translate into Western epistemologies—there is no language of spirit (Smith, *Decolonizing Methodologies* 43). Building on Stuart Hall's work, Smith observes the subtlety with which the Western cultural archive maintains itself by denying what does not fit its terms:

> Theories about research are underpinned by a cultural system of classification and representation, by views about human nature, human morality and virtue, by conceptions of space and time, by conceptions of gender and race. Ideas about these things help determine what counts as real. Systems of classification and representation enable different traditions or fragments of traditions to be retrieved and reformulated in different contexts as discourses, and then to be played out in systems of power and domination, with real material consequences for colonized peoples. (44)

The performance paradigm serves this managerial function when it structures spirituality in a system of representation or signification, forcing visibility and materiality rather than reckoning with spirituality (and performance) in the terms of people who sense a spiritual presence.

Two examples from well-known anthropological studies of indigenous rituals, discussed below, illustrate how performance as a structuring paradigm manages Western encounters with spirituality. In each case, interpretation of a ritual as performance works up to a point. At that point, the performance paradigm cannot quite manage the spiritual epistemology at work in the ritual. In the first example, the paradigm cracks; in the second it shatters.

Edward Schieffelin reckons with spirit in the performance paradigm in his description of séances held by the Kaluli people of Papua, New Guinea, in the 1970s. In his encounter with spirit-calling, he posed the logical first question a theater anthropologist would ask of a ritual: "In what sense is a spirit séance a 'performance'?" (Schieffelin 60). The question makes some epistemological assumptions: that performance is a cross-cultural mechanism for presence and that bodies are present for observation so what can be seen is the limit of presence. Performance, as a presumed framework, provides a way to encounter spirit-calling without actually having to accept spirits. Reading the séances as performance thus made the appearance of spirits (which otherwise could not be accounted for) manageable. The performance paradigm allowed for spirits as fictions, perhaps believed by some people to be real but illusions nevertheless. The Kaluli performance of a séance *produces* spirits in the same way the play *Hamlet* produces the specter of a dead parent for an audience's visual consumption in the Western intellectual tradition. Spirits are assumed to be as real as their theatrical or ritual production makes them.

Rendering spirituality as performance here makes it present as matter. By making spirituality material, the performance paradigm denies the fundamental nonmateriality of spirits called in the séance, bracketing spirituality as belief or illusion. Still, though the paradigm cannot fully accommodate it, Schieffelin's effort is to recognize and come to terms with the séance as a localized form of knowledge through a familiar epistemology. To get out of the familiar, the question "In what sense is a spirit séance a 'performance'?" becomes "In what sense of performance is there spirit?"

The second example comes from Robert R. Desjarlais's description of his apprenticeship with shaman Meme Bombo, of the Yolmo people (*Ylmo wa*) in the Helambu region of north-central Nepal. Desjarlais's encounter suggests a more membranous approach to spirituality in spirit-calling rites (143). "I have been trying to understand," he writes,

> if, how, and to what extent his spirit-calling rites work to rejuvenate a spiritless body. My understanding is that the rites do, at times, have a positive effect, tending to work through indirect, tacit means—the less obvious aspects of ritual—to negate a sensibility bound by loss, fatigue, and listlessness and create a new one of vitality, presence, and attentiveness. Simply put, Meme changes how a body feels by altering what it feels. His cacophony of music, taste, sight, touch, and kinesthesia activates the senses. The activation has the potential to "wake up" a person,

> alter the sensory grounds of a spiritless body, and so change how a person feels. (Desjarlais 143)

This encounter tolerates possibilities for sensation and sensibility that cannot be contained in or as performance. Desjarlais's willingness to engage the sensory dimension of the Yolmo spirit-callings challenges the rules of "dominant anthropological interpretations of ritual healing, which tend to privilege the symbolic, intellectual, and social features of such healings," and leads him to ask what "spiritlessness" means among the Yolmo to better understand how specific rites come to revive bodies (143–44). Though performance is still the template for whatever is going on in the spirit-callings, Desjarlais is willing to let the convention that the séance is *only* a performance open up enough to take seriously the internal transformations the séances can generate.[12] He takes spirit-calling on its own terms.

In these encounters with spirit in anthropological fieldwork, the customary frame of performance does not quite contain the observers' perception that something else might be operating. Yet accepting spiritual presence remains an epistemological gap the observers do not quite cross. A sense of spirit remains a mark of Otherness. That Otherness can be observed with respect, no longer demeaned as "primitive" or "backward," but not accepted as knowledge. The performance paradigm remains the material container for what has no language. Spirits are left behind with the peoples to whom they belong, managed by field notes written in a language that has no terms for spiritual knowledge with, as Smith reminds us, real material consequences.

Practices like Collective Awakening bring those spirits home, so to speak, not in the critical analysis of notebooks but in practice. That is what makes them so profoundly disturbing to critical interpretation. Analytical rigor demands critiquing such practices to expose the ways practitioners gloss cultural difference, naively insist on a common humanity, generalize their individual experiences as universal, ignore historical conditions through which spiritual practices have been colonized and appropriated, and erase issues of ethnicity, class, and gender in the effort to promote pan-religious spirituality.

Taking spirituality seriously as an axis of inquiry should not become uncritical advocacy. Certainly the conflation of ancient or indigenous cultures with nature, and nature with spirituality, raises concerns that should not be ignored. Not the least of these concerns is the specter of "primitivism" so rigorously exorcised over the last four decades. Statements from *Music as Medicine* such as "Indigenous cultures have a long history of looking beyond the physical world for social and spiritual guidance" and "[Africa's] connection to nature, her community and her creativity in expression are all aspects of human spirituality many have forgotten" raise these concerns (Klabunde 64, 69). It is important to at least acknowledge, however, that such statements by practitioners might be more than the utopian dreams of cultural tourists, the facile pronouncements of spiritual dabblers, or wide-eyed affectations of people entranced by exotic spiritual traditions. Such critiques too easily fall into the bias against spirituality rather than engaging with whatever challenging perspectives such practices might offer.

For example, the background for the first-person perspective of Klabunde's book is informed by his immersion in specific musical traditions, spiritual traditions, and languages of West African drummers (131). Like anthropologists Schieffelin and Desjarlais, Klabunde spent several years in African villages, and like his scholarly counterparts, he is keenly aware of his own position as a white man from the United States studying shamanism in Africa. In his workshops and concerts, Klabunde speaks in anecdotes about the poverty, violence, and killings he witnessed during his studies, as well as his observations of the effects of Western industry, particularly pharmaceuticals, in Africa. In language similar to Somé's, Klabunde speaks of being told by his teachers to take spirit drumming back to the United States to cure the cultural sickness in the West that causes pain in Africa.

Unlike his anthropologist counterparts, he went as a practitioner to learn *from* shamans, rather than to *observe* them with the critical distance of someone who must account for spirits in a framework that rejects their existence. This distinction separates the academic (that which studies) from the vernacular (that which is studied), placing managerial authority in the former. Is a practice like Collective Awakening too easily dismissed because its practitioners embrace in cultural Others what does not belong in modernity? An alternative approach to critical inquiry, developed by M. Jacqui Alexander in *Pedagogies of Crossing*, addresses this question.

RETHINKING CULTURAL HYBRIDITY AS THE MOVEMENT OF SPIRITS

In her analysis of the transmission and transformation of African religions in nineteenth-century Trinidad, Alexander works against critical analysis conventions that enclose and isolate spirituality, resisting recognizing it as a mode of knowing. Alexander takes spirituality on its own terms. In her historical project, spirituality is an agent in the slave crossing. Working from primary documents, she argues that, in diaspora, people do not carry the sacred in objects and rituals in order to fix memories of a lost past or community (a conventional view in which the performance of religion testifies to a lack or absence—that which is left behind). Her argument is that rituals and spiritual practices are not recuperative devices to ease the present by remembering the past, but that the sacred itself is in constant transformation as people move from place to place.[13] In the violence of the slave crossings to Trinidad, she does not see rituals as reconstructed memories but as "multiple avatars of the same Sacred force," with which "collectivities develop different relationships to the same multilayered entity as Sacred energies," and through which people "engage the different inventions of the social" (Alexander 292). The social, she suggests, emerges from the sacred.

Alexander's project is concerned with how Western historical accounts of the crossing rewrote the Africans' spirituality. She demonstrates how the conventions of Western knowledge could not see that African spirits *moved* to Trinidad during the slave crossings. Alexander points to the ways Western histories classified and categorized spirituality according to practices and beliefs observed in geographic locations or specific groups of people. This analytical strategy, she argues, tries to localize the sacred rather than allowing for the sacred as a moveable, migratory, active presence. The unexamined strategies of conventional historical analyses render the sacred material—specific to local customs, a function of social organization, or read in expressive forms (such as rituals). This conventional bracketing of spirituality qua spirituality limits access to how the sacred moves from place to place and from social group to social group.

Alexander's project is to work with this well-established process of classification and categorization to develop an alternative writing of the history. In the violent relocation of African people into the plantation system of Trinidad, she argues, spirits were not brought into being or remembered in the practices people developed, but travelled along with the people. With an entirely rational approach to the writing of this history, Alexander traces the movement of African spirits in the diaspora, their disappearance and reappearance in different forms with different names. Spirits, she maintains, are not bound to the names scholars, theologians, or practitioners give them but have independent existence as they move from place to place in the diaspora.[14] Sacred energies emerge, disappear, and reemerge in the ways people envision them and sense their presence as active participants in the material world.

Alexander thus opens a discourse on spirits and a spiritual dimension that acknowledges a nonmaterial dimension to the material conditions in which people lived. The sacred is not an imaginary construct of a cultural or social situation, nor is the sacred brought into being by the performance of rituals, statues and objects performing cultural codes, the charisma of individual priestesses or shamans, or even by devotional practices. Spirituality, in Alexander's analysis, is a kind of energetic property that emerges in cultures. The names and qualities of African spirits found in the historical record of the diaspora trace this migration of spirits associated with the African homeland:

> Some energies have been fused; others apparently atrophy in certain places while becoming dominant in others. Yemayá, the goddess of the Ocean seems to have "disappeared" in Haiti, yet homage to Agwe the sea god and Mambo La Siren, the mermaid sister of the two Ezilis, Freda Dahomey and Dantò, attest to the sustained metaphysical significance of water in both systems. Yemayá reigns in Candomblé and Lucumí, assuming the position that had been accorded her River sister Oshún in Yorubaland, the recognition that it would have been impossible to have survived the Crossing without her. (Alexander 292)

If spirituality migrates as an energetic property of the material world and is always available for people to sense through the cultural practices they develop, the view that performance marks loss, lack, or displacement has less power. Alexander writes that the Crossing, which violently severed people from their religious beliefs and practices, did not relegate spirituality to the reconstitution of memories to keep a lost past alive. She states that the Crossing was not required for African spirits to express their beingness. Material expression and embodiment were not methods of preserving a religious past remembered from before the Crossing. Rather, a divine or sacred presence moved *with* the people across time and geography, reconstituting itself in the everyday material realities of a new cultural world. Alexander writes that *in spiritu*,

> there was a prior knowing, a different placement in the human idiom of constricted time. Still, the capacity to operate outside of human time

> does not mean that Divine energy has no facility within it. In this sense, there is no absolute transcendence—no transcendence, in fact—for if there were, there would be no intervention in, and no relationship with, the material, the quotidian, the very bodies through which divinity breathes life. Indeed, the Divine knits together the quotidian in a way that compels attunement to its vagaries, making this the very process through which we come to know its existence. It is, therefore, the same process through which we come to know ourselves. (293)

Alexander's analysis does not lapse into perennialism. Spirituality can be many things in social practice: an experiential condition, a mode of engagement with everyday life, a human capacity, or a sense of a metaphysical reality. In practice, people might be accessing different spirits or spiritual energies. Conversely, it is equally possible that the variety of practices accesses one common spiritual presence with different aspects. Spirituality is always, she rightly insists, grounded in social practices, and in that sense can quite reasonably be considered performative. By taking the textual evidence of spiritualities seriously in this historical context, however, Alexander is able to analyze not what spirituality *is* but how spirituality *moves*. Alexander offers a methodological template that differs radically from the analysis of social practices as only and entirely material, while simultaneously avoiding reducing spiritual sensibilities to emotional affect.

Alexander's project is specific to the ways African bodies moved in the plantation economy of colonial Trinidad, between "European and African systems," and between being understood as the "repository of sin" and "the direct instrument of the Divine." Her project seeks "to move beyond the more dominant understanding of African spiritual practice as cultural retention and survival" proscribed by analyses of religion as functional and to find "the spiritual as epistemological, that is, to pry open the terms, symbols, and organizational codes" by which people made sense of the world and by which memory brings spiritual practices into being, transforms them, or hides them (Alexander 293). Her questions for the archive of nineteenth-century Trinidad, which accepts the reality of spirits in that time and place, challenge rules of analysis that bracket spirituality as symbolic or superstitious, or deny spirituality in this context.

The analytical strategies by which Alexander accepts people's sense of the ineffable within a rigorous historiographical critique and gives spirituality credibility as yielding a particular kind of knowledge suggests possibilities for studying spirituality as a component of modern, technologically advanced cultures. She allows a more flexible approach to cultural hybridity than that which discredits spirituality as not belonging to the West while accepting spirituality in Othered cultures.

I want to be absolutely clear here that I am not equating or comparing modern spiritual practitioners in the United States with people forcibly brought from Africa and forced into slavery in the 19th century. There is a radical difference between the violence of Alexander's account and the ease of today's spiritual practitioners. I am pointing here to Alexander's thesis and method as a model for working outside the problem of a paradigmatic rejection of spirituality, which I am suggesting limits interpretive possibilities for vernacular spiritual practices today in the West.

Alexander quotes words of a contemporary *espiritista* (healer-medium), Maria: "'Yo soy mis santos; mis santos soy yo' (I am my saints, my saints are me)" (293). Alexander is willing to take claims such as Maria's seriously and to consider them evidence of spiritual energies emerging through cultural practices and in people's sensations of themselves and their worlds. She thus asks questions that generally fall outside the critical frameworks that organize paradigms such as performativity: "How does one come to know oneself through and as Saints or Spirits? How does one not know oneself without them? What kind of labor makes this intelligibility possible?" (293). Her questions for this historical archive suggest paths of inquiry into the cultural work today's vernacular spiritual practices are doing. *Espiritista* Maria's expression of embodied spirituality, of a self that is spiritual, is very similar to the sensations of a spiritual self that Klabunde and McPherson describe.

Klabunde senses the presence of African spirits who have migrated to the Tucson mountain ranges from Africa. His drumming and meditation practices, as he understands them, open portals for communication with those spirits. The music he plays on instruments with which those spirits are familiar brings people into contact with the energetic qualities of a spiritual dimension. Following Alexander, if spirituality can be worked into discussions of such sensations as a part of cultural analysis, rather than bracketed or Othered by conventions of classification and categories that exclude it, then the seemingly performative writing, speaking, and events of contemporary vernacular practitioners may be evidence of the movement of spirits through cultural practices in the contemporary Western world. The question is whether we can take these spirits as seriously as Alexander takes the spirits of the Crossing, or whether spirituality must remain culturally Other and temporally distant.

Alexander's thinking shifts the epistemological ground of historical inquiry. The orientation she takes to spirituality, coming out of her work on nineteenth-century Trinidad, sets a precedent for integrating experiential spirituality and analytical-interpretive inquiries. Spirituality, as an energetic property of the material world and the human body, can also be the foundation for ways of knowing, which in turn govern how people understand how their embodied practices and the objects and texts that inhabit their worlds. Spirituality then becomes an aspect of the material world, neither a separate, transcendent domain nor entirely a private mental experience. Alexander writes:

> The designation of the personal as spiritual need not be taken to mean that the social has been evacuated for a domain that is ineluctably private. While different social forces may have indeed privatized the spiritual, it is very much lived in a domain that is social in the sense that it provides knowledge whose distillation is indispensable to daily living, its particular manifestations transforming and mirroring the social in ways that are both meaningful and tangible. Indeed, the spiritual is no less social than the political, which we no longer contest as mediating the traffic between the personal and the political. (295–96)

Is the a priori sacredness Alexander acknowledges in this historical account necessarily limited to peoples Othered by time and distance? Can theoretical paradigms that defer meaning and reduce subjectivity to culturally situated identities or affects adjust to, in Seligman's words, "a greater appreciation of what externality or otherhood can mean—not in its trendy postmodern guise, but as the essence of a heteronomously constituted self" (*Modernity's Wager* 70)? This greater appreciation requires reconsideration of the "postmodern guises" that mask the ways spiritual practitioners constitute their work and themselves in the social world.

The overlap between spirituality and consumer capitalism is one of the primary lines of critique that dismantle experiential spirituality. This line of critical analysis has methodological affinities with the paradigm of performativity in part because consumer capitalism produces the demand to perform, make things visible, be heard, adopt a socially recognizable style, and fill spiritual lack with material objects.

The engagement of cultural idioms in the effort to make spirituality intelligible is not only the labor of "showing doing," of performance, however. What we see as performance might well be the labor of making spirituality intelligible with whatever material resources are available. A Dancemeditation Alembic concert or Collective Awakening sacred drumming ceremony might invite analysis of *how* the sacred is evident. We might well ask: "How does spiritual work produce the conditions that bring about the realignment of self with self, which is simultaneously a realignment of oneself with the Divine through a collectivity" (Alexander 298)? These are the very capacities vernacular practices cultivate in the physiological interior of their bodies and which they make intelligible in the interaction with cultural resources.

CONSUMING SELVES, SENSORY STIMULATION, AND THE SENSE OF SPIRIT

Somé, as noted above, calls the West a "show-off culture" because it identifies power in performance. Performativity, as an analytical paradigm, validates this cultural propensity for "showing." The logic of production and consumption is also the logic of performativity. Consumer capitalism relies on the production and consumption of material goods—it values what can be seen, what can be "performed."

This line of thinking also posits spiritually oriented people as participating in "consumer religions," consuming "products for gathering and enhancing sensations" associated with spirituality (Possamai, "Alternative Spiritualities" 31). An array of consumer goods, from yoga mats to aromatherapy oils and chakra-balancing CDs to zazen cushions, falls under the critique that such goods reinforce individualized experiences of corporeal sensations, which people then accept uncritically as authentically spiritual. Spirituality, in this view, becomes another performable commodity subject to the mechanics of reproduction that characterize modernity and define postmodernity.

A culture driven by this circulation of goods relies on performance to show its products, create desire, and remind people of a lack that must be filled. Performativity, as an analytical paradigm, supports capitalism's imperative for the display of objects and bodies: bodies and objects cannot *not* perform. The intellectual move to insist on the performativity of vernacular culture perpetuates this logic. It also elevates an essentially bourgeois concern with being looked at and with being evaluated for one's material possessions and physical appearance to the status of a theoretical apparatus that values the visible.

Familiar formulations such as "spirituality as performance" or "performing spirituality" presume that texts and objects produce spirituality and participate in discourses on spirituality. The circulation of goods in the marketplace (CDs, DVDs, workshops, veils, drums, etc.) thus appears to invalidate the spirituality that practitioners claim. Without question, the cultural work spiritual practitioners like Klabunde and McPherson do involves commerce and commodification; they participate in the mechanisms of consumer capitalism. Their workshops, retreats, private teaching, CDs, DVDs, websites, blogs, and books ensure that their practices and ideas circulate. The Internet, auto and air travel, rented studio space, the sound systems and lights they use for concerts, PayPal, cash, and credit cards are the lymph carrying their sense of spirituality through material culture.

If these spiritual practitioners engage a modern culture steeped in the overt performativity of political campaigns, reality television, advertising, and self-presentation, "in which signs and symbols are innovated at a rapid flow" and ideas are "dispersed through many networks," their bodies appear as sites at which multiple spiritual traditions and borrowed cultural idioms intersect with indiscriminate, imperialist, and playful postmodern fluidity (Possamai, *Religion and Popular Culture* 64). The hybrid cultural identities possible in the global circulation of spiritual products—from dancing Shiva statues to rosaries—are easily read as a soteriological response to postmodern insecurities and the Western crisis of inauthenticity (Vannini and Williams 1). Spiritual practitioners' products, we can assume from the perspective of this viewpoint, reproduce that inauthenticity. Their claims of authentic spiritual experience automatically implicate these modern metaphysicals in systems of oppression: in the oppression of those from whom spiritual practices are taken and in the exercise of the privilege that takes and absorbs those practices according to its own values (Alexander 297–98).

Analyzing spirituality as the end result of people's imaginative interpretations of external sensory stimuli manages the sense of spirit by conveniently reducing it to sensory stimulation. For an example of a conventional critical reading, consider a person buying a bundle of sage in a natural foods market. The person accepts the label's explanation that sage was a sacred plant for Native Americans. The explanation gives the dried leaves meaning (even if the buyer cannot tell desert sage from bay leaves). The person takes the bundle home, ceremonially burns it, and smudges a room in which an unpleasant event took place the day before. The sensation of breathing in the smoke combined with beliefs about spirituality produces a sensation (perhaps burning, perhaps pleasant) and stimulates the sense of smell. With the meaning attributed to the sage, the person believes that the room is cleared of the spirits or energies from the previous day and the body-mind cleansed of the memory.

A critical perspective recognizes that the stimulus itself does not in fact cleanse the mind or body, though the person may believe it does and, through that belief, derive some emotional or psychological benefit. This line of analysis's managerial terms render bodily sensation a less sophisticated mode of engagement with the self and world than linguistic expression and reactions to external stimuli more significant than what McPherson and Klabunde would call sensing with "inner eyes."

Dancemeditation and Collective Awakening can certainly be viewed as performing a widespread interest in subjective well-being, which often equates spirit with products such as the sage. To an extent, their products and services also construe spirituality as a familiar kind of physical and psychological well-being. Both practitioners emphasize relaxing the body and mind, coming to a feeling of inner peace, increasing self-knowledge, and a holistic synthesis of mind, body, and spirit. They participate in a milieu of "holistic approaches to physical exercise and spiritual growth, and 'trademark' exercises" that appropriate spirituality into a "contemporary cultural fascination with neurobiology and health (sciences)" (Karjalainen 212, 200). When domesticated and medicalized, these practices seem to serve the ends of consumer capitalism by producing products that construct desire and drive a market (Heelas, *Spiritualities of Life* 199–201). The critique of consumer capitalism and the alterity of spirituality in Western thinking align. The representation and reproduction of Sufism and African shamanism as vehicles for spirits in the modern, urban West can thus be interpreted as simply displacing an imagined originary, authentic, or perennial spirituality with products and performances that invoke a discourse on spirituality—matter that serves the lack of spirit.

The critique of spirituality as a consumer product easily manages people's sense of an ineffable presence. In this line of critique, spirituality cannot belong to societies driven by consumer capitalism. In an ironic and subtle attachment to modernity's rejection of religion, the critique itself relegates spirituality to premodern societies by assuming that spirituality cannot belong to the West. Dancemeditation and Collective Awakening must be read as reproducing the imagined spirituality of Othered cultures in readily recognizable and normalized forms—CDs, books, DVDs, workshops, retreats, cruises, and so on. The very normalcy of these expressions makes spirituality tangible, portable, and objectifiable. This critique can easily insist that this production undercuts spirituality as a credible foundation for people's sense of themselves and the world they live in (see chapter 1).

Paradoxically, the critique of vernacular spirituality in the West is constructed by the dualism built into the Western intellectual tradition. That dualism situates spirituality outside the mundane world of society, culture, and economics in languages of transcendence and privacy, as well as outside the West. The definition of spirituality as transcending the mundane is a function of the critical apparatus, not necessarily the way a spiritual practice might operate.

This critical frame presents participants in the spiritual marketplace as having tainted their potential for countercultural resistance with consumer capitalism. It cannot show spirituality and so shows instead what it knows: purveyors of spiritual practices promoting techniques for a more comfortable experience of self, failing to do the cultural work of social transformation.[15] Heelas summarizes the problem with this quest for well-being in the guise of spirituality:

> The creativity of capitalist enterprise is witnessed in the proliferation of "new" mind-body-"spirituality" provisions within subjective wellbeing culture, aimed as a seductive bait to fuel the purchase, to fuel consumption; holistic activities are served up as a promising means to the end of recharging, reenergizing, "empowering" managers for commercial wealth-creation, shareholder, ends; publishers try to ensure that mind-body-spirituality books are composed and presented to maximize sales. (*Spiritualities of Life* 199)

Indeed, in his assessment of critiques on how alternative spiritualities are enmeshed in the cycle of marketing and purchasing, Heelas observes that practitioners "generally avoid the language of consumption like the plague" (*Spiritualities of Life* 83). In this frame, the spiritualized selves people cultivate appear to be empty bodies longing for authentic experience and sensory stimulation. For Jeremy Carrette and Richard King, then, the "privatized psychological formation" that characterizes contemporary spiritual practices is ultimately

> *not a cure for our sense of social isolation and disconnectedness but is, in fact, part of the problem.* Private spirituality, as opposed to an understanding of spirituality as linked to issues of social justice, is dangerous precisely because it conceals the underlying ideological effects of individualism. Psychologists rightly observe the problems of "meaningless" values in consumer culture, but they unwittingly offer yet another consumer product as an answer to that void. (58)

The critique of sacralized selves in consumer culture, however, sets up a tautology in which spirituality as an internal sense *cannot* be credible. It makes consumer culture the credible site for analysis, where desire is produced and displaces meaning.

The logic of the critique, so unlike Alexander's, first defines the sacred by its categorical distinction from the mundane, evaluates internally sensed spirituality *in the terms of the mundane,* and denies the possibility for a sense of spirit to enter the social sphere. Critical assessments of spirituality in consumer culture turn on the very spirit-matter binary that is so entrenched in the Western intellectual tradition, as well as a suspicion of what cannot be explicitly shown in the domain of the social. The logic undergirding the phrases "performing spirituality" or "spirituality as performance" here assumes both the failure of the Christian monotheism's transcendent spirituality and the modernist denial of spirituality.

The critique of sacralized Western selves immersed in the waters of consumer capitalism provides an important and necessary caution to any investigation of contemporary spirituality. Spiritual kitsch, quick fixes, and easy wisdom are for sale everywhere, as my early forays confirmed (see preface). The energetic properties and spiritual epistemologies Alexander found in the archive of nineteenth-century Trinidad have little traction in this discourse. The logic at work makes it impossible to take the sense of spirit on its own terms, or see the ways the cultivation of that sense may be envisioning social justice and community; instead, spiritual practices are emptied of the experiential content while the goods available for enhancing spirituality are held up as proof of that emptiness.

The assumption that sensory affect fills in for people's sense of spirit reinforces the point made in chapter 1: analytical perspectives forged in an intellectual tradition that brackets spirituality occlude people's sense of spirit. Sensation, in this paradigm, is assumed to be a process of moving external stimuli inward by consuming products already associated with spirituality and (frequently) specific cultural and religious valences (such as incense, drums, candles, veils, prayer beads, meditation mats, special clothing, statues, and icons). These are assumed to produce anticipated sensations that people then interpret as spiritual (e.g., inner calm, communication with spirits, a sense of love or peace, altered consciousness, the sense of "oneness," etc.) (Possamai, "Alternative Spiritualities" 31).

From within a practice, however, spirituality may be a more profound experience than the sensory stimulation for sale in the marketplace suggests. There may be more going on than the critique of contemporary well-being spirituality allows. For example, when describing mystical experiences grounded in physical sensation, Klabunde says that external stimulation of the senses does indeed produce illusory sensations and he offers a caution:

> If I weren't careful, it would have been easy for me to consider these sensations to be the goal of the experience. We should always remember that any sensations we experience associated with our participation in the spiritual realms are not the goal of our experience; they are the byproducts of being a human being with a nervous system. The human experience embodies sensations, and while they may be valuable in our existence in the physical world, they are merely sensations and having them should not be taken as reaching a deep spiritual place. That being said, I did recognize them as markers of being on the right track. Pleasant sensations such as euphoria are often felt when we connect to our spirit and allow it to guide us as we navigate multiple realities and dimensions. (56–57)

Klabunde's words readily acknowledge sensory stimulation and emotional affect as illusory even though their effects may be pleasurable and, for that matter, neurologically verifiable. Klabunde's assertion that sensory affect is illusory is not a distrust of the senses or internal sensation, but an acknowledgment of their limits. Lines of inquiry that address the social, material aspects of spirituality avoid people's claims of "a beautiful connection with the divine" and "the sacred wisdom" of an inner being (Klabunde 57). That the multiple realities and spiritual realms are as real for Klabunde as the drums he plays and the van he drives to transport his instruments remains a seemingly unbridgeable conceptual chasm.

Spirituality as a "source of values and meaning beyond oneself, a way of understanding, inner awareness, and personal integration" looks very much like a Western yearning "for a reconstructed interior life, deliberate and formative efforts aimed at forging an integrated self and transcending the limits of the given" among people who already know themselves to be commodified and their identities constructed by external forces (Roof 35). Putting spirituality in the exchange dynamics of objects or services in order to prove its vacuity ultimately sustains the terms of a critical discourse suspicious of both spirituality and capitalism, rather than engaging people's sense of spirit (see chapter 1).

The consumer marketplace is what allows people like McPherson and Klabunde to move their sense of spirit beyond private experience into communities—and to infuse the mundane with spirit. While we might recognize and frame this movement as the "showing doing" of performance, there may be a very different negotiation going on between people and the materiality of bodies, texts, and objects. A critical lens that brings production and consumption to the foreground immediately reduces spirituality to the mundane, rather than examining how people's sense of the numinous informs the mundane. Reducing spirituality to the matter of everyday life manages experiential spirituality in familiar terms, but in doing so occludes more complex interpretations of material culture. The critical challenge is to consider that spiritual practitioners might engage the materiality of culture, money, and social identities differently than a narrow definition of spirituality as transcendence allows.

A spiritual orientation to culture and the body works against the devaluation of internal, corporeal-mental sensations and the critical methods that manage spirituality in terms of the visible and the material. An approach that takes people's sense of ineffable presence as the foundation for such consumer products reverses the conventional critique of spirituality as consumerism, instead emphasizing how people press the consumer market into service of their sense of something beyond its materiality. Consumption does not invalidate the sense of spirit, but may be a conduit for that sense.

THE POWER OF NOT SHOWING

The performance paradigm problematizes the hybridity of cultural idioms, engagement with consumer culture, and investment in internal sensibilities in Western vernacular spirituality. Practices like Dancemeditation and

Collective Awakening, however, problematize the managerial function of performativity as a critical apparatus. The anthropological encounters with séances and healings discussed above give firsthand accounts of events that produce a kind of force that is not explained by the play of representation. In either context, spiritual practices push back against conventional models for analyzing culture and behavior, forcing the lens to refocus and demanding that the critical frame recognize the possibility of what Alexander calls "Sacred energies" at work in the world.

Yet spiritual practices operate in a culture that demands performance—a "show-off" culture—and readily deploy the conventions of performance. But the spirituality itself is not for show, even when a concert format or carefully produced DVD or CD frames the music or dance as a performance. Following Somé, what is important about Dancemeditation or Collective Awakening in the act of performance is the practitioners' sense of the a priori presence of the numinous—the movement of what Alexander calls "Sacred energies"—through the matter of bodies, language, and culture (292). As they meet the performative expectations of the broader culture, the cultural work these practices do proposes a role for an inner, spiritual life.

The sense of spirit Klabunde and McPherson describe is predicated not on the sense of emptying out, which Somé identifies as a problem with Western thinking, but on a copious sense of presence. Somé holds that the power of ritual knowledge depends on a presence that is *not* shown. This proposition goes against the binding of knowing to showing and of showing to presence. "Performances" organized by a sense of spirit might well be starting with an assertion of power that *cannot* be shown. What does the possibility of the unshown suggest for performativity?

The anxiety around this question is the anxiety around spirituality in general: as a kind of authentic experience, a dimension of reality, knowledge that cannot be verified, or a perspective that sees an ineffable dimension to the social world. The conventions of the performance paradigm put people's sense of spirit into a system of knowledge oriented toward the public spheres of politics, economics, and social structures. The possibility of a reality that cannot be shown destabilizes the paradigm precisely because for practitioners what spirituality posits as real does not require bodies and objects or the symbolic systems of consumer culture.

The issue is not how spiritual practices perform in the cycle of production and consumption defining modern cultures, but how a spiritual sensibility engages the cycle. They shift focus from the production of objects and practices that symbolize, represent, or perform spirituality for profit to the presence of spirit in the mechanisms of production. Meredith McGuire locates spirituality solidly in the material and the everyday. She makes the case that participation in consumer culture is an inevitable component of everyday life. At the level of the individual practitioner, what might look like "selling out" to a Western marketplace saturated with global kitsch and an ethos of inauthenticity might also be interpreted as a process by which people are organizing the materiality of everyday life around a sense of the numinous. By expanding and extending spiritual practices into the public spheres of social interaction, through media and the marketplace, spiritual practitioners may be introducing different ways of engaging with, and thinking about, what we would otherwise take as performance.

MIGRATIONS OF SPIRIT FROM THE SELF TO THE SOCIAL

Though spirituality is sometimes viewed as anti-institutional or is compared to the institutional status of religion, contemporary spiritual practices readily incorporate, trademark, apply for nonprofit status, buy retreat properties, and rent spaces from which to operate.[16] The CDs, DVDs, and books the practitioners circulate are the agents of their cultural influence. The effects of individual gnosis and personal transformation also work their way into the broader culture in ubiquitous linguistic formulations, such as "mind-body-spirit," "inner peace," "transformation," and "connection."

Jennifer Porter notes that in contemporary spiritualities, "to be referential is not to be inauthentic, it is simply to be contextualized in the cultural milieu of the times" (275). That these practices do not set themselves apart from a global market economy does not automatically devalue the experiences people claim; rather "it is entirely within patterns of cultural consumption that indicators of personal, social, political, and spiritual meaning are to be found" (Porter 276). They may be invitations to unconventional modes of thinking, being, and doing.

Heelas goes as far as to find an active cultural politics in the emphasis on internal sensation and well-being in contemporary spirituality. He notes the standard argument against the social value of such practices, which claims "that contemporary forms of holistic, wellbeing-focused spiritualities of life are ineffectual—for what they do for the person; and, more glaringly, for what they contribute to relational, social or cultural life" (*Spiritualities of Life*

196). Heelas argues for interpreting people's cultivation of spiritual selves in a broad, more optimistic, category of "holistic spiritualities of life." In what he calls "expressive" spirituality, the sense of spirit moves outward from individuals in ways that have positive effects in and on relational, social, and cultural life.

Heelas's view of contemporary spirituality resonates with Alexander's migratory "Sacred energies." In Heelas's perspective, spirituality is not localized to individuals' experiences but moves energetically "from the self to the relational; to the public realm; into use" (*Spiritualities of Life* 201).[17] Heelas argues that the sense of spirit flows "into the spiritual person's self-expression with others and their interactivity (the inter-dynamic). It thereby enters into 'public' contexts, like teaching in schools. Spirituality flows to 'encompass,' to 'incorporate' what it touches" (201). Holistic spirituality "flows" through the materiality of contemporary culture, expanding the material presence of performance—the CDs, DVDs, books, artifacts, and concerts practitioners might sell, and in the work practitioners like McPherson and Klabunde do in schools, community centers, retreat centers, and through public framed performances. Spirituality can be treated as a particular kind of active engagement with the social, material world.

David Tacey sees the potential for vernacular spiritual practices to speak back to the consumer culture in which they participate and challenge modes of thinking that bracket or dismiss spirituality. Tacey cites the failure of cultural materialism, which promised a "better and more humane world," but made us "victim to new kinds of enslavement and oppression, and old mythology has become reality as giants (in the form of monstrous corporations) stalk the earth" (19). Tacey positions spirituality as a human sense or quality not fully present in dominant paradigms that look for liberation in social or political change. Against the conventional suspicion of religion as inherently conservative and anti-intellectual, Tacey says yes, we may need to look beyond the human to discover a more humane world:

> Paradoxically, it may be the extra-human and the spiritual that delivers the liberation and justice that we seek. We might need to draw from the transcendental and its lofty ideals so that we can become more fully human. Certainly, it has become increasingly difficult for people to have a faith in politics, science or humanism. . . . We can no more invest our hopes and dreams in utopian political programs.
>
> The state or political cause has little to offer the desire for liberation

> and freedom, for unconditional love and support. The secular world is running on empty, and it has run out of answers. Every one of our institutions has "experts" and futurists who claim to see the way through this depressed phase to a brighter future, but few of us are taken in by their claims. In this depleted state, with less to believe in, we are ready to reconsider what we had once thrown out: religion and spirituality. (19)

Heelas also argues that contemporary spiritualities run "'counter' to a number of key features of capitalistic modernity" rather than being completely consumed by the desire to consume (*Spiritualities of Life* 201). Heelas's approach counters the "reduction to consumption" habit of analysis and proceeds "on the grounds that what experiences of mind-body spirituality and associated values *can* bring to life-in-experience goes beyond the simply (or largely) consumptive" (202).

Spiritual practices are not benign participants in modernity's lost wager, the forfeit of "our idea of the sacred on beliefs in individual rights, rooted in reason" to the opposing fundamentalisms of enlightened reason and religiosity (Seligman, *Modernity's Wager* 12). Contemporary vernacular spiritualities may be speaking from an investment in adaptive modes of thinking, feeling, and acting that engage resources available in a wide range of spiritual and religious traditions. Properties of consciousness, as Michael Winkelman reminds us, "are not just the properties provided by brain structures; they are derived from interrelations of systemic properties of the brain with symbolic information and meanings provided by learning and culture" (24).[18] Performance may be the *process* through which people negotiate the materiality of culture and a sense of ineffable presence.

Countering the critique of self-absorbed individualism often levied at alternative spiritualities, Jeffrey Kripal, in *The Serpent's Gift*, suggests that although contemporary spiritualities draw "profoundly on the symbols, myths, rituals, and revelations" available in world religious traditions, their own gnostic insights are simultaneously at odds with religious and cultural orthodoxies (13). Those insights presume

> a certain individualism, an inviolable intellectual and moral integrity, and a privileging of individual conviction, dream, conscience, and vision over any and all authorized truths or revelations, even as it recognizes, through reason, that its own individual convictions have been nurtured and formed by community and tradition. (13)

The neurological pathways activated in the sense of self overlap with those of religious experience (see chapter 3). That overlap suggests that the emphasis in contemporary Western spiritualities on the sensations of the self cannot be attributed only to Western individualism or "feel-good" solipsism, but is affected by cultural values.

If there is indeed a modern malaise for which cultivating a sense of the ineffable offers a corrective, Marilynn Robinson suggests that that malaise might result from "the exclusion of the *felt life of the mind*" from the ways we construct and validate knowledge. Not investing knowledge paradigms like performativity with a felt life of the mind in effect accepts "spiritlessness" as a cultural norm. Against critical tendencies grounded in a sense of loss and lack, she asserts that subjectivity "is the ancient haunt of piety and reverence and long, long thoughts . . . literatures that would dispel such things refuse to acknowledge subjectivity, perhaps because inability has evolved into principle and method" (Robinson 35).

Vernacular spiritual practices may cultivate the sense of an essential or authentic self, which is clearly not the identity-self of critical discourses. This sense of a spiritual self challenges the perspective emptying out the self to privilege multiple, socially constructed identities. In practice, a spiritual self may be fluid, malleable, and transformable, but it is concerned with the sense of the numinous rather than the performance of identity. The speaking subject demanded by performativity becomes receptive subjectivity in which listening and interiority are more powerful than visible or audible expressions. The promise is not a transformative epiphany, but a life praxis that construes the world as spiritually alive.

Selves informed by a sense of spirit may be more complex than critiques of identity politics suggest (Seligman, *Modernity's Wager* 70). The self is not a symbolic code to be deciphered but a complex, shifting site of sensations and consciousness. This self is not experienced as a stable subject, nor is its subjectivity limited to changes in affect. McPherson and Klabunde describe experiencing a fundamental dissonance between their cultural, social, and intellectual environments and some internal impulse that moves them into unfamiliar cultural territory. The appeal to non-Western, indigenous, or ancient traditions allows them to negotiate that dissonance between an internal sense of a spiritual self and the expectations of a culture that marginalizes religion and spirituality and in which those very terms are contested. They crafted ways of thinking, making a living, being in their bodies, and communicating that aligned their internal lives with their life praxis.

SPIRIT MIGRATIONS INTO MODERNITY

Practices such as Dancemeditation and Collective Awakening press performance into service of spirituality. In the case of Klabunde, taking African spirituality on its own terms rather than as an anthropological study of ritual-as-performance yielded a critique of his home culture even as he works within it. Klabunde's critique of Western individualism, far from championing the primacy of personal experience or the pursuit of generalized well-being, echoes Seligman's wager. Klabunde writes:

> Americans define themselves by and place value on individual freedoms rather than prioritize the role of the individual within a communal context. Individual rights take precedence over the needs of the community. This is significant because a culture that prioritizes interconnections between community members also develops a natural connection with the earth and the spiritual realms. . . . a spiritual ideology that places emphasis on interconnection also develops a social structure that provides a foundation and support system for such interconnection. Modern-day humans relinquish their connection to the spiritual for the continuance of the status-inspired Euro-American tradition. (105–6)

McPherson is keenly aware that her intensive study of Sufism at summer retreat camps in New Mexico through the 1980s was a luxury of the economic times and that "a black sheep scion of Reynolds tobacco money" had donated the land for the camp she attended (42–43). She is also aware of it being situated in the Arabic and Persian politics and culture in the 1980s, as well as the perceived threat posed by both the alterity of Islam and nonreligious spiritualities to a predominantly Christian country:

> America in the 1980s was rife with anxieties about cults. Concern skittered across my parents' faces. In particular, my father, who'd spent some years in Tehran during the Shah's ascendency before the Ayatollah Khomeini's right wing swing, took issue with my pro-Islamic stance. He observed the suppression of women under Khomeini's Islamist rule, while I observed a naïve, apparent empowerment of women under a Moslem teacher. We were both right and both wrong, of course, and we were both Westerners seeing what we hoped or feared in a culture we would never fathom. (McPherson 54)

Critical awareness surrounds, but does not define, the spirituality at work in the practice she adopts.

McPherson relates her first encounter with *cultural* difference as *spiritual* difference and how that encounter changed her understanding of performance. During her tenure at the Victoria College of Arts in Melbourne, an Indian dancer with whom she had been taking Bharata Natyam classes announced that, having been accepted by a guru to learn the dance of the Goddess Durga, he would be returning to India. She writes of the shift in her understanding of dance as performance:

> He was not going to India to learn a role in any theatrical sense but for spiritual mentorship, and this sacred rite of passage would be danced. Bound by my Western-ness, and despite frustration with my dance education's limitations, I'd assumed that the spiritual guru-disciple relationship was the prerogative of other cultures. In the West, except for the Shakers, dance was secular. It was Art, a voice for the human condition and capable of expressing abstraction that indicated transcendence, but it was not a form of workshop or mystical union. The latter was the purview of monks and nuns whose robes erased their aging bodies; in my mind, dance had always been the province of young bodies.
>
> . . . His dance, because it was his spiritual path, was a life-long pursuit. He would not retire and hang up his toe shoes. He would not sit back, read novels, and never again stir his limbs. At midlife, he was poised to leap from the shell of preparatory youth into effulgent maturity. His body would evolve, his gestures ripen, syrup simmering in his veins until wisdom sparked from every glance and footstamp. My cells tingled with this harbinger of unfamiliar realness. (McPherson 28)

While performing bodies and the cultural idioms they engage can be read and decoded as signs in a signifying system, what is at stake for a spiritually oriented practice is the phenomenon that moves through the materiality of bodies: the sense of embodied presence in whatever a numinous dimension of life might be.

Seligman observes that "we are all so thoroughly modern, hence autonomous, that we have become blind to alternative phenomenologies, which are, however, increasingly attractive to more and more people in the West as they experience the expressive muteness of the autonomous self" (*Modernity's Wager* 70). If they can be accepted as presenting alternative phenomenologies with their own epistemological dynamics, perspectives such as those articulated by McPherson and Klabunde revitalize the materiality of performance and invite reexamination of the performance paradigm.

MOVING INTO THE TERMS OF THE NUMINOUS

Language, in the epistemological systems of the Western tradition, functions as the conduit for knowledge; however, the internal processes of language are intertwined with those that produce the sensations of spirituality. In what Jorge N. Ferrer identifies as "the participatory predicament," spiritual knowing is distinct from abstract cognition or sensory data processing. It can also provide a foundation for cultural engagement that can, in turn, ground knowledge claims such as those articulated in *Skin of Glass* and *Music as Medicine*, which involve more "subtle forms of consciousness." Participatory knowing engages sensibilities people identify as spiritual, "from somatic transfiguration to the awakening of the heart, from erotic communion to visionary cocreation, and from contemplative knowing to moral insight" (Ferrer 137). I have proposed that when that knowledge informs what we take to be performative, we are obligated to invest intellectual energy in understanding how it works, even if that means rethinking the assumption that performance is the primary, constitutive action that constructs the social world.

These practices propose a bidirectional infusion of spirit into the physical body and the materiality of the phenomenal, observable world. This is not the Eucharistic transformation of matter into spirit in the Western Christian tradition and ritualized in the incarnational aesthetic that persisted from the medieval churches through the European Enlightenment (see chapter 1). This bidirectional infusion of spirit into matter works as a quotidian synthesis of spirit and matter lived out in practice, where myths are retold, rituals invented, drums beaten, veils twirled, and money exchanged. But the sense of spirituality does not depend on the performativity of objects, language, or bodies to confirm its presence.[19] The numinous, sacred, or ineffable dimension is always present as long as it can be sensed, and it can be sensed whether or not performance makes it visible. Spirituality, as *Skin of Glass* and *Music as Medicine* formulate it, does not conform to the rules of operation that govern performativity. For spiritual practitioners, in a reversal of what is now a cliché of postmodernism, it is always already there.[20]

Vernacular practices such as these accept spirituality crossing the domains of consumer capitalism and the objectivity of scientific proof, rather than problematizing contradictions between the physical and metaphysical, natural and supernatural, tangible and ephemeral, or sacred and profane. The inner life that these practices and their products cultivate invests in *being in* sensations of ineffability and allowing those sensations to take on forms of cultural expression. This process, I suggest, is not performance in the conventional use of the term. If those sensations infuse what we conventionally interpret as performance, we might ask ourselves how to expand our understanding of the matter they present to us.

The longing for and experience of an authentic inner life these practices present are sincere. The absence of creedal or doctrinal statements of belief removes the problem of doubt or loss of faith. It is committed to unquestioned presence. Its language is not that of difference but of synthesis and compatibility. Its sensibility is toward the numinous, and its vision looks inward to a holistic self, while its practice extracts the sacred from the materiality of culture.

What we observe as performance in the ways these practices cultivate consciousness to be receptive to unorthodox sensibilities is a register of what practitioners know to be spiritual in nature and origin. Analytical and interpretive paradigms like performativity will always be concerned with the origin of that knowledge in an inaccessible self, the unverifiability of the ineffable, and the presumed immunity of "my experience" to rational critique, debate, resistance, or argument.[21] Nevertheless, the expressive forms these practices produce suggest lines of serious inquiry into contemporary vernacular spiritualities, including rethinking the limits of performativity as a paradigm and performance as a cultural practice grounded in representation, referentiality, and the dualism of observer-observed.

If these kinds of internal experiences cannot be observed as either culturally produced performances of spirituality or representations of physiological activity, what is available for study are "perceptions of sacredness and their implications for people's lives" with openness to the possibility that people who experience and view life through a spiritual lens might bring a different paradigm to performance (Pargament 14). A spiritually oriented performance appears at the intersection of spiritual sensibilities, the interior processes of the human body, and the body's engagement with the cultural idioms shaping sensations into the expressive forms and language that communicate.

Cultivating the capacity to sense the self as a holistic body-mind-spirit in vernacular spiritual practices reflects, or perhaps is prompting, a shift in methods for interpreting culture. As methods for integrating biological bodies, mental processes, and social systems gain strength in academic inquiries, spirituality may emerge as a site for serious, rigorous inquiry, not only as performative social practice but in practitioners' terms. A different schema emerges to account for the process of performance.

1. Spiritual practices recruit neurological processes and pathways that support specific internal sensations.
2. People recognize those sensations as spiritual through cultural idioms (such as veils and indigenous instruments) and practices that support those internal mental-physiological conditions and allow people to develop and deepen them (such as drumming or dancing).
3. Performance makes the exchange between interior processes, internal sensations, and cultural idioms possible.
4. Performance makes the exchange accessible to others, whether or not they share the same understanding of the internal sense of spirit.

The expressive forms through which practitioners engage the sense of the numinous may be an adaptive mechanism that reconciles an internal sense of spirit and self with the interiority of the body and the human impulse for expression and action in the material world.

SPIRITUAL SELVES IN COMMUNITY

Far from advocating a self-interested investment in sensory stimulation that stops at the boundary of one's skin, as spiritless critiques of Western vernacular spirituality would suggest, Klabunde specifically cites a lack of attention to community in Western cultures, which relational spirituality addresses. "Service," he writes, "is the fabric of community; the role of the individual is always to be in service to the community" (Klabunde 194). He observes that "Western culture does not support community" but supports individuals who align themselves with causes or agendas or who match culturally sanctioned "specific ideas of normalcy" (Klabunde 194–95). He writes:

> The reality of community in the West is one of a narrow focus on individualism and consumption, and this breeds negative and unproductive

> emotions that hinder our spiritual growth. Stress and emotional and mental illnesses are often a direct result of the loss of community. . . . This is our challenge, to develop and walk a deep spiritual path while being bombarded with messages that tell us we ought to be looking outside ourselves for meaning, purpose, happiness, contentment and joy. (Klabunde 197)

Klabunde's insights yield a cogent critique of Western individualism and consumption from an orientation in spiritual practice.

Spiritual practices are not free of clashes and tensions with social conventions and imposed identities. As a white woman in the contemporary West, McPherson notes the contradiction in her own adaptation of Sufi whirling. Her experiential gnosticism combined with the influences of Western feminism put her at odds with the very mystical tradition that provided the symbols, myths, rituals, and revelations upon which she bases her spiritual practice:

> As a teacher, I am updating the historically male Sufi tradition, remaking it in the shape of a woman. Journey into the body with curiosity and acceptance, I say. Understand that the body is the Original Gift. Beyond the dichotomy of good and bad, its urges and motions just are. Experience. Wonder. A body is a teacher. This attitude will bring its genius out of hiding. Part of my maturing as a Sufi teacher has been to own this approach knowing that, though not traditional, it lifts the dark veils. (McPherson 171)

Here, the intersection of a sense of the numinous, the cultural specificity of Sufism, and the presumptive authority to change tradition complicate spirituality as a cultural negotiation.

Performativity is embedded in a sociology of knowledge that occludes spirituality as a foundation for formulating knowledge. The personal, interior experience these contemporary practices cultivate requires valuing the sensations of the body "as genuine (re)sources for knowledge and experiences" (Karjalainen 199). Privileging a nonphysical aspect of one's body and recognizing a noncomputational aspect of the mind rearranges the hierarchy of sensibilities privileged in Western culture. Spiritual practices like Collective Awakening and Dancemeditation destabilize this hierarchy. As their books indicate, these practitioners in particular critique the way knowledge is organized in the culture in which they function—their spiritual practices are critical practices. Adapting organizational schemas for moving, sensing, and thinking from other cultural traditions, like African shamanism and Sufism, allows them to introduce spirituality into their narratives and practices when conventional organizations of knowledge (such as that of performance studies) cannot.

For Klabunde, spirits move through the sounds of drums and indigenous instruments, and the people playing them. For McPherson, ineffable forces motivate physical movement and spiritual insight. The focus on the body's interior and the link practitioners make between self and spirit are crucial elements in the epistemologies that inform their events and language. They may use the cultural codes and discourses upon which the performativity paradigm depends for analysis, just as they might produce aesthetic affects or emotional responses. I have suggested that what they appear to perform cannot be bound to material culture or the body precisely because they understand it to be spiritual in origin and nature.

The argument here does not free contemporary vernacular spiritual practices from critique, or assume an authentic or perennial spirituality at work in them. However, vernacular voices speak back to the performance paradigm in ways worth noting. A dialogue with vernacular culture, as scholars of lived religion have shown, yields a compelling interrogation of how spirituality constitutes a kind of knowledge people express in social practice and how people adapt their minds, bodies, and cultural resources as they cultivate a sense of spirit. Such a dialogue presumes, at minimum, a willingness to accept that there may be more to matter than meets the eye, if not to take people's accounts of spirituality as worthy of investigation.

Whether performance, as a paradigm for analyzing social interaction, can or should adapt to a reliance on sensation (rather than psychoanalysis) as a model for an inner life, and whether the ineffability of internal experience has a place in an analysis of material forces constituting selves and communities, remains an open question. However, if performativity, as a paradigm, only addresses how performance constructs spirituality—"spirituality as performance"—then the intricate ways spirituality redefines the performative will remain unavailable. Engaging the epistemologies these particular practitioners present goes against (in ways I think are productive) the foundational assumptions holding up the performance paradigm. In those epistemologies, the mental processes participants in these practices cultivate are not representational or referential. The bodies they inhabit engage cultural codes but are not bound to cultural or social identities. The subtle sensations they cultivate require a kind of consciousness that is distributed throughout the body and (the sticking point) beyond the body.

Spiritual practices may posit spirituality as not only a kind of inner knowing but as the foundation for a better society, which is the same aim as political, activist performance. The self that spiritual practices cultivate may not be the decentered self of postmodernism, fragmented by overlapping identities, but a process, a doing of being. This self may also be communal, relational, and actively engaged in the material world. Taking seriously the spiritually oriented engagement with culture that these practices propose undercuts a critical framework that dismisses the veracity and efficacy of these practices' cultivated sensibilities. For practices such as these, productive inquiries might question what it means when the self is experienced in relationship to a dimension of spirit as well as the domain of the social. That contemporary life might be infused with something inherently spiritual could be the most compelling and destabilizing idea these practices offer to interpretive critiques grounded in methodologies of materialism.

WHEN SPIRIT CONSTRUCTS PERFORMANCE

The practices described in chapter 2 draw cultural idioms—in these examples, African drumming and Sufi dance—into the body, where internal sensations of the numinous, the ineffable, the sacred, or the divine can be cultivated and extended back into the culture through expressive forms (Heelas, *Spiritualities of Life* 202). Those forms, I have argued, require an epistemology that allows for ineffability, multiple modes of sensing, ambiguity, and creative, conscious interpretation of subjective experience within an analytical and critical framework. That epistemology must also take spirituality as constitutive of legitimate modes of knowledge, in non-Western or indigenous cultures and in the contemporary West.

The orientation to actions, bodies, words, and objects as infused with spirit and the sense that physical and spiritual presences are aspects of each other undoes the expectations of performativity. In practice, people like McPherson and Klabunde intervene in a system of knowledge that produces presence through performance. For them, there is no *thing* to be performed, only something to be sensed with the combined capacities of mind and body. For practitioners, the material products of spiritual practices have aspects that are not accessible through the lens of performativity unless inner sensations of spirituality have credibility. McPherson writes self-reflexively of this nonperformative presence in the context of the "selling" spirituality:

> I've been a Sufi teacher for almost twenty years. I undo, uncover, remove, kindle, erase and rouse, a contrast to my early teaching years when I ladled steps, repertoire and concepts into the eager bodies of young dancers-to-be. Then, leaning against a steady rock of information, which endowed me with institutional weightiness, I watched them scrutinize themselves in the mirror, tweaking their sinews as I had done years before. Now, I close my eyes, always looking at emptiness, and students follow me as I move and breathe, drawing us into the simplicity of moving and breathing. I settle into a flow of focus. My student's wild nonrealities eddy around me. I respect them by trying not to believe what they imagine me to be, a difficult task since I was once mostly a reflection of others. Every so often a recurring anxiety invades my steady now-ness. Perhaps my students, wanting something for their money, aren't so sure why they pay me for providing an expensive Nothing. I haven't much to say in defense of this exchange except that Nothing is hard to come by. (203–4)

Amid the performative din of modern culture, the capacity to experience nothing, to show no thing, is the presence of spirit.

From this perspective, spiritually oriented performance may not be the sign of a lost or desired experience but evidence of people's sense of what is real. Taking spiritual practices as performative requires shifting from models that read symbol systems (language, aesthetic conventions, cultural codes) as unstable and adaptations of cultural idioms (indigenous instruments, veils, burning sage, prayers to the earth, etc.) as appropriations. Such a perspective requires understanding spirituality as the quality with which people engage culture (their own and others) and their bodies (their own in solitude and with others in community). Performance can be viewed as the material form of that engagement. From this perspective, performance is an organic, circular process rather than bodies, texts, and objects "doing." Performance becomes the membrane across which spirituality and material culture mix seemingly incompatible properties: visibility and invisibility, solidity and ineffability, mystery and intelligibility.

CHAPTER 5

Reorienting Performance

DISRUPTION BY ENCHANTMENT

Performance, as a critical and interpretive paradigm, structures a way of seeing, thinking, and constituting knowledge. The intersection of people's internal sense of spirit with the performance paradigm has been the overarching concern of this book. At stake has been the status of ineffability, the numinous, spirits or a spiritual dimension as a structuring principle for what we observe in the materiality of performance. Minds and bodies acclimated to sensing spiritual presence might operate differently with regard to a sense of self, performance, and interpreting sociocultural demands than current theoretical frameworks allow. Such a sense might ask for reconsidering the conceptual architecture of performance, for example the gap between representation and referent, or the translation between embodied performance and text. What do we do when people's spirituality refuses to allow the critical terms of performance to structure their experience (see chapter 2)? What norms does the performance paradigm reinforce that may not be normative in spiritual practices (chapters 3 and 4)?

Chapter 3 looked into the physical body. Western modernity has had a fascination with the body as a theoretical category and object of inquiry. Even as language became the technology for constructing bodies in performance and literary studies, cognitive neuroscience worked toward a view of the mind and language as embodied.[1] Mark Johnson observed, "In order to have human meaning, you need a human brain, operating in a living human body, continually interacting with a human environment that is at once physical, social, and cultural" (155). The exploration of a subjective "inner life," once the intellectual territory of the humanities, is now more likely to happen in neuroscience and cognitive science. In a cultural context that privileges computational thinking, people's persistent sense of the numinous has become a curious line of research. Chapter 3's discussion suggested that the neurological activity allows for significant overlap between the capacities that support symbolic representation and logical thinking, but also those mental sensations associated with spiritual experiences.

I have not argued that people's sense of spirit is, or is not, reducible to physiology or to culture, but rather tried to make the issue of reduction irrelevant. If bodies are natural and social, experienced and constructed, then we can see performance as the membrane between people's internal sensibilities and material culture. What are the possibilities if we do not think of human capacities as biological or sociocultural first, but begin with people's capacity for sensing spirit first? How would that change how we see, hear, and interpret performance?

Performance, since Brecht, delights in showing the workings of representation, of the illusion, without leaving the frame of theatrical. Neuroscience, too, has this quality. We can see the processes of the mind, the mechanics that produced the illusion of weird, uncanny, anomalous experiences. Neuroscience, like performance, relies on representation. We come to know the mind by the technologies that make the working brain visible in readouts, graphs, and images of light. These technologies for visibility are immersed in social relations no less than the technologies through which Collective Awakening and Dancemeditation do their own cultural work.

Neuroscience, like performance, relies on representation and people's engagement with symbol systems for knowledge, not on access to a reality beyond those systems. In either framework, religion and spirituality can be understood, appropriately, as hermeneutic processes:

> Whatever else religion is about and regardless of theoretical ideas guiding research on it, religion is fundamentally about meaning. Humans apparently are built with a tendency to represent one thing with another; to assess information relative to a larger, more global idea; to use that idea to shape the interpretation of incoming information to guide behavior and establish a sense of consistency in their mental representation of life and their position in it. (Paloutzian, Swenson, and McNamara 154)

As frameworks for what we can know, neuroscience and the performance paradigm both assure us that we are secure in matter, and that illusion (however productive, meaningful, and useful) is a choice. Neither framework need directly confront a reality of spirit and the sense of spirituality beyond the materiality of the body and social sphere. The conclusions people draw from the embodied sense of that reality thus present significant challenges.

Chapter 4 looked to the materiality of culture. Deep within the structuring assumptions of the critical methods we use to observe culture lurks a strong antipathy to considering spirituality as part of the modern West or of an intellectual project. Attending to spirituality in contemporary vernacular practices "challenges a view of modernity as disenchanted and thus as opposed to past of distant cultures that are 'still' enchanted" (Meyer 87). In the lingering biases against taking spirituality seriously in the global North-West, spirituality has been explored in other cultures, often as a defining criterion of that Otherness. Performativity, as a paradigm, keeps spirituality at a safe distance by interpreting symbols, myths, and rituals as signifiers for spirituality. Though spirituality is everywhere in Western vernacular culture, from a critical stance, spiritual practices remain sites of distrust, illusion, and skepticism.

This is the framework in which Jane Turner struggles with performance ethnography in Bali. She recounts struggling with how not to turn the gaze of a Western tourist on Balinese cultural practices (even as those practices might be constructed as such for her gaze). Turner sees the performance of religion with a keen, well-trained fear of "the dangers of imposing meaning on my experiences and not interpreting events through a lens of Western culture" (61–62). She wants to be simultaneously inside and outside the spirituality she encounters, yet spirituality has no epistemological status in her critical paradigm. This is Turner's dilemma:

> While spirituality in the West might be argued to be a separate part of our epistemology, in Bali it is embedded in both everyday and ritual practices. Performance in particular is imbued by a strong sense of spiritual effect and, in some instances, spiritual possession. (62)

Performativity itself might be the imposition. The paradigm in which she is working constructs the gap a Western performance ethnographer cannot quite cross. Spirituality, from this stance, cannot be managed as a discursive proposition; thus it cannot be rendered as knowledge. It sits outside the paradigm, even as it beckons the ethnographer's acknowledgment.

In a profound way, however, spirituality is already embedded in the epistemology of performance. To a significant degree, Christianity has shaped ideas about religion, spirituality, and performance. The paradigm of performativity has a distinctive affinity with Christianity's reliance on representation, *imitatio*, and reenactment of historical events for knowledge of a transcendent Spirit. Indeed, it could be argued that performativity has its distant intellectual origins in the efforts of medieval Christians to reconcile their readings of Aristotle with their God.

Jill Stevenson analyzes "the strategies that evangelical performative media employ to reconfigure aesthetic information in ways that will support certain evangelical Christian epistemologies" (3), acknowledging that "while certain evangelical denominations or groups of believers may embrace a performative genre, others may reject or simply ignore it" (4). Stevenson's rich and detailed readings of passion plays, biblical theme parks, Holy Land recreations, and creationist museums as "evangelical dramaturgy" start with the performance paradigm—the material, the visible. Performance here is both a standard model and, I would argue, inherent in this particular religious epistemology.

Christianity hinges on belief in Christ, which is known by showing the fact of Christ's resurrection as body and spirit by representational means. Thus, the familiar parameters of Western drama (representation, realism, enactment, spectatorship, presence, affect, narrative, dramaturgy, visual aesthetics, and genre) appropriately frame Stevenson's analysis of how performance constructs belief and a sense of God's presence (4). Belief is intertwined with interpreting signs, and performance is both a framework identifying spirituality and a hermeneutic practice. Christian spirituality, which is part of the intellectual tradition that gave rise to performativity, is in many ways aligned with the paradigm in ways other formulations of spirituality may not be.

T. M. Luhrmann's study of American evangelical Christianity at the Vineyard Church in Chicago emphasizes how the performative quality in Christian epistemologies of the numinous emerges from the spirituality itself. Evangelical Christianity invites you to sense God "as if he were real in the flesh and standing by your side, with love. The challenge is to learn how to do that" (Luhrmann 38). The imagined fleshiness of God, the embodied presence of the numinous, also invites pretending "in order to make the pretense into a reality" (Luhrmann 73). This particular orientation to representation often renders Christian spirituality invisible. As Luhrmann makes clear, however, this is not the "as if" that is the essential relational dynamic of theatrical performance (see Mason on Stanislavsky) or of dramaturgical play (see Schechner, "Restoration of Behavior"). Rather it is a movement toward the experience of spirit in one's own flesh, God's voice in one's own mind, God's love in one's own heart. Luhrman's ethnography demonstrates that these senses are the foundation for people's claims about the material world, by which people know the objective reality of the numinous—"God's supernatural presence" (100). Evangelical worship songs represent in words and sound that feeling of bringing the transcendent into the body: "You, the singer, feel [the supernatural substance of God] in your body, like bones in your thighs and blood in your arteries" (Luhrmann 5).

In Luhrmann's accounts of evangelicals, knowing the numinous is feeling God's unconditional love (102). Stevenson's account suggests that Christian spiritual knowledge is performative on its own terms, which are aligned with the expectation for knowing via representation. This is the expectation Turner questions in her encounter with a sense of spirituality that does not quite conform to performance. My argument has focused on how spiritual practices in the modern, global North-West also may not perform according to expectations for showing, narrative, affect, play, imitation, representation, signification, realism, spectatorship, and reading. There may be a different presence to be discerned in and around the materiality of the performance.

SPIRITUALLY ENGAGED PERFORMANCE

Here I have proposed that what we observe as performance fuses the interior of the body where people sense spirituality as a presence with the body that is physically available in material culture; fuses knowledge articulated in texts with the formation of language in the body; and fuses sensory input into the body with sensations that collapse a distinction between physical and mental processes. In this reckoning's narrow focus on the performance paradigm and two vernacular spiritual practices, many issues in the study of vernacular spirituality remain untheorized.

Contemporary Western spiritualities encompass a vast array of beliefs and practices, from "the imagined pacific spirituality of yoga, meditation, and the like" to "transnational religious pilgrimages and stories of traveling spirits, spirit possession, and 'getting the Holy Ghost'" (Bender and McRoberts 14). Bender and McRoberts problematize the category of spirituality in relation to religion and the secular as a domain of experiences and practices that "reflect and articulate registers of feeling, desire, and motivation (and experiences of agency)" (19). The methodological moves they track "bring spirituality into focus in its own terms, rather than as merely one of religion's many others" and, as I have suggested, as a criterion for cultural Otherness (Bender and McRoberts 20). The methodological disruptions they offer propose spirituality as a field of inquiry in its own right, in and around the study of religion, religious traditions, and secularity.

The study of spirituality on its own terms and as private experience can provide a critical foundation for better assessing performative acts in the social sphere, the domain of performance. Simon Dein outlines the shift from conceiving of religious experience as precultural and individualistic to sociocultural constructs that function ideologically. "Future research on religious experience," he suggests, "needs to move beyond quantitative/qualitative studies of individual experiences to examine the cultural contexts which construct them in the first place, how they inform discourse about them and to examine the ways in which that discourse is ideological" (Dein 7). Resituating spiritual and religious experience in the specific cultural contexts through which people's sense of the numinous gives rise to ideologies (a significant concern in performance studies) requires attention "to the particular configurations of power, autonomy, authority, etc., that emerge through spiritual discourses, experiences, and rituals" (Bender and McRoberts 18).

As scholarly positions such as these indicate, vernacular spiritual practices may be socially, politically, and culturally engaged. The discourses and knowledge they produce out of the materials of their social construction, however, emerge from sensibilities that may not be readily apparent. Their expressions may reveal alternative modes of representation crucial to their ideologies. What, for example, does a political commitment to social justice mean to someone who senses the presence of benevolent spirits active in an urban landscape, or who senses each individualized social self as having a spiritual as well as material body? Sensibilities such as these, and the particular configurations of knowledge they generate, may also alter familiar paradigms for analyzing social practice. One of those paradigms is performance. If performances of spirituality seem to mark a lack, loss, aporia, or unfulfilled desire, it may be due to the failure of interpretive frameworks to account for what might be present in people's spiritual practices.

This book has not been intended as an apologia for "New Age" or "alternative" spirituality as distinct from religious spirituality, nor is the intent here to validate particular experiential truth claims. The critique of unchurched spirituality as experiential (spiritual shopping, anti-intellectualism, solipsism, self-centeredness, cultural borrowings by people of privilege, nostalgia for an idealized premodernity, the appeal of "feel good" philosophies of life, etc.) is not unfounded, and indeed many of these criticisms could be levied at people's participation in organized, institutionalized religions as well. In a culture that markets everything from soft drinks to software as experience, it should not be surprising that spirituality, institutionalized or not, comes to people as embodied experience. The concern here has been that experience serving as the measure of authenticity in vernacular culture is too easily and authoritatively dismissed. That performance practices themselves (music and theater in particular) have been associated with producing "spiritual" experiences (that is, referencing the numinous) does not suggest the displacement of spirituality from religion to the social, but the persistence of some experiential dimension that has no other name in the Western tradition.

A DIFFERENT PRESENCE

Performativity is a kind of consciousness that takes people out of the self, demands action for affect, and derives its power from the ability to elicit responses. Performance always calls attention to the performer and itself, even when it tries to hide or expose the mechanics of this calling. *Skin of Glass* and *Music as Medicine* suggest that the call of spirit is oriented differently, calling attention to a different logic.

Current paradigms might insist that an essential self, self-transcendence, and transcendent reality are illusions produced by the brain, culture, social norms, and discourses. But people continue to create meaning, construct knowledge, and, most importantly, live according to their embodied experiences. The mental and physical capacities people cultivate in practices (academic as well as spiritual) yield conceptual possibilities that extend into and affect material culture. We need to take seriously how the sense of spirituality shapes conceptual possibilities. Whether or not there is a spiritual dimension to the material world or spirituality is a fantasy for which people invent performative practices, we must recognize that there are people situated in a culture that privileges performance, materiality, and rationality making a committed effort to cultivate very different modes of sensing and thinking. They are doing this at an internal level of experience, while their life praxis engages conventions of writing, production, and performance familiar to their home culture even if they might locate spiritual practice in non-Western, premodern cultures.

If we take people's sense of an ineffable presence seriously, which performance and theater scholars such as David Mason, Jill Stevenson, and John Fletcher are doing, we might be able to tease out ways of perceiving, sensing, and formulating knowledge that will tell us more about the historical moment in which we live—if we are willing to engage them. We might, in the face of Stephen Pinker's pointed criticism of academic privilege, establish a dynamic conversation with vernacular culture rather than sustaining an uncritiqued critical stance.[2] Is the fact that these practitioners find something different from the cultural norms shaping their bodies and minds as performative a site for criticism or celebration? Is the critical demand that the world perform a desire for entertainment that distracts us from inquiry into the conditions of being human? Does the construction of tight, tautological circles to circumscribe culture and cognition (as though these were natural states of being) mask a longing for something more significantly human and profoundly Other in an otherwise indifferent world?

Jeff Kripal observes, "The present models of the human being dominant in the social sciences and humanities are seriously inadequate to the kinds of weird, uncanny, anomalous experiences that pepper, indeed *define*, the history of religions" ("Mind Matters" 220). I have suggested that vernacular spirituality, not excluding spirituality as experienced within religious traditions, yields a different orientation to knowledge as well as to the material world of bodies and culture. With this in our embodied minds, we might then ask some very challenging question of the performance paradigm. What if performance simply fails to appear in the presence of spirit? Which is more disturbing: the illusion that spirituality is real and can be explained away by analyzing its origins in the body and culture, or the fear that it isn't, so we defer to analyzing it as a cultural or neurological phenomenon? What would it mean to be agnostic about theater or performance? What would it mean to say, "I don't believe in performance" with the same ease as "I don't believe in ghosts"?

Spiritual practices may posit rules of engagement with the material world that are not bound to the familiar critical categories of gender, class, ethnicity, and cultural or social identities. We can map those categories onto the practices and their practitioners, but the map will be familiar. A critical stance manages this unfamiliarity in a language of cognition (belief, faith, myth), embodied display (ritual, ceremony, performance), and the authority of observation (participant-observation, audience, spectator). Moving into unfamiliar territory requires accepting the immateriality of spirit as an ontological and experiential condition for practitioners—a reality on the order of social class, gender, and ethnicity—and trying to work out how the matter we observe is transformed by that experiential condition.

Performance can construct a theoretical orientation from which it is too easy to overlook the ways people create intriguing, challenging realities as they engage their minds, bodies, and cultural resources. What orientations to culture and bodies do not show up in a performative perspective on the world? How might we recognize these unfamiliar realities? Basic strategies for a reorientation in performance begin to emerge. We can ask what knowledge informs the performance and identify modes of knowledge that do not correspond to a performative model; how performance is structured by that knowledge; how cultural idioms (be they textual, iconographic, gestural, etc.) function, and how those idioms collaborate with, rather than construct, the sensations of spirituality; or what relationship to language, everyday life, crafted events, and objects spiritual practices develop and how that relationship challenges our perspective. We can consider performance not only as a process of meaning-making but as an articulation of meaning inherent in the sensations identified as spiritual (this last is the most difficult). This is the point at which "knowledge that," "knowledge about," and "knowledge of" intersect with "knowledge from."

Disciplines like performance studies, straddling the social sciences and humanities, are poised to go beyond critical analyses of how we construct meaning in the act of performance to the qualities and characteristics of the experiential phenomena from which what we interpret as performance emerges. For performance studies, the first set of questions involves the ways a given practice or tradition understands the act of being physically present to others before assuming we know what "performance" is or means. Further, the normative claims people make in the actions of their bodies and the formulation of their texts across practices and traditions will reshape the analytical categories that structure the concerns of a paradigm such as performativity. Love, for example, might emerge as an analytical category in practices such as those described here and in Luhrmann's analysis of the Vineyard Christian Fellowship. How might love structure the performative?

LOOKING OUT FROM THE MIRROR OF REPRESENTATION

In the current intellectual context of critique and skepticism, the mirror of representation is assumed to constitute the real. Trying "to get *behind* the mirror in order to see the seer and observe the observer" is a kind of heresy, as Jeff Kripal points out ("Mind Matters" 221). Yet the quest for "direct knowledge of consciousness, much less the true nature of reality itself," sits outside humanities inquiry, its possible outcomes already foreclosed upon, the quest itself a modern myth ritualized in critical practice (Kripal, "Mind Matters" 221). As Kripal points out, a materialist orientation is itself a metaphysical commitment to reveal certain kinds of knowledge and to resist others. He continues with the observation that the "metaphysical commitments to contextualism and materialism" shared by many contemporary intellectuals deny "that the human species shares common forms of consciousness, agency, and moral integrity, and that these are transmissible and replicable and not simply epiphenomena of local political, economic, and social practices" (Kripal, "Mind Matters" 222). Such commitments see "only the infinitely recursive reflections in the mirror of language, history, culture, and identity. There is only the mirror. There is no behind the mirror" (Kripal, "Mind Matters" 222).

The spiritual orientation of people like McPherson and Klabunde does what current analytical paradigms cannot accomplish. Do practices such as those developed by McPherson and Klabunde shatter the postmodern mirror? What, in this context, do we make of McPherson's fierce effort to pry her eyes away from the mirror of the dance studio and not to see herself as a reflection of others, to "face a different sort of mirror, one that refracts the naked glimmer of self" (203, 204). Or of Klabunde's sense that the sounds he generates reflect a collective consciousness and open a person's consciousness to the perception of infinity (66)? From this orientation to performance, the concern is the quality (or perhaps qualia) of immediate, direct internal sensations, rather than how those sensations are mediated by culture and language. Have we abdicated a responsibility to pursue the integrity of such claims when we encounter them in vernacular culture?

Perhaps it is precisely the willingness of practitioners to extend their experiential spirituality in performative ways—concerts, CDs and DVDs, veils and drums for sale—that shatters the mirror of representation and reconfigures it as a membrane. Immanence and transcendence, like religion and secularity, are aspects of each other. For Adam Seligman, what is left of the sacred is in fact left to representation, even what of the sacred may be inside the self (*Modernity's Wager* 67). The Western self—long problematized as individual, subjective, inward facing, and invested in its privatized experience—finds external expressions for the felt sense of the sacred driven inward by the critique of the self in performance (68). Thus, reworking "New Age" and "alternative" spiritualities from mere techniques of the self in an intellectual context that cannot see beyond matter, Seligman suggests that we can "theorize the rise of contemporary pagan cults, witchcraft, and the like as very much a reaction to the interiorization of all expressive moments (of ultimate concerns) and the need precisely to find an external, objectified form outside of oneself to express states of feeling that have for too long been deemed an internal affair" (68). For practitioners, the sensations of spirituality in such external expressions are not imaginary, but require the doing of being to give them material form without betraying them.

Performance might be an inquiry into how to experience being human. We need as many ways as possible to understand how people come to experience that oscillation between interior and exterior, immanent and transcendent, something beyond and in the material world, words made flesh and flesh made words, the universal and the particular, self and identity. This is the challenge of writing about what sits outside the boundaries of cultural analysis. Perhaps spirituality can be subsumed under the rubrics of performativity, contained in the matter of culture and framed as representational practice. But this perspective comes at a loss. The commitment to studying vernacular culture also requires an awareness of the assumptions guiding cultural criticism, telling us what to take seriously and what to dismiss. When the insistence on performed identity occludes a sense of self as an essence, critiques of cultural hybridity and appropriation occlude processes in which new ideas and practices are generated, experiential subjectivity is neglected, the emphasis on seeing material culture obscures the subtle, internal sensibilities and thoughts that move people to *create* material culture, we have reached a critical impasse. The formulations of knowledge that come out of spiritual and religious practices may be the source of theories that allow us to rethink the boundaries of performance.

PRESENCE AND THE MEMBRANE OF PERFORMANCE

I have suggested that an orientation to the numinous might involve ways of engaging with the world that do not assume performance as a structuring principle for words and actions. Chapter 2 situated two specific vernacular spiritual practices in the cultural context of the contemporary United States and, in describing those particular practices, suggested that an internal sense of a numinous presence informs what appears as the materiality of performance. Spirituality emerged as a kind of relationality, a way of engaging with the self, the world, other people, and the numinous, rather than as the *performance of* spirituality or *discourse on* spirituality. Spirituality appeared as movement between mind and body, subject and object, self and other, ineffability and matter, representation and referent. Performance emerged as the membrane that allows that movement to be seen.

There is a temptation to explain spirit as a function of matter, whether of human physiology or material culture, because that is what we know we can know (or at least argue about). The ways these particular practices integrate mental, physical, and spiritual capacities and articulate that integration as knowledge suggest the need for paradigms that can link mental and physical action—the "doing" of performance—with spirituality. The physical activities and narratives people create to accommodate a register of mental and physical sensations as spiritual suggest a willingness to name and frame that register in ways analytical paradigms do not. There are thought processes at work, ways of thinking, of interpreting and analyzing culture that speak back.

Do we fail to see humanity in our midst in the effort to distance spiritual practices precisely *because* they seek a stable, knowable self that navigates and ameliorates culture and identity, seek transcendent and immanent values and meaning, assume not a random proliferation of significations but real presence, refuse to rend signifier from signified, and take internal experience as an unmediated source of knowledge?

I have argued here that the experiential synthesis of mind, body, and spirit in vernacular practice has produced a form of knowledge, articulated in language and framed performances. They do not start from emptiness, do not lack, and are not abject unless (or until) an analytical paradigm makes them so. That knowledge is certainly subject to critique. Nevertheless, this is a functional knowledge grounded in the consciousness of sensations and the sense of consciousness. This vernacular epistemology is developing at a significant pace in Western cultures. That knowledge is performative, but the question is *how the materiality of performance is conditioned by people's orientation to the numinous.*

People's sense of spirit asks us to value an inner life in which the numinous, the sacred, an ineffable presence is real. What does this mean for the materiality of performance? The sense of the heart opening is one of the most prominent images in *Music as Medicine* and *Skin of Glass.* The sense of receiving, giving, and living in the condition of love is understood to be a physical, mental, emotional, and perceptual reality. That reality appears as a presence radically and recognizably different from socially constructed meanings and discursive constructions. A hermeneutics of sensation collapses, an analysis of signification dissolves. This love is the very condition of being and knowing a numinous dimension to the world and self. The word *love* here is ambiguous not because it has multiple contested meanings but because of its precision as a sense of being. Love's presence is a vibration, a motor running in the center of the chest, sugar syrup exploding, fire burning, divinity prying at the walls of one's heart, a feeling that cannot be remembered with one's mind, a sense that cannot be understood (Klabunde 20; McPherson 216). These words are not a discourse on love, and the sense is not a performance. There is a presence to be known and this sense of an ineffable, numinous, sacred, embodied presence knows the materiality of performance.

Notes

Preface

1. For the conceptual ground of this stance, see Lyotard.

2. For religion in the performance paradigm, see Grimes.

3. Working groups in the International Federation for Theatre Research and the American Theatre and Higher Education organization are currently involved in lively discussions about the interrelationship of four key terms: religion, spirituality, performance, and theater.

4. For an excellent essay that puts the terms "materiality" and "spirituality" in tension, see Miller.

5. Barbara Ehrenreich reflects on the encounter with mystical experience and the possibility of forms of consciousness eluding what we can observe.

6. As this book is in its final revisions, spirituality is entering the scholarly lexicon with less trepidation and fewer apologias. In 2014, Linda A. Mercadante's ethnographic analysis of "nones" in *Belief without Borders* and Kelly Besecke's nuanced exploration of reflexive spirituality in *You Can't Put God in a Box* speak directly to the reckoning with spirituality in current paradigms. For spirituality and religion, see Mercadante's Introduction, 1–19.

7. The inquiry could also be reversed by studying performance practices and their audience/spectators as a source for the sense of a numinous dimension to the world, but that is another project.

8. For performativity as a paradigm, its contested and problematized domains, and the kaleidoscopic paradigms that shift within it, see McKenzie 29–53.

9. For an introduction to the interdependency of secularity, religion, and spirituality, see Bender and Taves. The sections "From Secularization to Secularism: The Secular-Religion Binary and the Challenge of Spirituality" (3–9) and "The Embrace of Paradox: Modern Spirits and Enchantments" (15–28) describe the discursive foundation of this

study. The latter section introduces key issues raised here—authenticity, experience, and authority—within this intellectual context. Jeremy Carrette and Richard King trace historical uses of the term "spirituality" to its current incarnation as a kind of cultural-transcending experience happening within a modern, individual self (30–53). For an overview of distinctions between religion and spirituality, see Zinnbauer and Pargament.

10. Thanks to Professor Haiping Yan for this observation.

11. For this tautology and a reimagining of performance studies through Jacques Derrida's notion of haunting, see Powell and Shaffer.

12. See Auslander. Texts included in this volume cover the years 1908 to 2003.

13. For a perceptive discussion of the trouble with spirits in performance ethnography, see Jane Turner. For postmodernism as a simplified ideology in American popular culture and its antipathy toward the truth-claims of religion, see Mercadante 29.

14. For vernacular culture as a text to be decoded, underpinning that which drives the study of culture as performance, see Roland Barthes's *Mythologies.*

15. See Paul Heelas's discussion of the significance of experiential claims to inner life spirituality in *Spiritualities of Life* 144–46.

Introduction

1. See the Pew Forum for Religion and Public Life report from December 9, 2009 ("Many Americans Mix Multiple Faiths: Eastern, New Age Beliefs Widespread"), which documents the prevalence of overlapping spiritual and religious practices, the coexistence of contradicting beliefs, and combining elements from multiple religious traditions in American approaches to religion. See also the April 7, 2009, report, "Faith in Flux: Changes in Religious Affiliation in the U.S.," which emphasizes shifts toward disaffiliation with religious traditions, concluding that the shifts are not due to scientific explanation replacing religion, spirituality, or superstition, but to people's sense that religious institutions and teachings are not tenable. The Pew Forum report on December 18, 2012, "The Global Religious Landscape," reported that 6.7% of the world's population identifies as "other" or "folk religion" and 16.3% as unaffiliated with any religious tradition. For current and past reports, see http://www.pewforum.org/CategoryIndex.aspx?id=80. Though the terms "religion" and "spirituality" are still contrasted as categories or seen as subsets of each other depending on the context, emerging studies recognize that these terms do not necessarily operate in any particular categorical relation to each other. See Bender and McRoberts 1.

2. For example, the belief that the self itself is sacred "accounts for the remarkable diversity at the surface of the spiritual milieu—which is inevitable when people feel they need to follow their personal paths and explore what works for them personally—and at the same time provides ideological unity and coherence at a deeper level" (Aupers and Houtman 205).

3. In this familiar binary, spirituality is associated with internal sensations of the sacred or divine, such as mystical experiences, whereas religion implies participation in institutionalized traditions and belief systems. Data on how people distinguish between spirituality and religion is dependent on the survey instruments themselves. Raymond F. Paloutzian, Erica L. Swenson, and Patrick McNamara point out that survey instruments may construct religion as a subset of spirituality or spirituality as a subset of religion. They note that "measures of religiousness ask about things such as belief in certain teachings, participating in religious services, and supporting institutional religious programs. Measures of spirituality ask about things such as connecting with whatever is of the highest meaning to oneself, a sense of striving for oneness, and transcending one's own limitedness" (153).

4. For foundational texts on religion in the social sphere, see Durkheim on religion and social cohesion; see Weber for the "disenchantment" associated with modernity and capitalism.

5. Religion and secularity are, as Mark C. Taylor makes clear, interrelated perspectives on culture. Taylor observes, "What neither secularists nor religionists realize is that secularity is a *religious* phenomenon—indeed, religion as it has developed in the West has always harbored secularity, and secularity covertly continues a religious agenda. In other words, secularity and religion are coemergent and codependent" (132).

6. For a summary of sociological perspectives, see Besecke, "Seeing Invisible Religions" 91; and in the same volume, Hammer.

7. For a summary of the qualities that identify spiritual practices as New Age or alternative, especially in relation to the secularization thesis, see Partridge 1:29–34. For examples of practices and venues in this broad genre, see Partridge 1:32–33 and 2:4–5; Besecke, "Seeing Invisible Religions" 89–90; Heelas and Woodhead 29–30.

8. For a general overview of spirituality in the marketplace, see Wade Clark Roof's classic, *Spiritual Marketplace: Baby Boomers and the Remaking of American Religion*, and Possamai, *Religion and Popular Culture.* On secularization, see Partridge 1:1. For the cultural politics of modernity, see Heelas, *Spiritualities of Life*. For broader cultural shifts that emphasize holistic well-being, also see Heelas, especially 61–67.

9. The classic twentieth-century text on this affective dynamic is Susanne Langer, *Feeling and Form.*

10. For the classic exegesis on art as inherently spiritual, see Wassily Kandinsky's 1911 treatise *Concerning the Spiritual in Art.* Olivier Messiaen's *Quartet for the End of Time,* for a musical example, invokes the biblical book of Revelation (10:1–2). Messiaen shifts the musical structure of time with rhythmic patterns from Indian music, and in its last movement seems to extend indefinitely into an eternal and ultimate silence. The piece was written during the composer's internment in a German prison camp (1940–41).

11. See Zarrilli.

12. For the internal incoherence of postmodernism and the limits on its liberatory motivations as an intellectual movement, see Slingerland 99–102. See also Latour 3–5.

13. For resistance to normative commitments and paradoxical inconsistency to which postmodern thinkers held unacknowledged normative commitments, see Slingerland 101. For the bracketing of metaphysics in these domains of inquiry, see Lee Irwin's introduction, "Esoteric Paradigms and Participatory Spirituality in the Teachings of Mikhael Aivanhov" 197–99. Irwin is interested in the potential of metaphysical experiences for personal transformation, not the interplay between internal experience of the metaphysical and the material, observable world.

14. For an excellent overview of this process, see Reinelt.

15. For recent studies that address this issue and other complexities of spirituality and belief in religious performance (Christianity), see Fletcher; Stevenson. For the complexities of Christian Evangelicalism as lived religion, see also Luhrmann.

16. For a discussion of the epistemological assumptions underpinning the move toward understanding the exchange between internal processes (mind) and the world (external stimulation), as well as the problems of a representational (essentially theatrical) model for mental processes, see Varela, Thompson, and Rosch 134–45.

17. On materialism, see Mark C. Taylor 595.

18. Partridge takes this perspective, resisting the secularization thesis, in *The Re-enchantment of the West*, vol. 1. See also Heelas, *Spiritualities of Life* 195.

19. For art as expression moving from human emotion and conceptual capacities outward into aesthetic forms, and on art as a distinct category of human production, see Langer, *Feeling and Form: A Theory of Art. Feeling and Form*, as aesthetic criticism, has lost its status amid the focus on vernacular culture in performance criticism and postmodern and poststructuralist concerns for how knowledge is constructed, constituted, and transmitted. *Feeling and Form* is now out of print.

20. See Barua. See also Slingerland's discussion of phenomenology's attempt at non-representational engagement with the phenomenal world, which he criticizes for not putting the body in the mind (88–89). For Raymond Gibbs's summary of phenomenological approaches to the "felt sensations in mental life and bodily actions," which remain grounded in a tripartite division between corporeal sensations, mental processes, and an external world, see *Embodiment and Cognitive Science* 25. On Gerardus van der Leew, see LaMothe.

21. For a summary of the legacy of symbolic and pragmatist accounts of religion and the constructivist model in anthropology and religious studies, see Slingerland 228–29. For the "intellectualist-pragmatist" theory and its predictions that scientific explanations will overtake the need for religious accounts of natural phenomena, see Slingerland 230–31. For a critique of the theoretical assumptions limiting new naturalist approaches to religion and the call for "subtler, more conceptually spacious, and arguably more empirically responsive . . . understandings of human behavior, cognition and culture," see Barbara Herrnstein Smith 48. For an assessment of New Naturalist explanations, with a focus on Pascal Boyer's *Religion Explained*, see 30–58 and 62 in Smith.

22. See Partridge 2:6–7; Ferrer and Sherman; and Heelas and Woodhead.

23. The introduction to Russell T. Hurlburt and Eric Schwitzgebel's *Describing Inner Experience: Proponent Meets Skeptic* provides a good overview of the taxonomic difficulties inherent in discussing an "inner life." For the shortcomings of any terminology for the phenomenon or phantasm of "internal experience," see page 15. For a brief historical overview, see pages 3–5. For the ambiguity of cognitive processes and feeling in people's descriptions of internal experience, see page 18.

24. "Bodily awareness in emotion experience is based crucially on cognitive attributions of the cause of bodily arousal. An emotion is arousal plus a cognitive label for it in terms of anger, sadness, joy and so on. In some cases, people misattribute arousal to some source that is not responsible for what they are consciously feeling" (Gibbs 250).

Chapter 1

1. For ways of interpreting religious experience as private or public, as emotional affect or linguistic thought, as sui generis or a cultural manifestation, see G. William Barnard's discussion of Wayne Proudfoot's seminal *Religious Experience* in his review article, "Explaining the Unexplainable: Wayne Proudfoot's 'Religious Experience,'" 232.

2. For the premium placed on personal experience as authoritative of spiritual realities in these practices, see Partridge 1:71–77.

3. For the foundational text on the social construction of religion, see Durkheim. For a helpful introduction to issues of internal experience, claims to unmediated experience, and performance, see Smart. For the Protestant orientation to interiority and the necessity of transcendence for representation, because something *outside* the self must be represented, see Seligman, *Modernity's Wager* 67–68.

4. For a summary, see LaMothe, *Between Dancing and Writing* 21–64; Proudfoot 3–5.

5. For a summary, see Charles Taylor 43–65, especially 63.

6. See Taves, *Religious Experience Reconsidered* 3–4.

7. For a summary of this trajectory from Kant, see Proudfoot 6–40.

8. See Taves, *Religious Experience Reconsidered* 4. For an analysis of James's assessment of internal religious experience as cognitive and precognitive feeling in the context of the neurology of religious experience, see Azari, "Religious Experience" 69–74. For James and the establishment of internalized religion as an object of study in the discipline of psychology, see Jay 102–10. For a critique of functionalism, the outward turn to behaviorism in psychology, and the reliance on representational brain scans in neurophysiology as systems of knowledge that avoid the elusiveness of introspection, see Lyons.

9. On individualism (especially of morality and sensation) and materialism in modernity, see Heelas, *Spiritualities of Life* 196–98. For the goal of "keeping religion at bay" in modernism, see Possamai, *Religion and Popular Culture* 31–33. For the social construction of internal authority from Émile Durkheim, see Hammer 51.

10. For the habits engendered by critical theory's stance toward nature, politics, and discourse, see Latour 3–5.

11. For brief summaries of major religious theories, see Tweed 48–53, and of religious experience specifically, see Taves's introduction to *Religious Experience Reconsidered* 3–12.

12. Throughout this chapter, I share David Hufford and Mary Ann Bucklin's concern "with the way that modern intellectual attitudes toward spirit belief have stigmatized a broad range of spiritual experiences as pathological and the beliefs arising from those experiences as naïve or irrational" (26–27).

13. Cf. an earlier schematic that organizes performance as processes of representation; signification as that which exceeds, supplements, and fills in texts, as in the creation of characters (closely allied to representation and theater); and social role-playing, in Thompson.

14. For performance as crafted communicative or artistic skill, see Bauman. For an analysis of performativity as a paradigm to measure workplace efficacy, see McKenzie 55–94.

15. See Roof 81–86 for themes in descriptions of "spirituality."

16. For the hybridity of New Age or Alternative spiritualities, see Possamai, *Religion and Popular Culture* 50. For alternative spiritualities mainstreamed into corporate culture, even as New Age festivals celebrate their alterity to mainstream culture, see Possamai, "Alternative Spiritualities" 32. For a critique of individual agency in navigating this hybridity, see Hammer, especially 50–54.

17. See Dolan. Dolan looks at the ways theatrical performances create communities of feeling, "in which social discourse articulates the possible, rather than the insurmountable obstacles to human potential. . . . The aesthetics of these performances lead to both affective and effective feelings and expressions of hope and love not just for a partner as the domestic scripts of realism so often emphasize, but for other people for a more abstracted notion of 'community,' or for an even more intangible idea of 'human kind'" (2). Dolan is apologetic in recognizing her "use of metaphors of prayer or communion to describe performances that *I'd rather argue engaged civic participation than religious fervor*" (italics added) and that "religious" has been levied as a criticism of her recent work. Dolan's professed belief "in the spiritual aspects of utopian performatives," her longing to "articulate a spiritual effect in performance" opens to a sense of something "deeply spiritual, ineffable, and at the same time profoundly *human*" that yields ethics without religion (136). At the same time, however, in this elegant meditation spirituality must remain an epiphenomenon of performance, an effect produced by the material and communal engagement performance offers and an affect felt in service of social transformation that is always deferred (135–36). In contrast, the performances offered in chapter 2 start unapologetically from an embodied, felt sense of the ineffable. Performance is the epiphenomenon, the effect of that felt sense, not dependent upon aesthetic affect.

18. See, for example, Charles Taylor; Asad; and Steven D. Smith.

19. The prominence of sociological models is challenged by scholarly attention to lived religion. See Taves, *Religious Experience Reconsidered* 6–7; McGuire 20–21; Bender 7–12.

20. Phenomenology offers valuable insights into the limits of the visible and the ways a performing body is understood to constitute presence. The late work of Maurice Merleau-Ponty, *Visible and Invisible,* in particular wrestles with the encounter between what is available to the senses and what eludes the body's materiality (as the visible):

> Since the total visible is always behind, or after, or between the aspects we see of it, there is access to it only through an experience which, like it, is wholly outside of itself. It is thus, and not as the bearer of a knowing subject, that our body commands the visible for us, but it does not explain it, does not clarify it, it only concentrates the mystery of its scattered visibility; and it is indeed a paradox of Being, not a paradox of man, that we are dealing with here. (136)

21. Robert Orsi observes that the discipline of religious studies "exists in the suspension of the ethical, and it steadfastly refuses either to deny or to redeem the other. It is a moral discipline in its commitment to examining the variety of human experience, and to making contact across boundaries—cultural, psychological, spiritual, existential. It is a moral discipline in its cultivation of a disciplined attentiveness to the many different ways men, women, and children have lived with the gods and to the things, terrible and good, violent and peaceful, they have done with the gods to themselves and to others" (203).

22. The three terms most commonly associated with these experiences are "religious," "spiritual," and "mystical." General use of the terms is consistent with the following definitions.

> Religious experiences arise from following a religious tradition and involve a contact with the divine or a religious figure. Spiritual experiences are subjective experiences that do not arise from following a religious tradition. These experiences, however, can also bring the experiencer into contact with the divine or a transcendent reality. Mysticism refers to the pursuit of an altered state of consciousness that enables the mystic to communion with, or identify with a divinity or ultimate reality through an immediate, direct, intuitive knowledge and experience. (Beauregard 58)

> The term "religion" refers to that which has become *canonical,* meaning that at its core are writings, teachings and organizational structures which are viewed as somehow essential for devotees to connect with the sacred. "Spirituality" is a more inward concept in that it connotes one's personal sense of the sacred, and those places, practices and times that enrich that sense and promote growth towards a more continuous experience of the sacred. That sense is not merely intellectual but is primarily emotional. . . . "Mysticism" includes teachings and practices that encourage a quest to unite with the source of the sacred." (Lancaster 21)

23. For the history of the generative tension between religion and theology, see LaMothe, *Between Dancing and Writing* 19–20.

24. McKenzie observes, "Cultural performance, as studied by Performance Studies researchers, entails the embodiment of symbolic structures in living behavior and, crucially, the transformation of these structures through discourses and practices of transgressions, resistance, and mutation. The challenge is thus one of social efficacy" (130).

25. See McKenzie: "The concept of performance as the embodied enactment of cultural forces has not only informed many disciplines of study, it has also given rise to its own paradigm of knowledge, called in the United States and other English-speaking countries, 'Performance Studies'" (8).

26. Two essays from *Bodily Citations: Religion and Judith Butler*, Armour and St. Ville, when compared, illustrate the problem of dealing with spirituality as a kind of interiority when working from an intellectual foundation built on citational practices, mimesis, and semiotics. In "Materializations of Virtue: Buddhist Discourses on Bodies," Susanne Mrozik uses Judith Butler's work to "explicate and contest normative representations of body ideals in pre-modern South Asian Buddhist literature" (15). Reading the story of the Beautiful Woman, in which the Buddha in the form of a beautiful woman cuts off her breasts to feed a starving woman, Mrozik finds that "identification with an abject body image in the context of Buddhism is a conscious and intentional performance" of virtue and a newly sexed body (17). Rebecca Schneider's essay on citation, "'Judith Butler' in My Hands," points to the "particular Western architectonic of (theatrical) perspective that continues to play out in much work on performativity" (227). Even as Mrozik recognizes that Buddhist "abjection" and sexing of bodies works through different processes than those Butler proposes, the architectonic, theatrical perspective Schneider identifies structures her reading of the Beautiful Woman. In these readings, the materiality of the text constructing the sexed body and the legacy of psychoanalysis pathologizing interiority occlude understanding the attention to virtue as an internal quality to which bodies respond. Spirituality is somewhere outside this architecture. For a critique of psychoanalysis and embodiment in Butler, see Rothenberg.

27. As Adam Seligman points out in *Modernity's Wager*, in the foundations of a social approach to religion it "was Durkheim's insight that the symbolic (his concern was with forms of solidarity) takes the place of the thing itself as a locus of meaning and significance. It only exists if it exists 'out there'" (68).

28. For the marginalization of religious experience in the social sciences, see Dein.

29. For the distinction between affirmation and critique in the history of religious studies, see LaMothe, *Between Dancing and Writing* 19–20.

30. Evidence that children believe in spirits, an afterlife, and other unverifiable concepts before indoctrination into belief systems yields the scholarly judgment that spirituality is naive, childish, prelinguistic, and primitive. See Bering 126–27. In contrast, see Irwin 197–98 for the effects of biological and cultural empiricism on "the epistemic import of subjective experience in modern thought."

31. Hufford and Bucklin take issue with "modern academic discourse" and its relation to notions of spirit, the spiritual, and spirituality. They acknowledge "belief in spirit(s) is problematic in modern discourse" and that "a wealth of data shows that belief in spirits is persistent and widespread among modern persons" (26). They note in scholarly analyses a "distinctively modern separation of the spiritual from the observable world" that was "part of the construction of religion as affective rather than cognitive, in contrast to science, the domain of rationality and the observable" (33). In modernity, they observe,

> we find assumptions that are biased not only against the validity of belief in the existence of spirits but against the idea that such belief can be rationally warranted. These assumptions are found in theology as well as in philosophy and developing fields devoted to the study of humanity. This bias is not in itself the widely imagined rift between science and religion, because it does not arise from science per se but rather from scholarly reflections about science. But these assumptions are an important source of the idea the such a rift exists. (31–32)

32. For the ways the study of religion in the American academy identified religious Otherness on a scale of primitive to modern with implied moral judgment, the influence of postcolonial and postmodern critiques on the study of non-Christian religions, the broadening of religion as spirituality in sociology and psychology, and the morality undergirding constructions of religious Otherness, see Orsi 186–87, 194–96, 197, 198–99. For an overview of the problem, see Hay.

33. For political conformity as the epistemological standard in postmodernism, and by extension performance studies, as evidenced by Jill Dolan's *Utopia*, see Slingerland 104–5. For a critique of the scholarly characterization of New Age and alternative spiritualities as individualistic, and the need to interrogate the social constructions and systems that support the "doctrine of self-spirituality," see Aupers and Houtman 205. See also Bender, especially 23–24 for the observation that contemporary spiritual practitioners are engaged with modern culture but "organized differently." For a perspective on the ways "inner-life spirituality" and the special value placed on the "subjective experiences of the inner self" that permeate contemporary culture, see Heelas, *Spiritualities of Life* 60–62.

34. For succinct analyses of the constitution and characteristics of "spiritual, not religious," see Possamai, *Religion and Popular Culture* 35–39; Partridge 1:46–50; Wuthnow, *After the Baby Boomers* 131–34.

35. For studies of how spiritual communities operate in mainstream culture in England, see Heelas and Woodhead, and in the United States, see Bender. For a succinct summary of the characteristics, resources, and practices that make spirituality "alternative," see Pike, *New Age* 14–38. For a review article of research on spiritual experiences, see Hood. For a summary of approaches to religiousness and spirituality, including prominent definitions and spirituality as an alternative to formal, institutionalized religion, see Zinnbauer and Pargament.

36. For "postmodern primitives" and the "postcultural West," see Bender 16 n. 43. For the romanticization of the premodern, see Partridge 1:77–78.

37. For the adaptation of spirituality into neoliberal economic culture, see Carrette and King. For holistic spirituality marketed as an antidote to "social and environmental maladies," see Partridge 2:18–21.

38. See Tacey 12–16, especially page 13.

39. See Roof; Carrette and King; and Bender.

40. See Possamai, "Alternative Spiritualities" 33.

41. See, for example, Edith Turner. For a more critical approach, see Geurts.

42. See, for example, the comparison between the psychological orientation to character in Konstantin Stanislavsky's work and the Indian devotional drama, *râs lila*, in Mason. Mason's study posits theater as presenting a fictional, alternative reality that is structured by religious belief and emotional response. Religious experience is a result of performers and spectators entering into a fictional representation, which is responsible for conditioning and eliciting a specifically spiritual response. Representation, character, narrative, and role-playing, all characteristics of Western realism, combine with religious belief in the creation of religious affect. In this fascinating study, Mason discusses religious experience and a religious worldview in theatrical form as a "paradox of fiction" (120–27), considers religious experience as role-playing within and informed by a religious worldview (127–33), and interrogates the conflation of stage realism in European and Indian traditions with living in religious commitment. Mason's interests revolve around emotional affect, religious feeling, and aesthetics. He explores in detail the tradition of Western realistic acting's emotional memory with the devotional memory invoked in a *ras lila* performance.

43. For a description of "wellbeing culture" and holistic spirituality as part of a general subjective turn in popular culture, see Partridge 2:17–20.

44. For religious experience as a component of individual psychology, a feeling with both subjective and objective aspects, and a social construction produced by activities such as rituals, see Rappaport.

45. Bender notes the frequency with which William James's *Varieties of Religious Experience* appeared on the bookshelves of the Cambridge metaphysicals she studied and the degree to which they assumed that her goal as a researcher was to validate and legitimate their experiential findings (69).

46. On this resistance, see the observations of Apache scholar Ines Talamantez, quoted in Donaldson 692.

47. For consciousness and experience, see Taves, *Religious Experience Reconsidered* 57–58, 63.

48. For examples of different models of organizing sensation and sensory data, see Geurts 7–10; and Desjarlais, especially 143–44. Geurts argues that the modern, Western five-senses model is itself a folk ideology:

> Despite the belief of many Euro-Americans, the five-senses model is not a scientific fact, and the enumeration of the senses has been a subject of debate among scholars and philosophers for many centuries. . . . From Aristotle to Aquinas and Descartes, however, cultural traditions have sustained a five-senses model that privileges mental representations and external modes of knowing. This construct, I argue, is essentially a folk ideology. (7–8)

49. For a trajectory that traces performance as a shift from theater to theory, see McKenzie 40–42.

50. The "really hard problem" of consciousness is, for Chalmers, "the problem of *experience*," the subjective aspect of information-processing that requires description by analogy:

> When we see, for example, we *experience* visual sensations: the felt quality of redness the experience of dark and light, the quality of depth in a visual field. Other experiences go along with perception in different modalities: the sound of a clarinet, the smell of mothballs. Then there are bodily sensations, from pains to orgasms; mental images that are conjured up internally; the felt quality of emotion, and the experience of a stream of conscious thought. What unites all of these states is that there is something it is like to be in them. (201)

51. Current frameworks for theorizing the inner workings of the mind fall into general categories of consciousness driving behavior and some forms of expression not directly accessible in language: cognitive processes (decision making, logical thought, symbolic reasoning, ideation, intentionality, language, concept formation), perception (apprehension and organization of information from the senses, conceptualization, identification of feelings and emotions, identification of qualia, recording and representing the world outside the mind), memory (recollection, reconstruction, and representation of events, images, facts, emotions), and the more ambiguous, liminal domain of the subconscious, unconscious, and dreams, which drive behavior and some forms of expression but are not directly accessible in language.

52. For an experimental perspective on the fallibility/infallibility problem in people's interpretation and reporting of internal experience, see Hurlburt and Schwitzgebel 41–53. The introduction provides a strong overview of the taxonomic difficulties inherent in discussing an "inner life." For the shortcomings with any terminology for the phenomenon or phantasm of "internal experience," see page 15. For a brief historical overview, see pages 3–5. For the ambiguity of cognitive processes and feeling in people's descriptions of internal experience, see page 18.

53. For theatrical consciousness as a distinctly European and modern phenomenon that yields an intellectual view of humans and human culture as performative, see Egginton.

54. For the nuances of the distinction between theatricality and performativity, see Power; Reinelt.

55. As Orsi notes, however, "Confessional pedagogy slips its nose into the academic tent through the opening created by postmodernism" (194). For the position of Christianity and an excellent summary and analysis of religion as an academic discipline in the American academy in general, see Orsi 177–204.

56. See Power 119.

57. For the detrimental effects of postmodernism's inherent dualism on humanities scholarship, see Slingerland 74–98.

58. I have argued elsewhere that the logics of spirituality or religious belief may yield radically different understandings of how performance works. In the case of Christianity, for example, the view of performance as a representational practice is structured into the theology. God can be represented as real and present in people's everyday lives in the materiality of performance (for example, the theatrical reenactment of biblical events). Performance works well as an analytical paradigm for this religious tradition in part because Christian theological thinking is woven into the Western intellectual tradition that gave rise to theories of the world as performance. The idea of a transcendent deity operating in the material world operates with similar assumptions about representation and deferred referents, whereas a sense of spirituality might not depend on those assumptions. For how analytical commitments to material culture and representation struggle with spirituality, see Dox.

59. See Egginton 44–45 for medieval Catholic and sixteenth-century Protestant metaphysics of presence.

60. For the argument that theatrical representation creates presence and for the critique of presence in poststructuralist performance criticism, see Power 119–46.

61. See Roof; Carrette and King.

62. For a critique of Western postural yoga as "an individualized spirituality of the self, or . . . repackaged as a cultural commodity to be sold to the 'spiritual consumer,'" see Carrette and King 115–20.

63. On representations of spirituality, see Roof 67–72; on consumerism, see Heelas, *Spiritualities of Life* 97–112.

64. See Iwamura.

65. Hufford and Bucklin observe "the distinctively modern separation of the spiritual from the observable world" that "was part of the construction of religion as affective rather than cognitive, in contrast to science, the domain of rationality and the observable" (33).

66. See Bauman.

67. For a discussion of this rift, see LaMothe, *Between Dancing and Writing* 21–64.

68. For a historical sketch and critiques of introspection as both a phenomenon and foundation for inquiry, see Wallace, *The Taboo of Subjectivity* 76–89.

69. For the relationship between experience, cognition, and embodied meaning, see Taves, *Religious Experience Reconsidered* 64–68.

70. See Seligman, "Ritual and Sincerity" 104–5.

71. For a summary of theories about the relationship between myth and ritual, see Bell 3–19.

72. See the 1972 documentary film *Marjoe*, in which Christian evangelical Marjoe Gortner exposes his theatricalized faith-healing as faithless and manipulative. On Australian Jose Alvarez going undercover for James Randi as a self-proclaimed guru who channeled a 2,000-year-old spirit named "Carlos" in 1988, see Carroll. For a more recent example, see the 2011 documentary, *Kumare: A True Film about a False Prophet*, in which American filmmaker Vikram Gandhi sets out on a Carlos-like social experiment but ends up speculating on the effects alternative spiritualities can have on people.

73. See Wakin, "Lincoln Center" and "White Light." See also Steve Smith.

74. For the psychoanalytic assessment of the "oceanic feeling" associated with religious experience as primitive and ego-oriented, see Freud 28–39. For the significance of water as an immersive medium in a contemporary world of simulation, see Helmreich.

75. See Wallace 17–56.

76. For consciousness and experience in neurosciences, and the stances taken by constructivists and perennialists on the issue of experience in religious studies, see Taves, *Religious Experience Reconsidered* 57–63.

77. For the social function of symbolic language and rituals that express and preserve the positive qualia of neurological events, see James and Engebretson 223.

78. Mark C. Taylor, for example, offers a model in which human consciousness constantly creates and resolves differences and the workings of the mind are simultaneously subject and object (58). Language loses its representational function, and, "while appearing to represent the world . . . is a play of signs unanchored by knowable referents" (15), as is the case with the spiritually oriented performances described in chapter 2.

79. For the ways people link spirituality with artistic expression and practices, see Wuthnow, *Creative Spirituality*. Wuthnow also acknowledges that the effort to recognize spirituality in corporeal practices in academic inquiry still comes up against the dichotomy in Western thought between spirituality and materiality. Though he acknowledges that current scholarship can now "view the spiritual life in active, rather than passive, terms" and that people actively seek out activities that generate experiences they interpret as spiritual, that dichotomy is still a problem (Wuthnow, *After the Baby Boomers* 112).

80. For example, one definition of spirituality might privilege consciousness. For Philip Hefner, "The spiritual refers to the way in which our *consciousness is organized* (another of Csikszentmihalyi's ideas), so as to enable us to put our knowledge and experience of the world together in coherent ways that support values, viable lifestyles, and moral behavior. Spirituality refers to the organization of our consciousness that makes

richness of life possible, for individuals and communities" (124). Another might assume a sacred or divine realm. Pargament identifies spirituality as the "search for the sacred," with psychological, social, physical, or material goals (12–13).

81. In *Religious Experience Reconsidered,* Taves urges attention to cross-disciplinary research design that can address spiritual experience with greater precision: "Experience—whether religious, spiritual, or mystical—is definitely a phenomenon for study within this new [interdisciplinary] paradigm, but the implications of the paradigm for setting up experientially related objects of study that can be examined across disciplines have not been adequately worked out. Without further refinement at the design stage, it will be difficult to connect different lines of research" (8). Like Slingerland, but for different reasons, Taves seeks "methodological bridges across the divide between the humanities and the sciences" by focusing on "the interaction between psychobiological, social, and cultural-linguistic processes in relation to carefully specified types of experiences sometimes considered religious" (*Religious Experience Reconsidered* 8).

82. Taves's approach to inner experience opens space for humanities scholarship: "By locating how we come to know our own and others' experience through processes that are simultaneously embodied and interactive, we can make a concept familiar to scholars of religion usable across disciplines and further a process of conceptual integration that is presupposed in the natural sciences but less well advanced elsewhere" (*Religious Experience Reconsidered* 14).

83. For the distinction between spiritual experience and pathologies see Giordano and Engebretson, "Neural and Cognitive Basis of Spiritual Experience." For case studies in schizophrenia, obsessive-compulsive disorders, and dementia, see also McNamara. For a review article on spirituality and mental illness, see Miller and Kelly.

84. See also Certeau 80–82.

85. For a critique of Buddhism adapted to New Age individualism and the contradiction between Western constructions of self and atman, see Carrette and King 95–108. For a similar analysis of how this statue might function in the cultural context of a country in which Buddhism is the dominant religious practice, not a potentially exoticized import, see Scott.

86. For sincerity as the antidote to habitual ritualization, see Seligman, "Modernity and Sincerity."

87. See Orsi's analysis of Catholic devotion to the Virgin Mary for an example of how people construct religious experience despite prevailing devotional norms imposed by religious discourse (62).

88. For similar approaches see Heelas, *Spiritualities of Life*; and Tacey.

Chapter 2

1. Dancemeditation could be situated in a range of contemporary practices loosely recognized as "somatic spirituality" or "embodied spirituality." Such practices seek a ho-

listic perception of being human, sometimes positing a distinctly spiritual dimension, but more often locating spirit as an aspect of a person's human capacity for sensation and perception. These frequently include aspects of Jungian psychology and combinations of physical systems such as hatha yoga, Tantra, Sufism, shamanism, and Taoism to integrate the body and the mind with spirituality. They are closely allied with transpersonal psychology. See, for example, Washburn.

2. Collective Awakening could be situated in modern shamanism, which seeks to reconstitute shamanism as a technique for accessing spirit worlds, usually for healing purposes. For core shamanism as developed by Michael Harner in *The Way of the Shaman*, see the Foundation for Shamanic Studies. Popular magazines for practicing shamanism include *Shaman's Drum: A Journal of Experiential Shamanism and Spiritual Healing* and *Sacred Hoop*. On the more extreme end of modern shamanic practices and spiritual tourism, there is the pursuit of enlightenment through visions produced by a potent herb grown in Peru and Columbia, *ayahuasca*. See Weiskopf. Klabunde dissolved Collective Awakening in 2013 and continues his work as a teacher.

3. This chapter takes an emic approach to these practices, based on observation. I am not an adherent of either practice. No formal interviews were conducted with practitioners, though I have talked and corresponded with Martin Klabunde and Dunya Dianne McPherson. Both practitioners were aware of this book project during my observations and gave their consent. No interviews or conversations were conducted with participants and no record made of any inadvertent conversations. Every effort has been made to ensure that no participants in any events can be identified based on information provided in this chapter. Chapters 3 and 4 take an etic approach, juxtaposing theoretical models through which these practices can be interpreted.

4. http://www.dancemeditation.org/about/dancemeditation.

5. http://www.youtube.com/user/DunyaDancemeditation.

6. http://www.collectiveawakening.us.

7. http://blog.dancemeditation.org/alembic-performance/.

8. A recent testimonial from a Dancemeditation student-practitioner mirrors McPherson's self-perception: "'I used to think Dunya led. Then I thought she facilitated. Now I know that what she truly does is *reveal essence*.'—Dr. Scott Elkin, physician, psychiatrist, personal trainer." The idea that performance reveals essence has little traction in performance theory. If such practices were considered performative, this quality would be dismissed despite its centrality to the way performance is understood within the practice. http://www.dancemeditation.org/events?view=detail&id=42.

9. "Humility . . . [i]s being willing to become a 'nobody[.]' This culture has taught us very specific definitions of independence, success, and ambition. Redefining these concepts can be a part [of] developing a new belief system that provides a foundation for our spiritual goals" (Klabunde 237).

10. For McPherson's image of skin as a membrane in sexual intimacy, see 187.

11. These two practices could be contextualized by other spiritualized dance or

music such as, for example, Wilbert Alix's "Trance Dance International" (www.trance dance.com/wilbertalix.do) and Gabrielle Roth's (d. 2012) 5 Rhythms Trance Dance (www.5rhythms.com).

12. See Roof.

13. Tam Tam Mandingue USA is a 501(c)(3) nonprofit organization and the worldwide headquarters of Tam Tam Mandingue international network of schools founded by Mamady Keita in 1991. See www.ttmusa.org.

14. www.engobeartstudio.com.

15. http://www.razoo.com/story/Dsa and https://www.facebook.com/Dancemeditation/info.

16. Pierre Bourdieu allows for agency in how people construct the world visions they carry out under the structural constraints of their histories, collective practices, and material forces conditioning what people take as "common sense" and constituting life praxis. See Bourdieu. Slingerland credits Bourdieu with taking seriously "prelinguistic, tacit forms of embodied knowledge that are more basic and pervasive than either abstract reason or explicit social discourse" (94). He finds in Bourdieu a similar limitation to that which I am identifying in performance studies: "The basic problem is that Bourdieu fails to really take embodiment seriously by allowing the body to play an *active* role in the structuring of human consciousness. For all his talk of the body, it is for him ultimately nothing more than a passive storehouse for socially constructed *habitus*." In short, Bourdieu merely extends mind as the tabula rasa waiting for inscription to the body-mind with agency to operate within social structures (94–95).

17. For Collective Awakening's classes, events, flyers, newsletters, instruments for sale, CDs, and mission, see http://www.collectiveawakening.us/. I have attended Collective Awakening classes, workshops, concerts, meditation sessions, and trance dance events in Tucson, Arizona, since 2008.

18. For 2012 flyers of events cited here, see http://www.collectiveawakening.us/index.php/events/private-events.

19. http://www.dancemeditation.org/about/dancemeditation.

20. http://blog.dancemeditation.org/.

21. For recent workshops, see the Events tab on the Dancemeditation website.

22. http://www.dancemeditation.org/training.

23. http://www.dancemeditation.org/events?view=detail&id=62.

24. http://www.dancemeditation.org/events?view=detail&id=44.

25. My discussion of these two books focuses on how a spiritual orientation alters the materially oriented paradigm of performativity, and will not cover the numerous and significant differences in the authors' formulations of spirituality and their spiritual practice. These are rich illustrations of how people develop spiritual lives in contemporary vernacular culture. Each warrants far more comprehensive interpretation than this chapter affords. A comparative study would be very useful as a model for refining a critical understanding of how people constitute and value spirituality as nonreligious

life praxis. A study of differences might analyze practices like Collective Awakening and Dancemeditation along axes such as the role of a master (as an internal sense, a spiritual guide, a human teacher); cosmologies and maps of the body; the intersection of spirituality with psychology (the dominant cultural paradigm for an inner life); "essence" as a sense of self and perception of universal principles; how the practices identify and subvert the perceived imperatives of Western culture (e.g., cultural normalization of "stress," "speed," "ego," "rational thinking," and "fragmentation" requiring a "holistic" approach to being human); the construction of hermeneutic narratives around illness or physical injury; what "healing" means and how it is accomplished; how spirituality is gendered in the discourses; how or if a spiritual practice speaks to the characteristic problems religion (evil, afterlife, beginning and end of the world, the existence of a deity); and the precise foundational principles a practice constitutes as spiritual knowledge. Other questions might address whether such spiritual practices begin to take on some of the defining characteristics of religion (e.g., organization, hierarchies, truth-claims) and can be considered new religious movements (as opposed to spirituality without religion).

26. Yoga Tree Studio, December 17, 2011, Tucson, AZ.

27. "We can infuse sound with our intentions of gratitude, compassion, forgiveness, humility and unconditional love. These are powerful tools that can heal and transform. This is sound with a soul!" (Klabunde 49).

28. Dunya Dianne McPherson, *Dancemeditation with Dunya: Sand Tracings I & II*, Dancemeditation, 2009, DVD.

29. This statement was given in response to a new student's comments on a winter weekend retreat at the Margaret Austin Center in Chappell Hill, Texas, which I attended in 2000. See http://www.dancemeditation.org/community/dunya/writings/32-heart-opening.

30. In this memory of leading a ten-day Winter Movement Monastery, McPherson describes how sensing the numinous is embodied and a particular kind of consciousness that is both individual and collective:

> I went into the circle to lead because no one else seemed to be catching on fire. At first neither did I. The suddenly I emptied into the risk of the Unknown. I found myself struggling to stop my mind from controlling the movements' progression. I focused instead on what was trying to come in. I was afraid of the Unknown. I might be too exposed, alone or abandoned; I didn't know if the group would journey with me; perhaps I hadn't prepared them sufficiently for this event. At length my mind stopped dithering.
>
> The unfolding was, in the initial stages, spinal vibration. I noticed its unkempt nature, not my usual up and down progression in a ladderly fashion. Motions eddied in one spot or another without proprioceptive logic. The movement mesh wasn't chaotic—it was a schizophrenic overlay. One part of the spine jerked and spat while another part careened like a cobra; sometimes the same area of the spine fought

> to express several conflicting patterns. I knew I had entered into the Room, the Moment, the Present—the place where the night could fulfill its purpose. We all participated consciously in the collective event directed by an over-arching cosmic source. (*Skin of Glass* 151)

31. Sacred Movement Arts Center, Paige, Texas, August 7, 2011.

32. For Klabunde's performance flyers see http://www.collectiveawakening.us/index.php/performance.

33. Yoga Tree Studio, December 16, 2011, Tucson, AZ.

34. Concert, December 16, 2011, Tucson, AZ.

35. For visuals of a previous Alembic performance and commentary, see http://blog.dancemeditation.org/2009/03/alembic-at-the-metro/.

36. See also http://www.dancemeditation.org/events?view=detail&id=42.

37. Reorienting performance theory to include people's sense of the numinous requires a shift in how we perceive performance as material, visible, and socially constructed. McPherson describes the experience of performing a solo concert in which her sense of spirituality orients her interaction with the materiality of performance (front stage and backstage, props, makeup, an observing audience). This orientation to performance is important to a wide range of contemporary vernacular practices and warrants consideration in its own terms:

> I move into the unconscious space outside the carpet border. I am a faceless everywoman. I pound against the wall, the wailing Wall, the Limits, the Edge. I whirl off the carpet into the eternal Cosmos. Returning to the carpet, I pace the parameters, crossing from corner to corner in steps and rhythms. The carpet is the known, seen life, the recognizable part of self. I stand in the center and vibrate while lines of gravity chart the planetary center, elliptically charging and discharging. Finally, I take my two veils, brilliant rainbows of color, and travel back and forth from carpet with its patterns of flue and red, to bare wood floor, weaving the worlds. . . . The threshold between the two worlds is both an impenetrable wall and a skin so sheer it cannot be seen or felt. I track back and forth over the doorsill, invisible strings flowing through my body, weaving skeins of the Real and the Apparent until they make one fabric. Later, while removing my make-up backstage, I see the residue of my dance in the mirror—my shining eyes. In the center of each blue iris is a thick golden drop, a honey tunnel to the Beloved. (McPherson, *Skin of Glass* 211)

38. Klabunde describes receiving and rejecting a record contract and listening to "inner wisdom for guidance and direction" (137). For the detailed narrative, see 134–35.

39. The sense that "all is one" comes up frequently in contemporary, vernacular spiritualities. This sense may be privileged because it fits well with liberal humanism's vision of a common humanity and the all-encompassing spiritual unity envisioned by Western monotheism. What is important here, I am suggesting, is not deconstructing the legacy to invalidate the sense or formulation of "oneness," but the fact that people cultivate and

value that particular sensibility as spiritual. From a Marxist perspective, practices that purportedly offer a view of "reality as it is" simply fetishize the construction of a different model of reality. See Frantisek Zizek on Western Buddhism as commodity fetishism, 13–16, especially 15.

40. It is worth noting that though both shamanism and Sufism are traditionally the province of male practitioners, Wing Man Law is a constant presence in Collective Awakening. Based on the accounts in *Skin of Glass*, McPherson's cohort in Adnan Sarhan's Sufi Camp was largely female, as are practitioners of Dancemeditation, based on observations of workshops, Alembic performances, and instructional materials.

41. The practices described in chapter 2 require sincerity in ritual, in contrast to the perspective taken by Adam Seligman in the essay "Ritual and Sincerity," which posits ritual as those performative cultural habits (including religion) that evacuate sincerity and to which sincerity poses an antidote.

42. For the importance of altered states of consciousness in shamanism, see Winkelman, "Cross-Cultural Assessments" 143–44. Winkelman discusses the centrality of visionary experiences in which people contact animal or human spirits and spirit worlds (often called soul journeys or mystic flights) to shamanic practices. Alternate states of consciousness in shamanism are "typified by the soul-flight experiences, involving natural symbolic systems for self-representation that are found cross-culturally in out-of-body and near-death experiences. The homologies reflect their innate basis in psychophysiological structures as forms of self-representation that are a natural response of the human nervous system" (Winkelman, "Cross-cultural Assessments" 151).

> British shaman Dr. Zoe Bran gave a first-person account of a shamanic out-of-body soul journey in an unpublished paper titled "Spirit and Shaman: Altered Consciousness and the Development of Creativity," at the University of Kent's 2011 conference, "Daimonic Imagination: Uncanny Intelligence." The last six minutes of the thirty-five-minute oral presentation were devoted to a recording of a shamanic journey experienced by the speaker. The entire presentation is available at http://www.youtube.com/watch?v=0ndIX_xBj0A. For Dr. Bran's description of shamanism, see http://www.youtube.com/watch?v=bmeHmb78VCI. Taking this presentation of shamanism as if it is informed by an orientation to, in Dr. Bran's words, "the nature of reality" rather than reading it as a performance immediately shifts perceptual possibilities.

43. For a review of the ways spirituality sits outside contemporary Western knowledge paradigms, see Huston Smith's chapter "Higher Education: Excluded Knowledge" in *Beyond the Postmodern Mind* 73–102.

Chapter 3

1. Playshop drumming workshop, Yoga Tree, Tucson, AZ, December 17, 2011.

2. Neurologically, religious experience and temporal lobe epilepsy are sometimes in-

distinguishable, to the extent that temporal lobe epilepsy has been cited as the neural substrate for mystical experiences. See Paloutzian, Swenson, and McNamara 155. See, in the same volume, Schachter. See also Beauregard.

3. Summarized in brief from McNamara's list, these properties are a sense of self-integration and oneness with others, transcendence of space and time, positive mood, the sense of the sacred, inner wisdom or insight, the capacity for holding opposing ideas, ineffable experiences, positive changes in behavior and attitudes, sense of personal power, enhanced mental and psychic abilities, changes in expressions of sexuality, an increase in reading and writing, increased sensitivity to music, increased sensitivity to visual images and metaphors, ritualization (as "the propensity to perform ritual actions *when religious experiences are heightened*" as distinct from performing empty habitual actions), and encounters with "God or spirit beings" (15–16). Each of these properties is evident in the practices discussed in chapter 2.

4. See Gallese, Eagel, and Migone.

5. Dissociation refers to experiences that are perceived as disconnected from culture, social roles, concepts of self, and cognitive frameworks organizing reality; a distinctly different kind of consciousness or perception; and the experience of an alternative mental schema for interpreting the world. See McClenon. Dissociative states can result from inhibitions of parts of the brain or neural networks that prevent coherent syntheses of information or sensations (deafferentation). See D'Aquili and Newberg 41–42.

6. A physicalist model takes spirituality as an emergent phenomenon with a "definite biology" that "serves some functional purpose for the individual." See McNamara 9, 10.

7. The perceptual capacities of the brain produce the spirit world. "The spirit world," Michael S.A. Graziano asserts, "by its very nature, by its dependence on social perceptual constructs, is a creation of the brain. It is a perceptual illusion" and "a natural extension of the way the human brain is wired" (50, 47).

8. Spirituality may not serve an evolutionary or adaptive function. "Even if there are clearly identifiable neurophysiological correlates or causes of a particular pattern of thought, emotion, or behavior," Lee A. Kirkpatrick asserts, "it does not follow that the function of the module is to produce those effects. Observed effects may well represent one or another sort of *by-product* of a system designed to do something else" (161).

9. The materialist perspective, as John R. Searle summarizes in his review of David J. Chalmers's *The Conscious Mind: In Search of a Fundamental Theory*, "is to say, yes, mental states really do exist, but they are not something in addition to physical phenomena; rather they can be reduced to, and are forms of, physical states."

10. "Cognitive scientists generally wish to uncover the neural and cognitive mechanisms that presumably subsume perception, thought, language, emotion, and consciousness" (Gibbs 39).

11. Carol Rausch Albright observes that "to identify mind with brain may seem threatening because it implies that our sense of self-determination is an illusion: if our neurons actually control us, then we do not really control ourselves. This belief has not

entirely disappeared, even within neuroscience, but is in fact a gross oversimplification of what goes on" (174). For a polemic against the threat of reducing human experience to neurology, see Tallis.

12. For this history, see Gutierrez.

13. For the role of emotion in religious experience at the level of the body, see Sachs Norris, "Religion, Neuroscience and Emotion."

14. See Taves, *Religious Experience Reconsidered*, 64–65 for the phenomenologically grounded approach in which "mind, experience, and language all arise through the interaction between brain, body, and world." As Gibbs observed in 2005, "Many philosophers and cognitive scientists now reject person-world dualism and advocate that persons be understood, and scientifically studied, in terms of organism-environment mutuality and reciprocity" (16).

15. Reviewing foundational early theories of embodied cognition by Mark Johnson, George Lakoff, and Antonio Damasio leads Slingerland to the conclusion that "there is strong evidence for the claim that sensory-motor patterns are cognitively active and being directly recruited—albeit perhaps in a 'bleached out' form—in the processing of conceptual metaphors," which guide feeling as well as perception and cognition. See Slingerland 173, 185. "Mind" can thus describe an expansive range of processes, not excluding those associated with spiritual experiences, but also not independent of physical bodies.

16. For summaries of Damasio's embodied emotions, thought, and self in earlier writings, see Gibbs 21; Slingerland 43–46. For Johnson's earlier writings, see Slingerland 162–66 and 170–74.

17. For how theater is a useful but limited metaphor for describing how the mind unifies and makes sense of internal sensations, sensory perceptions, and memories, see Baars 39–61.

18. For foundations in enactive cognition outside the Western tradition, see also Varela, Thompson, and Rosch 217–35.

19. For a summary of presentational and representational modalities of symbolic consciousness, including the sensorimotor-imagetic basis for symbolic cognition, as developed from George Lakoff and Mark Johnson in *Philosophy in the Flesh: The Embodied Mind and Its Challenge to Western Thought*, see Winkelman, *Shamanism* 38–45, and on mimesis, 45–47.

20. McNamara notes two particularly well-supported theories of the self in psychological literature: the self as a collection of schemas and the self as story (24).

21. McNamara argues "that religious practices help to build up a centralized executive Self by reducing the discrepancy between and ideal Self and the current Self." Decentering the self in spiritual practices, of which Collective Awakening and Dancemeditation could be examples, takes the volitional functions of the prefrontal cortex "'offline' out of working memory, for repair and construction." In this process, a person's "sense of agency or volition is inhibited," resulting in a sensation of being freed from the constraints of self-organization one has constructed (46).

22. Giordano and Engebretson note that "discontinuity in the coordination of the left and right medial temporal cortices may produce sensations of a physical (or nonphysical) 'presence' that, through concomitant amygdalar-hippocampal activation, is often cognitively conjoined to emotional and/or memory states and may be construed in personal (e.g., presence of relatives or conspecifics), cultural (e.g., presence of archetypal figures/characters), and /or religious (e.g., deific presence) contexts" (219).

23. Giordano and Engebretson note that a representational sense of self-awareness operates from the left temporal cortex, which is also the region from which communicative and primary linguistic capacities operate. Thus, neural connectivities across this region "may subserve both the ideative and communicative components of self-representation" (219).

24. McNamara suggests that "the most important regions of the brain for studies of religious expression appear to be a circuit linking up the orbital and dorsomedial prefrontal cortex, the right dorsolateral prefrontal cortex, the ascending serotoninergic systems, the mesocortical DA system, the amydgala/hippocampus, and the right anterior temporal lobes" (127).

25. Physical responses to music, from dancing to changes in heart rate or blood pressure, are also "mediated through the right hemisphere's vital connection with subcortical centres, with the hypothalamus, and with the body in general," according to Iain McGilchrist (73). This suggests the kind of overwhelming spiritual sensations Klabunde describes.

26. For a schematic overview of the neurological circuits associated with meditative states and spiritual experiences, noting initial activity in the right hemisphere, see Newberg, "Religious and Spiritual Practices" 15–31, 19, and "Neurobiology of Spiritual Experience" 191.

27. For shamanic visions, trances, and altered states as an integrated mode of consciousness, see Winkelman, "Cross-Cultural Assessments" 150–51.

28. Sebastian Schüler works through an integrated model of embodied experience without assuming religious experience as a cross-cultural phenomenon but acknowledging the somatic and cognitive processes.

29. Giordano and Engebretson note that the attentional capacities associated with spiritual experience and cultivated in these practices involve the prefrontal cortex, which suggests that the networks engaged both produce and facilitate cognitive awareness of spiritual experiences. That is, they engage "'top-down' physiological mechanisms." Such experiences may also involve sensory input (such as beating drums, handling a veil, inhaling the smoke of burning sage, feeling one's feet on the floor, etc.), which can "serve as 'bottom-up' body-brain/mind events" available to consciousness through attentional networks (218–19).

30. Chapter 1 addresses the production of knowledge schemas in the modern Western intellectual tradition that occlude or dismiss spirituality. For other ways spiritually oriented people parse their engagement with the natural and social worlds, the internal

processes of rational thought and cognition, and the physicality of the human body, see Wuthnow, *Creative Spirituality*, chapters 6 and 7.

31. The availability of neuroscience research has prompted a turn to the workings of the human brain in theater and performance studies. For the application of cognitive science to the interaction of body, mind, and culture in a spectator-performer model of performance, see McConachie. McConachie's important book takes theatrical performance as its starting point and examines theater through current research in cognitive science. This line of inquiry seeks to better understand the biological basis for theater (including memory, perception, emotion, and feeling). Using cognitive science in McConachie's study reinforces rather than challenges the performative model for interpretation or analysis of culture and behavior.

32. See Mason.

Chapter 4

1. For a summary of the literature on this perspective, see Aupers and Houtman.

2. See Adam Possamai on cultural appropriation of indigenous cultures, in *Religion and Popular Culture* 52–55.

3. On the political consequences of neopagan practitioners appropriating Native American ceremonies and the complexities of cultural strip-mining, see Pike, *Earthly Bodies* 134–35.

4. See Seligman, "Ritual and Sincerity" 125.

5. M. Jacqui Alexander notes that African cosmologies were subordinated to European systems of knowledge, which were derived from the synthesis of Neoplatonism with Christianity, distrust of the body, and reliance on symbols to signify a transcendent ideal. She writes,

> It is not that (post)modernity's avowed secularism has no room for the Sacred (witness the Bush administration's avid mobilization of faith-based initiatives in the service of renewing American imperialism), it is rather that it profits from a hierarchy that conflates Christianity with good tradition while consigning "others" to the realm of bad tradition and thus to serve as evidence of the need for good Christian tradition. (296)

6. For a lively assessment of this condition and how living in a performance-based culture affects the sense of self as always performing, which I suggest these spiritual practitioners resist in how they conceptualize their practices, see Zengotita.

7. For a critical analysis example on the performance of authenticity as affect, which could be applied to Collective Awakening's framed events, see Albrecht.

8. For the power, prevalence, and provenance of psychology as a popular discourse that constructs people's sense of self, identity, intimacy, and an inner life, in which vernacular spiritualities participate, see Illouz.

9. Cultivating an internal sensation of a spiritual self can also be a strategy for escaping the pressure of social self-presentation (Roof 58).

10. Klabunde related that drummers with whom he apprenticed in Uganda perceived the United States as a "sick" culture in need of healing in order to stop its political and economic incursions into Africa. They urged Klabunde to teach their drumming in the United States to bring about that healing. (Personal correspondence.)

11. Another perspective would be to see Western culture as constructing individual identities and blinded by individualism, unable to recognize something phenomenologically different from the self—a truly supernatural or transcendent Other. Seligman claims that to recognize the eternal, as these practices do, is also to recognize the constitutive role of expressive activities (the performative) in producing that other dimension. Here, the inner sense of a wholly other dimension to the material world, cultivated in practices like Dancemeditation and Collective Awakening, is a modern convention. Yet the *ways* these practices engage dance and music in service of a spiritual reality do recuperate for modern culture a sensibility too often denigrated as primitive:

> Thus we come to a paradox: that the same externality which, in the form of worldly existence, presents itself as chaos to be tamed and overcome is, in other forms—of transcendent God, supernatural deities, liberal morality, that which tames, mediates, and orders the contingencies of the world. Ritual systems, I contend, recognize this reality in ways that we moderns, with our purely internal systems of morality, do not. There adheres to the former an understanding that those dynamics through which a self is constructed exist in things done out-there, in the world. Instead, we denigrate such systems as primitive, as somewhat lower down on an imputed moral scale, and as stages on the way to our own developmental apex. (Seligman, *Modernity's Wager* 69)

12. For the physiology of spiritual transformation, see Andrew Newberg, "Neurobiology of Spiritual Transformation."

13. For how spirits sit in bodies across cultures, see Paul Christopher Johnson.

14. In the synthesis of African spiritualities with Christian monotheism in the United States, the Hebrews' narrative of enslavement and escape to a promised land evoked the theological narrative of crossing into liberation after death. This is another type of spiritual migration, in which African spiritualities fused with an eschatological vision of hope and transcending suffering.

15. Paradoxically, sacralizing the self often involves demonizing the very social and economic structures supporting the marketing and travel that sustains practitioners' lives and work. Aupers and Houtman understand this demonizing as evidence of an essentially dualistic worldview in which a spiritual life is the antidote to the mundane domain of a regimented work life (205). Yet as corporations incorporate quasi-spiritual practices, such as using Buddhist-inflected Mindfulness Based Stress Reduction to enhance efficiency and productivity, the cultural work of vernacular practices such as those

described in chapter 2 become increasingly mainstream. See Possamai, *Religion and Popular Culture*; Aupers and Houtman. As Mira Karjalainen suggests, in the process, "Some spiritual or physical aspects remain, while some get omitted or altered" (212).

16. See Bender.

17. The belief that the self itself is sacred "accounts for the remarkable diversity at the surface of the spiritual milieu—which is inevitable when people feel they need to follow their personal paths and explore what works for them personally—and at the same time provides ideological unity and coherence at a deeper level" (Aupers and Houtman 205).

18. See Rappaport's discussion of postmodern science and natural religion (456–59).

19. For a materialist perspective on religious or spiritual experience as emergent from social systems, see Boyer.

20. For the impulse to create certitude when the stable reference point of an originary moment slips away in religious and structuralist approaches to human experience, see Mark C. Taylor 304.

21. See Cabezón.

Chapter 5

1. McGilchrist, drawing on Lakoff and Johnson, notes "the flight of language from the enchantment of the body during the last hundred years" which in neurological terms he interprets as "part of a much broader revolt of the left hemisphere's way of conceiving the world against that of the right hemisphere" (120).

2. See Steven Pinker's argument in his popular book *The Blank Slate: The Modern Denial of Human Nature*. Chapter 12 concludes, "The view that humans are passive receptacles of stereotypes, words, and images is condescending to ordinary people and gives unearned importance to the pretensions of cultural and academic elites" (218).

Bibliography

Albrecht, Michael Mario. "Acting Naturally Unnaturally: The Performative Nature of Authenticity in Contemporary Popular Music." *Text and Performance Quarterly* 28.4 (2008): 379–95.

Albright, Carol Rausch. "Spiritual Growth, Cognition, and Complexity: Faith as a Dynamic Process." *Spiritual Transformation and Healing: Anthropological, Theological, Neuroscientific, and Clinical Perspectives*. Ed. Joan D. Koss-Chioino and Philip Hefner. Lanham, MD: Altamira, 2006. 168–87.

Alexander, M. Jacqui. *Pedagogies of Crossing: Meditations on Feminism, Sexual Politics, Memory, and the Sacred*. Durham: Duke UP, 2005.

Andrieu, Bernard. "Brains in the Flesh: Prospects for a Neurophenomenology." *Janus Head* 9.1 (2006): 135–55.

Armour, Ellen T., and Susan M. St. Ville, eds. *Bodily Citations: Religion and Judith Butler*. New York: Columbia UP, 2006.

Asad, Talal. *Formations of the Secular*. Stanford: Stanford UP, 2003.

Aupers, Stef, and Dick Houtman. "Beyond the Spiritual Supermarket: The Social and Public Significance of New Age Spirituality." *Journal of Contemporary Religion* 21.2 (May 2006): 201–22.

Auslander, Philip. *Performance: Critical Concepts in Literary and Cultural Studies*. London: Routledge, 2003.

Azari, Nina P. "Religious Experience as Thinking That Feels Like Something: A Philosophical-Theological Reflection on Recent Neuroscientific Study of Religious Experience." Diss., University of Denver, June 2004.

Baars, Bernard J. *In the Theater of Consciousness: The Workspace of the Mind.* Oxford: Oxford UP, 1997.

Barnard, G. William. "Explaining the Unexplainable: Wayne Proudfoot's 'Religious Experience.'" *Journal of the American Academy of Religion* 60.2 (Summer 1992): 231–56.

Barthes, Roland. *Mythologies: The Complete Edition in a New Translation.* Trans. Richard Howard and Anne Lavers. New York: Hill and Wang, 2012.

Barua, Archana. *Phenomenology of Religion.* Lanham, MD: Lexington Books, 2009.

Bauman, Richard. "Performance." *Folklore, Cultural Performance, and Popular Entertainment: A Communications-Centered Handbook.* Ed. Richard Bauman. Oxford: Oxford UP, 1991. 40–49.

Beauregard, Mario. "Neuroscience and Spirituality." *Neuroscience, Consciousness and Spirituality.* Ed. Harald Walach, Stefan Schmidt, and Wayne B. Jonas. New York: Springer, 2011. 57–73.

Bell, Catherine. *Ritual: Perspectives and Dimensions.* Oxford: Oxford UP, 1997.

Bender, Courtney. *The New Metaphysicals: Spirituality and the American Religious Imagination.* Chicago: U of Chicago P, 2010.

Bender, Courtney, and Omar McRoberts. "Mapping a Field: Why and How to Study Spirituality." Social Science Research Council Working Paper. October 2012.

Bender, Courtney, and Ann Taves, eds. "Introduction: Things of Value." *What Matters? Ethnographies of Value in a Not So Secular Age.* New York: Columbia UP, 2012. 1–33.

Bering, Jesse M. "The Cognitive Psychology of Belief in the Supernatural." *Where God and Science Meet: How Brain and Evolutionary Studies Alter Our Understanding of Religion.* Ed. Patrick McNamara. Vol. 1. Westport, CT: Praeger, 2006. 123–33.

Besecke, Kelly. "Seeing Invisible Religion: Religion as a Societal Conversation about Transcendent Meaning." *Religions of Modernity: Relocating the Sacred to the Self and the Digital.* Ed. Stef Aupers and Dick Houtman. Boston: Brill, 2010. 89–114.

Besecke, Kelly. *You Can't Put God in a Box.* Oxford: Oxford UP, 2014.

Blanke, Olaf, and Christine Mohr. "Out of Body Experiences, Heautoscopy, and Autoscopic Hallucination of Neurological Origin: Implications for Neurocognitive Mechanisms of Corporeal Awareness and Self-Consciousness." *Brain Research Reviews* 50.1 (2005): 184–99.

Borg, Jacqueline, Bengt Andrée, Lars Farde, and Henrik Soderstrom. "The

Serotonin System and Spiritual Experiences." *American Journal of Psychiatry* 160.11 (2003): 1965–69.

Bourdieu, Pierre. *The Logic of Practice*. Trans. Richard Nice. Stanford: Stanford UP, 1990.

Boyer, Pascal. *Religion Explained: The Evolutionary Origins of Religious Thought*. New York: Basic, 2001.

Bran, Zoe. "Spirit and Shaman: Altered Consciousness and the Development of Creativity." Presentation to the conference "Daimonic Imagination: Uncanny Intelligence." University of Kent, May 11, 2011.

Burns, Charlene P. E. "Cognitive Science and Christian Theology." *Soul, Psyche, Brain: New Directions in the Study of Religion and Brain-Mind Science*. Ed. Kelly Bulkeley. New York: Palgrave Macmillan, 2005. 174–96.

Cabezón, José Ignacio. "The Discipline and Its Other: The Dialectic of Alterity in the Study of Religion." *Journal of the American Academy of Religion* 74:1 (2006): 21–38.

Campbell, Colin. *The Easternization of the West: A Thematic Account of Cultural Change in the Modern Era*. London: Paradigm, 2007.

Carlson, Marvin. *Performance: A Critical Introduction*. 2nd ed. London: Routledge, 2004.

Carrette, Jeremy, and Richard King. *Selling Spirituality: The Silent Takeover of Religion*. London: Routledge, 2005.

Carroll, Robert. "Pranks, Frauds, and Hoaxes from Around the World." *Skeptical Inquirer* 28.4 (2004): 41–46.

Cave, David, and Rebecca Sachs Norris. *Religion and the Body: Modern Science and the Construction of Religious Meaning*. Leiden: Brill, 2012.

Certeau, Michel de. *The Mystic Fable: The Sixteenth and Seventeenth Centuries*. Trans. Michael B. Smith. Vol. 1. Chicago: U of Chicago P, 1992.

Chalmers, David. "Facing Up to the Problem of Consciousness." *Journal of Consciousness Studies* 2.3 (1995): 200–219.

Clarke, Isabel, ed. *Psychosis and Spirituality: Consolidating the New Paradigm*. Chichester, Sussex: John Wiley, 2010.

Clough, Patricia. *The Affective Turn: Theorizing the Social*. Durham: Duke UP, 2007.

Conquergood, Dwight. "Performance Studies: Interventions and Radical Research 1." *TDR* 46.2 (2002): 145–56.

Crick, Francis, and Christof Koch. "The Unconscious Homunculus." *The Neuronal Correlates of Consciousness*. Ed. T. Metzinger. Cambridge, MA: MIT P, 2000. 103–10.

Csordas, Thomas. *Body, Meaning, Healing.* New York: Palgrave Macmillan, 2002.

D'Aquili, Eugene, and Andrew B. Newberg. *The Mystical Mind: Probing the Biology of Religious Experience.* Minneapolis: Fortress, 1999.

Damasio, Antonio. *The Feeling of What Happens: Body and Emotion in the Making of Consciousness.* Orlando, FL: Mariner Books, 2000.

Dein, Simon. "Religious Experience: Perspectives and Research Paradigms." *World Cultural Psychiatry Research Review* 6.1 (2011): 3–9.

Demastes, William W. *Staging Consciousness: Theatre and the Materialization of the Mind.* Ann Arbor: U of Michigan P, 2002.

Derrida, Jacques. *Spectres of Marx: The State of Debt, the Work of Mourning, and the New International.* London: Routledge, 2006.

Desjarlais, Robert R. "Presence." *The Performance of Healing.* Ed. Carol Laderman and Marina Roseman. London: Routledge, 1996. 143–64.

Dolan, Jill. *Utopia in Performance: Finding Hope in the Theatre.* Ann Arbor: U of Michigan P, 2005.

Donaldson, Laura E. "On Medicine Women and White Shame-Ans: New Age Native Americanism and Commodity Fetishism as Pop Culture Feminism." *Signs* 24.3 (1999): 677–96.

Douglas-Klotz, Neil. "Missing Stories: Psychosis, Spirituality and the Development of Western Religious Hermeneutics." *Psychosis and Spirituality: Consolidating the New Paradigm.* Ed. Isabel Clarke. Chichester, Sussex: Wiley-Blackwell, 2010. 49–62.

Dox, Donnalee. "The Willing Sustenance of Belief: Religiosity and Mode of Performance." *Journal of Religion and Theatre* 8.1 (2009): 20–47.

Durkheim, Emile. *Elementary Forms of Religious Life.* New York: Oxford UP, 2001.

Egginton, William. *How the World Became a Stage.* Albany: SUNY P, 2003.

Ehrenreich, Barbara. *Living with a Wild God: A Nonbeliever's Search for the Truth about Everything.* New York: Twelve, 2014.

Ferrer, Jorge N. "Spiritual Knowing as Participatory Enaction: An Answer to the Question of Religious Pluralism." *The Participatory Turn: Spirituality, Mysticism, Religious Studies.* Ed. Jorge N. Ferrer and Jacob H. Sherman. Albany: SUNY P, 2008. 135–69.

Ferrer, Jorge N., and Jacob H. Sherman, eds. *The Participatory Turn: Spirituality, Mysticism, Religious Studies.* Albany: SUNY P, 2008.

Fletcher, John. *Preaching to Convert.* Ann Arbor: U of Michigan P, 2013.

Fraleigh, Sondra. *Dancing Identity: Metaphysics in Motion.* Pittsburgh: U of Pittsburgh P, 2004.

Freud, Sigmund. *Civilization and Its Discontents*. Trans. James Strachey. New York: Norton, 2005.

Gallese, Vittorio, Morris N. Eagel, and Paolo Migone. "Intentional Attunement: Mirror Neurons and the Neural Underpinnings of Interpersonal Relations." *Journal of the American Psychoanalytic Association* 55.1 (2007): 131–75.

Geurts, Kathryn Linn. *Culture and the Senses: Bodily Ways of Knowing in an African Community*. Berkeley: U of California P, 2002.

Gibbs, Raymond. *Embodiment and Cognitive Science*. Cambridge: Cambridge UP, 2005.

Giordano, James, and Joan Engebretson. "Neural and Cognitive Basis of Spiritual Experience: Biopsychosocial and Ethical Implications for Clinical Medicine." *Explore* 2.3 (2006): 216–25.

Gran, Anne-Britt. "The Fall of Theatricality in the Age of Modernity." *SubStance* 31.2–3 (2002): 251–64.

Graziano, Michael S. A. *God, Soul, Mind, Brain: A Neuroscientist's Reflections on the Spirit World*. Teaticket, MA: Leapfrog, 2010.

Grimes, Ronald L. "Religion, Ritual and Performance." In Religion, Theatre, and Performance: Acts of Faith. Ed. Lance Gharavi. New York: Routledge, 2012. 27–41.

Gutierrez, Cathy. "Spiritualism and Psychical Research." *Handbook of Religion and the Authority of Science*. Ed. James R. Lewis and Olav Hammer. Boston: Brill, 2011. 591–608.

Hammer, Olav. "I Did It My Way? Individual Choice and Social Conformity in New Age Religion." *Religions of Modernity: Relocating the Sacred to the Self and the Digital*. Ed. Stef Aupers and Dick Houtman. Leiden: Brill, 2010. 49–67.

Harner, Michael. *The Way of the Shaman*. 1980. New York: HarperCollins, 1990.

Harris, Sam. *Waking Up: A Guide to Spirituality without Religion*. New York: Simon and Schuster, 2014.

Hay, David. *Why Spirituality Is Difficult for Westerners*. Charlottesville, VA: Societas Essays in Political and Cultural Criticism, 2007.

Heelas, Paul. "On Making Sense of Spirituality." *Spirituality in the Modern World: Within Religious Tradition and Beyond*. Ed. Paul Heelas. Vol. 1. New York: Routledge, 2012.

Heelas, Paul. *Spiritualities of Life: New Age Romanticism and Consumptive Capitalism*. Oxford: Blackwell, 2004.

Heelas, Paul, and Linda Woodhead. *The Spiritual Revolution: Why Religion Is Giving Way to Spirituality*. Oxford: Blackwell, 2005.

Hefner, Philip. "Spiritual Transformation and Healing: An Encounter with the Sacred." *Spiritual Transformation and Healing: Anthropological, Theological, Neuroscientific, and Clinical Perspectives*. Ed. Joan D. Koss-Chioino and Philip Hefner. Lanham, MD: Altamira, 2006. 119–33.

Helmreich, Sefan. "Intimate Sensing." *Simulation and Its Discontents*. Ed. Sherry Turkle. Cambridge, MA: MIT P, 2009. 129–50.

Hogue, David Allen. "Healing of the Self-in-Contexts: Memory, Plasticity, and Spiritual Practice." *Spiritual Transformation and Healing: Anthropological, Theological, Neuroscientific, and Clinical Perspectives*. Ed. Joan D. Koss-Chioino and Philip Hefner. Lanham, MD: Altamira, 2006. 223–38.

Hood, Ralph W., Jr. "Mystical, Spiritual, and Religious Experiences." *Handbook of the Psychology of Religion and Spirituality*. Ed. Raymond F. Paloutzian and Crystal L. Park. New York: The Guilford, 2005. 348–64.

Hufford, David J., and Mary Ann Bucklin. "The Spirit of Spiritual Healing in the United States." *Spiritual Transformation and Healing: Anthropological, Theological, Neuroscientific, and Clinical Perspectives*. Ed. Joan D. Koss-Chioino and Philip Hefner. Lanham, MD: Altamira, 2006. 25–42.

Hurlburt, Russell T., and Eric Schwitzgebel. *Describing Inner Experience? Proponent Meets Skeptic*. Cambridge, MA: MIT P, 2007.

Illouz, Eva. *Saving the Modern Soul: Therapy, Emotions, and the Culture of Self-Help*. Berkeley: U of California P, 2008.

Irwin, Lee. "Esoteric Paradigms and Participatory Spirituality in the Teachings of Mikhael Aivanhov." *The Participatory Turn: Spirituality, Mysticism, Religious Studies*. Ed. Jorge N. Ferrer and Jacob H. Sherman. Albany: SUNY P, 2008. 197–224.

Iwamura, Jane Naomi. *Virtual Orientalism: Asian Religions and American Popular Culture*. New York: Oxford UP, 2010.

James, William. *The Varieties of Religious Experience*. Boston: Bedford / St. Martins, 2012.

Jay, Martin. *Songs of Experience*. Berkeley: U of California P, 2005.

Johnson, Mark. *The Meaning of the Body: Aesthetics of Human Understanding*. Chicago: U of Chicago P, 1999.

Johnson, Paul Christopher. "An Atlantic Genealogy of 'Spirit Possession.'" *Comparative Studies in Society and History* 53.2 (2011): 393–425.

Kandinsky, Wassily. *Concerning the Spiritual in Art*. 1911. Trans. M. T. H. Sadler. Mineola, NY: Dover, 1977.

Karjalainen, Mira. "Scientific Approaches to the Body in the Spiritual-

Physical Marketplace." *Religion and the Body: Modern Science and the Construction of Religious Meaning.* Ed. David Caves and Rebecca Sachs Norris. Leiden and Boston: Brill, 2012. 199–216.

Katz, Stephen T. "Language, Epistemology, and Mysticism." *Mysticism and Philosophical Analysis.* London: Shelby, 1978. 22–74.

Kirkpatrick, Lee A. "Religion Is Not an Adaptation." *Where God and Science Meet: How Brain and Evolutionary Studies Alter Our Understanding of Religion.* Ed. Patrick McNamara. Vol. 1. Westport, CT: Praeger, 2006. 159–79.

Klabunde, Martin. *Music as Medicine: Accessing Sacred Wisdom from the Master Within.* Collective Awakening, 2011.

Kripal, Jeffrey J. "Mind Matters: Esalen's Sursem Group and the Ethnography of Consciousness." *What Matters? Ethnographies of Value in a Not So Secular Age.* Ed. Courtney Bender and Ann Taves. New York: Columbia UP, 2012. 215–47.

Kripal, Jeffrey J. *The Serpent's Gift: Gnostic Reflections on the Study of Religion.* Chicago: U of Chicago P, 2007.

Kubiak, Anthony. "Virtual Faith." *Theatre Survey* 47.2 (2006): 271–76.

Lakoff, George, and Mark Johnson. *Philosophy in the Flesh: The Embodied Mind and Its Challenge to Western Thought.* New York: Basic Books, 1999.

LaMothe, Kimerer. *Between Dancing and Writing: The Practice of Religious Studies.* New York: Fordham UP, 2004.

LaMothe, Kimerer. "What Bodies Know about Religion and the Study of It." *Journal of the American Academy of Religion* 76.3 (2008): 573–601.

Lancaster, B. Les. "Cognitive Neuroscience, Spirituality and Mysticism: Recent Developments." *Psychosis and Spirituality.* Ed. Isabel Clarke. Chichester, West Sussex: Wiley-Blackwell, 2010.

Langer, Suzanne K. *Feeling and Form: A Theory of Art.* New York: Scribner, 1953.

Latour, Bruno. *We Have Never Been Modern.* Trans. Catherine Porter. Cambridge, MA: Harvard UP, 1993.

Luhrmann, Tanya. *When God Talks Back: Understanding the American Evangelical Relationship with God.* New York: Vintage Books, 2012.

Lyons, William. *The Disappearance of Introspection.* Cambridge, MA: MIT P, 1986.

Lyotard, Jean-François. *The Postmodern Condition: A Report on Knowledge.* Trans. Geoff Bennington. Minneapolis: U Minnesota P, 1984.

Mason, David V. *Theatre and Religion on Krishna's Stage: Performing in Vrindavan.* New York: Palgrave Macmillan, 2009.

McCarthy, E. Doyle. "Emotional Performances as Dramas of Authenticity." *Authenticity in Culture, Self, and Society*. Ed. Phillip Vannini and J. Patrick Williams. Surrey, UK: Ashgate, 2009. 241–56.

McClenon, James. "The Ritual Healing Theory: Therapeutic Suggestion and the Origin of Religion." *Where God and Science Meet: How Brain and Evolutionary Studies Alter Our Understanding of Religion*. Ed. Patrick McNamara. Vol. 1. Westport, CT: Praeger, 2006. 135–58.

McConachie, Bruce. *Theatre and Mind*. New York: Palgrave Macmillan, 2013.

McGilchrist, Iain. *The Master and His Emissary: The Divided Brain and the Making of the Modern World*. New Haven: Yale UP, 2009.

McGuire, Meredith B. *Lived Religion: Faith and Practice in Everyday Life*. Oxford: Oxford UP, 2008.

McKenzie, Jon. *Perform or Else: From Discipline to Performance*. New York: Routledge, 2001.

McNamara, Patrick. *The Neuroscience of Religious Experience*. Cambridge: Cambridge UP, 2009.

McPherson, Dunya Dianne. *Dancemeditation with Dunya: Sand Tracings I & II*. Dancemeditation. 2009. DVD.

McPherson, Dunya Dianne. *Skin of Glass: Finding Spirit in the Flesh*. Dancemeditation Books, 2008.

Mercadante, Linda A. *Belief without Borders: Inside the Minds of the Spiritual but Not Religious*. Oxford: Oxford UP, 2014.

Merleau-Ponty, Maurice. *Visible and Invisible*. Trans. Alphonso Lingis. Evanston, IL: Northwestern UP, 1968.

Meyer, Birgit. "Religious and Secular, 'Spiritual' and 'Physical' in Ghana." *What Matters? Ethnographies of Value in a Not So Secular Age*. Ed. Courtney Bender and Ann Taves. New York: Columbia UP, 2012. 87–118.

Meyer-Dinkgrafe, Daniel. *Theatre and Consciousness: Explanatory Scope and Future Potential*. Bristol, UK: Intellect Books, 2005.

Middleton, Deborah, and Franc Chamberlain. "Entering the Heart of Experience: First Person Accounts in Performance and Spirituality." *Performance and Spirituality* 3.1 (2012): 95–112.

Miller, J. Hillis. "The Material Working of Spirit." *Material Spirit: Religion and Literature Intranscendent*. Ed. Gregory C. Stallings, Manuel Asensi, and Carl Good. New York: Fordham UP, 2014. 154–74.

Miller, Lisa, and Brien S. Kelly. "Relationships of Religiosity and Spirituality with Mental Health and Psychopathology." *Handbook of the Psychol-*

ogy of Religion and Spirituality. Ed. Raymond F. Paloutzian and Crystal L. Park. New York: The Guilford, 2005. 460–78.

Mrozik, Susanne. "Materializations of Virtue: Buddhist Discourses on Bodies." *Bodily Citations: Religion and Judith Butler*. Ed. Ellen T. Armour and Susan M. St. Ville. New York: Columbia UP, 2006. 15–47.

Nabhan-Warren, Kristy. "Embodied Research and Writing: A Case for Phenomenologically Oriented Religious Studies Ethnographies." *Journal of the American Academy of Religion* 9.2 (2011): 378–407.

Nancy, Jean-Luc. *Corpus*. Trans. Richard A. Rand. New York: Fordham UP, 2008.

Newberg, Andrew. *Principles of Neurotheology*. Surrey, UK: Ashgate, 2010.

Newberg, Andrew. "The Neurobiology of Spiritual Transformation." *Spiritual Transformation and Healing: Anthropological, Theological, Neuroscientific, and Clinical Perspectives*. Ed. Joan D. Koss-Chioino and Philip Hefner. Lanham, MD: Altamira, 2006. 189–205.

Newberg, Andrew. "Religious and Spiritual Practices: A Neurochemical Perspective." *Where God and Science Meet: How Brain and Evolutionary Studies Alter Our Understanding of Religion*. Ed. Patrick McNamara. Vol. 2. Westport, CT: Praeger, 2006. 15–31.

Noë, Alva. *Action in Perception*. Cambridge, MA: MIT P, 2006.

Noë, Alva. *Varieties of Presence*. Cambridge, MA: Harvard UP, 2012.

Orsi, Robert. *Between Heaven and Earth: The Religious Worlds People Make and the Scholars Who Study Them*. Princeton: Princeton UP, 2004.

Paloutzian, Raymond F., Erica L. Swenson, and Patrick McNamara. "Religious Conversion, Spiritual Transformation, and the Neurocognition of Meaning Making." *Where God and Science Meet: How Brain and Evolutionary Studies Alter Our Understanding of Religion*. Ed. Patrick McNamara. Vol. 2. Westport, CT: Praeger, 2006. 151–69.

Pargament, Kenneth I. "The Meaning of Spiritual Transformation." *Spiritual Transformation and Healing: Anthropological, Theological, Neuroscientific, and Clinical Perspectives*. Ed. Joan D. Koss-Chioino and Philip Hefner. Lanham, MD: Altamira, 2006. 10–24.

Partridge, Christopher. *The Re-enchantment of the West*. 2 vols. New York: T&T Clark International, 2004.

Peters, Karl E. "Spiritual Transformation and Healing in Light of Evolutionary Theology." *Spiritual Transformation and Healing: Anthropological, Theological, Neuroscientific, and Clinical Perspectives*. Ed. Joan D. Koss-Chioino and Philip Hefner. Lanham, MD: Altamira, 2006. 134–51.

Pike, Sarah M. *New Age and Neopagan Religions in America*. New York: Columbia UP, 2004.

Pike, Sarah M. *Earthly Bodies, Magical Selves: Contemporary Pagans and the Search for Community*. Berkeley: U of California P, 2001.

Pinker, Steven. *The Blank Slate: The Modern Denial of Human Nature*. New York: Penguin, 2002.

Porter, Jennifer. "Implicit Religion in Popular Culture: The Religious Dimensions of Fan Communities." *Implicit Religion* 12.3 (2009): 271–80.

Possamai, Adam. "Alternative Spiritualities and the Cultural Logic of Late Capitalism." *Culture and Religion* 4.1 (2003): 31–45.

Possamai, Adam. *Religion and Popular Culture: A Hyper-real Testament*. Brussels: Peter Lange, Editions Scientifiques Universitaires, 2005.

Powell, Benjamin D., and Tracy Stephenson Shaffer. "On the Haunting of Performance Studies." *Liminalities* 5.1 (April 2009): 1–19.

Power, Cormac. *Presence in Play: A Critique of Theories of Presence in the Theatre*. New York: Rodopi, 2008.

Proudfoot, Wayne. *Religious Experience*. Berkeley: U of California P, 1985.

Rappaport, Roy A. "Religious Experience, and the Numinous in William James, Rudolf Otto, and Emile Durkheim." *Ritual and Religion in the Making of Humanity*. Cambridge: Cambridge UP, 1999. 374–80.

Reinelt, Janelle. "The Politics of Discourse: Performativity Meets Theatricality." *SubStance* 31.2–3 (2002): 201–15.

Robinson, Marilynne. *Absence of Mind: The Dispelling of Inwardness from the Modern Myth of the Self*. New Haven: Yale UP, 2010.

Rolston, Holmes III. "Genes, Brains, Minds: The Human Complex." *Soul, Psyche, Brain: New Directions in the Study of Religion and Brain-Mind Science*. Ed. Kelly Bulkeley. New York: Palgrave Macmillan, 2005. 10–35.

Roof, Wade Clark. *Spiritual Marketplace: Baby Boomers and the Remaking of American Religion*. Princeton: Princeton UP, 1999.

Rothenberg, Molly Anne. "Embodied Political Performativity in Excitable Speech: Butler's Psychoanalytic Revision of Historicism." *Theory, Culture & Society* 23.4 (2006): 71–93.

Sachs Norris, Rebecca. "Examining the Structure and Role of Emotion: Contributions of Neurobiology to the Study of Embodied Religious Experience." *Zygon* 40.1 (2005): 181–99.

Sachs Norris, Rebecca. "Religion, Neuroscience and Emotion." *Religion and the Body: Modern Science and the Construction of Religious Meaning*. Ed. David Cave and Rebecca Sachs Norris. Boston: Brill, 2012. 105–28.

Schachter, Steven C. "Religion and the Brain: Evidence from Temporal Lobe Epilepsy." *Where God and Science Meet: How Brain and Evolutionary Studies Alter Our Understanding of Religion*. Ed. Patrick McNamara. Vol. 2. Westport, CT: Praeger, 2006. 171–88.

Schechner, Richard. *Between Theater and Anthropology*. Philadelphia: U of Pennsylvania P, 1985.

Schechner, Richard. *Performance Studies: An Introduction*. New York: Routledge, 2002.

Schechner, Richard. "Living a Double Consciousness." *Teaching Ritual*. Ed. Catherine Bell. Oxford: Oxford UP, 2007. 15–28.

Schechner, Richard. "Restoration of Behavior." *Readings in Ritual Studies*. Ed. Ronald L. Grimes. Upper Saddle River, NJ: Prentice Hall, 1996. 441–57.

Schieffelin, Edward. "On Failure and Performance: Throwing the Medium Out of the Seance." *The Performance of Healing*. Ed. Carol Laderman and Marina Roseman. London: Routledge, 1996. 59–89.

Schneider, Rebecca. "'Judith Butler' in My Hands." *Bodily Citations: Religion and Judith Butler*. Ed. Ellen T. Armour and Susan M. St. Ville. New York: Columbia UP, 2006. 225–51.

Schüler, Sebastian. "Synchronized Ritual Behavior: Religion, Cognition and the Dynamics of Embodiment." *Religion and the Body: Modern Science and the Construction of Religious Meaning*. Ed. David Cave and Rebecca Sachs Norris. Boston: Brill, 2012. 81–101.

Scott, Rachelle M. *Nirvana for Sale? Buddhism, Wealth, and the Dhammakaya Temple in Contemporary Thailand*. Albany: SUNY P, 2009.

Searle, John R. "'Consciousness and the Philosophers': An Exchange." *New York Review of Books*, March 6, 1997.

Seaquist, Carl. "Mind Design and the Capacity for Ritual Performance." *Where God and Science Meet: How Brain and Evolutionary Studies Alter Our Understanding of Religion*. Ed. Patrick McNamara. Vol. 2. Westport, CT: Praeger, 2006. 205–28.

Seligman, Adam B. "Modernity and Sincerity: Problem and Paradox." *Hedgehog Review* 12.1 (2010): 53–61.

Seligman, Adam B. *Modernity's Wager: Authority, the Self, and Transcendence*. Princeton: Princeton UP, 2000.

Seligman, Adam B. "Ritual and Sincerity." *Ritual and Its Consequences: An Essay on the Limits of Sincerity*. By Adam B. Seligman, Robert P. Weller, Michael J. Puett, and Bennett Simon. Oxford: Oxford UP, 2008. 103–30.

Sheets-Johnstone, Maxine. *The Corporeal Turn: An Interdisciplinary Reader.* Exeter: Imprint Academic, 2009.

Slingerland, Edward. *What Science Offers the Humanities: Integrating Body and Culture.* Cambridge: Cambridge UP, 2008.

Smart, Ninian. "Understanding Religious Experience." *Mysticism and Philosophical Analysis.* Ed. Steven T. Katz. London: Sheldon, 1978. 10–21.

Smith, Barbara Herrnstein. *Natural Reflections: Human Cognition at the Nexus of Science and Religion.* New Haven: Yale UP, 2009.

Smith, Huston. *Beyond the Postmodern Mind: The Place of Meaning in a Global Civilization.* Wheaton, IL: Theosophical Publishing House, 2003.

Smith, Huston. *Why Religion Matters: The Fate of the Human Spirit in an Age of Disbelief.* New York: HarperOne, 2001.

Smith, Linda Tuhiwai. *Decolonizing Methodologies: Research and Indigenous Peoples.* London: Zed Books; Dunedin, New Zealand: U of Otago P, 1999.

Smith, Steve. "Muslim Troupe Arrives with Splash and Age-Old Ecumenical Traditions." *New York Times*, November 24, 2010.

Smith, Steven D. *The Disenchantment of Secular Discourse.* Cambridge, MA: Harvard UP, 2010.

Sofer, Andrew. "Spectral Readings." *Theatre Journal* 64 (2012): 323–36.

Somé, Malidoma Patrice. *Ritual: Power, Healing, and Community.* New York: Penguin, 1993.

Spezio, Michael L. "Narrative in Holistic Healing: Empathy, Sympathy, and Simulation Theory." *Spiritual Transformation and Healing: Anthropological, Theological, Neuroscientific, and Clinical Perspectives.* Ed. Joan D. Koss-Chioino and Philip Hefner. Lanham, MD: Altamira, 2006. 206–22.

Stevenson, Jill. *Sensational Devotion: Evangelical Performance in Twenty-First Century America.* Ann Arbor: U of Michigan P, 2013.

Tacey, David. *The Spirituality Revolution: The Emergence of Contemporary Spirituality.* London: Routledge, 2004.

Tallis, Raymond. *Aping Mankind.* Durham, UK: Acumen, 2011.

Taves, Ann. *Fits, Trances, and Visions: Experiencing Religion and Explaining Experience from Wesley to James.* Princeton: Princeton UP, 1999.

Taves, Ann. *Religious Experience Reconsidered: A Building-Block Approach to the Study of Religion and Other Special Things.* Princeton: Princeton UP, 2009.

Taylor, Charles. *A Secular Age.* Cambridge, MA: Belknap Press of Harvard UP, 2007.

Taylor, Mark C. *After God*. Chicago: U of Chicago P, 2007.

ter Borg, Meerten. "Non-institutional Religion in Modern Society." *Implicit Religion* 10.5 (2008): 127–41.

Thompson, Grahame F. "Approaches to 'Performance': An Analysis of Terms." *Screen* 26.5 (1985): 78–90.

Turner, Edith. *Experiencing Ritual: A New Interpretation of African Healing*. Philadelphia: U of Pennsylvania P, 1992.

Turner, Jane. "Embodiment, Balinese Dance Theatre, and the Ethnographer's Predicament." *Performance and Spirituality* 2.1 (2011): 60–84.

Tweed, Thomas A. *Crossing and Dwelling: A Theory of Religion*. Cambridge, MA: Harvard UP, 2006.

Vannini, Phillip, and J. Patrick Williams. "Authenticity in Culture, Self, and Society." *Authenticity in Culture, Self, and Society*. Ed. Phillip Vannini and J. Patrick Williams. Surrey, England: Ashgate, 2009. 1–20.

Varela, Francisco J., Evan Thompson, and Eleanor Rosch. *The Embodied Mind: Cognitive Science and Human Experience*. Cambridge, MA: MIT P, 1993.

Wakin, Daniel J. "Lincoln Center Fall Festival to Focus on the Spiritual." *New York Times*, May 13, 2010.

Wakin, Daniel J. "'White Light': Is It Driven by the Soul or by Sales?" *New York Times*, November 23, 2010.

Wallace, B. Alan. *The Taboo of Subjectivity: Toward a New Science of Consciousness*. New York: Oxford UP, 2000.

Washburn, Michael. *Embodied Spirituality in a Sacred World*. Albany: SUNY P, 2003.

Weber, Max. *The Protestant Ethic and the Spirit of Capitalism*. Trans. Talcott Parsons. New York, Scribner, 1930.

Weiskopf, Jimmy. *Yaje: The New Purgatory*. Bogata, Colombia: Villegas Editores, 2004.

Winkelman, Michael. "Cross-Cultural Assessments of Shamanism." *Where God and Science Meet: How Brain and Evolutionary Studies Alter Our Understanding of Religion*. Ed. Patrick McNamara. Vol. 3. Westport, CT: Praeger, 2006. 140–59.

Winkelman, Michael. *Shamanism: The Neural Ecology of Consciousness and Healing*. Westport, CT: Bergin and Garvey, 2000.

Wuthnow, Robert. *Creative Spirituality: The Way of the Artist*. Berkeley: U of California P, 2001.

Wuthnow, Robert. *After the Baby Boomers: How Twenty- and Thirty-*

Somethings Are Shaping the Future of American Religion. Princeton: Princeton UP, 2007.

Yarrow, Ralph, ed. *Sacred Theatre.* Bristol, UK: Intellect Books, 2007.

Zarrilli, Phillip. *Psychophysical Acting.* New York: Routledge, 2009.

Zengotita, Thomas de. *Mediated: How the Media Shapes Your World and the Way You Live in It.* New York: Bloomsbury, 2006.

Zinnbauer, Brian J., and Kenneth I. Pargament. "Religiousness and Spirituality." *Handbook of the Psychology of Religion and Spirituality.* Ed. Raymond F. Paloutzian and Crystal L. Park. New York: The Guilford, 2005. 21–42.

Žižek, Slavoj. *On Belief: Thinking in Action.* London: Routledge, 2001.

Znamenski, Andrei A. *The Beauty of the Primitive: Shamanism and the Western Imagination.* Oxford: Oxford UP, 2007.

Index